SHIP
AND AIRCRAFT
MORTGAGES

SHIP
AND AIRCRAFT
MORTGAGES

By

NIGEL MEESON
of Magdalen College, Oxford
and of the Middle Temple, Barrister

|L|L|P|

LONDON   NEW YORK   HAMBURG   HONG KONG
LLOYD'S OF LONDON PRESS LTD.
1989

Lloyd's of London Press Ltd
Legal Publishing and Conferences Division
One Singer Street, London EC2A 4LQ

USA AND CANADA
Lloyd's of London Press Inc.
Suite 523, 611 Broadway
New York, NY 10012 USA

GERMANY
Lloyd's of London Press GmbH
59 Ehrenbergstrasse
2000 Hamburg 50, West Germany

SOUTH EAST ASIA
Lloyd's of London Press (Far East) Ltd.
903 Chung Nam Building
1 Lockhart Road, Wanchai
Hong Kong

British Library Cataloguing in Publication Data
Meeson, Nigel
Ship and aircraft mortgages
1. Great Britain. Ships. Mortgages. Law
2. Great Britain. Aircraft. Mortgages.
Law
I. Title
344.103'965

ISBN 1–85044–104–9

Text set 10 on 12 pt Linotron 202 Baskerville by
Promenade Graphics Ltd., Cheltenham, Glos.
Printed in Great Britain by
WBC Print Ltd., Bristol

PREFACE

In 1920 a short book entitled *The Law relating to the Mortgages of Ships* by Benjamin Constant was published, but to my knowledge no similar book has been published in England since then, although other works have touched upon the subject. It appeared to me that after more than 65 years there was a place for a new and up-to-date account of the law of ship mortgages.

Although today there are other means of ship finance than the ship mortgage, and the majority of ship mortgages concern non-British tonnage, nevertheless the ship mortgage continues to have widespread appeal, and, where permitted by national law, English law will often govern the deed of covenants regulating a mortgage of a non-British ship. In addition, the English law of ship mortgages can provide a source of reference in other jurisdictions where national law may not provide a solution. I have included aircraft mortgages in this work for completeness, although their relative significance in the field of aircraft finance is not as great as their marine counterpart in the field of ship finance.

As the subject of ship and aircraft mortgages is the province mainly of commercial rather than property lawyers, the book begins in Chapter 1 by considering the legal nature of a mortgage as a security transaction. Chapter 2 considers ownership of ships and aircraft in some detail for two principal reasons. First, it is obviously vital for a lender to investigate the title of the borrower if he is to take a mortgage and, secondly, the law of mortgages has to be understood in its proper context as being a species of ownership.

Chapter 3 deals with the creation, transfer and discharge of mortgages as well as with the question as to what items are comprised within the mortgage other than the actual ship or aircraft and Chapter 4 deals with the sort of provisions to be found in a typical deed of covenants.

Chapter 5 examines the respective rights and liabilities of the mortgagor and the mortgagee, and Chapter 6 considers questions of priorities. Finally, Chapter 7 covers conflict of laws aspects of ship and aircraft mortgages.

A fortunate consequence of my tardiness in completing the manuscript has been that I have been able to include the Merchant Shipping Act 1988 which makes important changes regarding the nationality requirements for ownership of British ships, and for the first time introduces a system of registration of fishing vessel mortgages. However, this should not detract from recognition of the customary patience of the Publishers who were no doubt wondering at one stage whether they would ever see a manuscript.

In Canada a book entitled *Mortgages of Ships: Marine Security in Canada* by J. D. Buchan was published in 1986 and I am grateful to the Publishers for having obtained a copy, which has been useful in accelerating the research of Canadian cases.

I should like to thank Beverley, my wife, for her continued understanding and support during the protracted period I have spent trying to find time to write in addition to meeting the demands of practice. Finally, I have dedicated this book to our daughter Verity who was born in the middle of the preparation of this work.

The Temple   NIGEL MEESON
September 1988

CONTENTS

TABLE OF CASES

TABLE OF STATUTES

1

INTRODUCTION

GENERAL DEFINITION

A mortgage is a security transaction and is a form of "real"[1] security. It is a transfer of property or an interest in property as security for a debt. At common law the mortgage of a chattel transfers to the mortgagee all the property of the mortgagor by way of security and subject to redemption on repayment of the amount due from the mortgagor to the mortgagee in respect of which the mortgage was granted.

The purpose of the mortgagee taking the property is so as not to be left with only a personal remedy against the debtor, but to have a right against property of the debtor independent of the debtor's continuing solvency. Thus the effect of the mortgage is to appropriate the property mortgaged to meet the debt or obligation of the mortgagor in respect of which the mortgage was executed.

The essential feature of a mortgage is that it is only a security transaction; the property is redeemable by the mortgagor upon satisfaction of the debt which it secures, but on the other hand the property is realisable by the mortgagee if it is not. From the standpoint of the mortgagee he acquires a right by a mortgage to the ownership of property in a certain event, namely, on default of payment of principal and interest. From the standpoint of the mortgagor, whereas every mortgage implies a right of redemption so too does it imply a debt, and a personal obligation to repay it: see *King* v. *King*.[2]

MORTGAGE DISTINGUISHED FROM ABSOLUTE TRANSFER

The difference between an outright disposition and a mortgage is that the latter is by way of security only. What may appear on its face to be an absolute transfer of property may be proved by extrinsic evidence to have been intended as a security transaction and will be treated as a mortgage only. The courts will

---

1. As opposed to "personal" security or suretyship by a contract of guarantee.
2. (1735) 3 P.Wms. 358.

1

always look to the substance of the transaction[3] and will, where necessary, admit parol evidence to establish the true nature of any transaction. The burden of proof will be upon the person alleging that a transaction which appears upon its face to be an absolute disposition is, in fact, a security transaction.

MORTGAGE DISTINGUISHED FROM PLEDGE OR PAWN

In the case of personal property, it is important to distinguish a mortgage from a pledge or pawn. Where property is pledged or pawned by way of security, the transaction is one in which the possession of the chattel is delivered to the creditor and no property in the goods passes under the transaction. It is a bailment of the goods to the creditor to be retained by him until the debtor has discharged his obligation and is an incomplete transaction without the delivery of goods, actual or constructive, to the creditor.

It is generally said that where goods are pledged the pledgee obtains a "special property" in the goods, although the general property remains in the pledgor. However, in *The "Odessa"*[4] Lord Mersey stated[5] that this so-called special property was in truth no property at all.

The essence of the distinction is therefore that in a pledge the pledgee's security is dependent upon possession and an ancillary power of sale, whereas in a mortgage the mortgagee actually has title to the goods, subject to the mortgagor's right of redemption.

MORTGAGE DISTINGUISHED FROM LIEN

A lien is technically a right given by law to retain the possession of property until a debt is discharged. For example, a repairer's lien or an unpaid vendor's lien. It is also used to describe such a right conferred by contract. There may not necessarily be an ancillary power of sale to a lien and unlike a mortgage no title is vested in the lienee.

MORTGAGE DISTINGUISHED FROM CHARGE

Although the phrase "charge by way of legal mortgage" is used in the Law of Property Act 1925 in relation to mortgages of land,[6] a charge is in law a different species of security transaction from either a mortgage or a pledge or a pawn. If property is subject to a charge, it is appropriated to meet a debt or obligation,

3. *Re Watson, ex p. Official Receiver in Bankruptcy* (1890) 25 Q.B.D. 27.
4. [1916] 1 A.C. 145.
5. Ibid. at p. 158.
6. See section 87(1) of the Law of Property Act 1925.

but its efficacy is not dependent upon possession (as in the case of a pledge or a pawn) nor does any property therein pass to the chargee.[7] In the event the debt is not discharged, the creditor may enforce his security by means of judicial process. The process when applied to goods is called hypothecation. In times past, hypothecation was an important transaction in maritime law being effected by bottomry (of a ship) or *respondentia* (of cargo). Such transactions are now unlikely to arise in practice.

MORTGAGE OF CHATTELS

Morgages of personal property need not generally be in writing, subject to certain provisions in the Consumer Credit Act 1974 relating to "regulated agreements" under that Act which require writing. The Bills of Sale Acts do not require writing, but make provision for the form and registration of certain agreements which are made in writing. Mortgages of ships and registered mortgages of aircraft fall outside the scope of the Bills of Sale Acts[8] and those Acts will not be considered further in this work.

MORTGAGES OF CHOSES IN ACTION

Things in action, such as stocks and shares, book debts, insurance policies, freight and hire charges, can be mortgaged, and unless by some particular statute a specific method is prescribed this will be done by way of assignment. The Bills of Sale Acts do not apply to mortgages of things in action.[9] However, because the rule at common law[10] was that a chose in action was incapable of assignment without the consent, express or implied, of the holder of the fund to apply it in accordance with the assignment, mortgages of choses in action were equitable only prior to the passing of section 25(6) of the Judicature Act 1873, now section 136(1) of the Law of Property Act 1925 which provides:

Any absolute assignment by writing under the hand of the assignor (not purporting to be by way of charge only) of any debt or other legal thing in action, of which express notice in writing has been given to the debtor, trustee or other person from whom the assignor would have been entitled to claim such debt or thing in action, is effectual in law (subject to equities having priority over the right of the assignee) to pass and transfer from the date of such notice—
(a) the legal right to such debt or thing in action;
(b) all legal and other remedies for the same; and
(c) the power to give a good discharge for the same without the concurrence of the assignor;

7. See *Swiss Bank* v. *Lloyds Bank* [1982] A.C. 584 at pp. 594H–596A.
8. See section 4 of Bills of Sale Act 1878 and article 16(1) of the Mortgaging of Aircraft Order 1972.
9. See section 4 of Bills of Sale Act 1878.
10. *Lampet's Case* (1612) 10 Co.Rep. 46(b) at 48(a).

Provided that if the debtor, trustee or other person liable in respect of such debt or thing in action has notice—

(a) that the assignment is disputed by the assignor to any person claiming under him; or

(b) of any other opposing or conflicting claims to such debt or thing in action;

he may, if he thinks fit, either call upon the persons making the claims thereto to interplead concerning the same, or pay the debt or other thing in action into court under the provisions of the Trustee Act 1925.

MORTGAGE OF A SHIP

In *Keith* v. *Burrows*[11] the Court of Common Pleas considered in detail the nature of a mortgage of a ship.[12] The following extract from the judgment of the court provides a useful introduction and a summary of the impact of the provisions of the Merchant Shipping Acts on the general law:

The mortgage to the plaintiffs was in the statutory form, and by it the ship was mortgaged to them. The word mortgage is a well known word and signifies a transfer of property by way of security. (See 2 Black.Com. 158; Termes de la ley Mortgage.) A mortgage is a transfer of all the mortgagor's interest in the thing mortgaged, but such a transfer is not absolute; it is made only by way of security, or in other words it is subject to redemption. Unless therefore there is any statutory enactment to the contrary, the plaintiffs in this case acquired by their mortgage the whole of the mortgagor's interest in the ship, or in other words the legal title to the ship as security.

Such is prima facie the effect of the instruments of mortgage. But the statutes relating to ships must be examined with a view to determine what the consequences of registration or non-registration may be.

Under the old statutes relating to Merchant Shipping all transfers and mortgages were made by bill of sale, and such bill of sale had no effect whatever either at law or in equity until registration. (See the cases collected in *The Liverpool Borough Bank* v. *Turner*, 1 J. & H. 159; 2 De G.F. & J. 502; *Maclachlan on Shipping*, p. 39, 2nd edit.)

The Merchant Shipping Acts now in force,[13] however, make a distinction between transfers of ships otherwise than by way of security and mortgages, and there are different groups of sections with different headings applicable to these two different subjects: (see ss. 24–30 which relate to transfers and transmissions, and ss. 31–38, which relate to mortgages). Amongst other distinctions between these two modes of dealing with ships the following are the most noteworthy: A transfer (otherwise than by way of mortgage) must be by bill of sale (sect. 24), and must be produced to the registrar for registration (sect. 26), and the transferee, if not a corporation, must make a declaration that he is a natural born British Subject (sect. 25).

On the other hand a mortgage must be by a different kind of instrument (sect. 31), and there is no enactment requiring such instrument to be produced to the registrar (cf. sect. 31 & sect. 26), and the mortgagee is not required to make any declaration as to his nationality.

It is true that in *The Liverpool Borough Bank* v. *Turner* (ubi sup.), Wood V.-C. and Lord

---

11. (1876) 1 C.P.D. 722.

12. See also: *Wilson* v. *Heather* (1814) 5 Taunton 645; *Thompson* v. *Smith* (1815) 1 Maddock 395.

13. The case was decided under the earlier Merchant Shipping Acts. The text has, however, been amended so as to refer to the corresponding provisions of the Merchant Shipping Act 1894 for ease of reference and understanding.

Campbell held that an unregistered equitable mortgage of a ship could not be enforced. But in consequence of this decision [sect. 57] was passed, and the validity of an unregistered mortgage as against all persons except registered transferees or mortgagees can hardly now be disputed (see *Stapleton* v. *Haymen*, 2 H. & C. 918).

It appears from the Merchant Shipping Act [1894] itself, that a mortgagee has an interest in the ship capable of transmission by bankruptcy, death or marriage[14] (sect. 38); and on payment off of the debt secured by a registered mortgage and entry of the payment in the registry, the estate, if any, which passed to the mortgagee vests in whom the same would have vested if the mortgage had not been made (sect. 32).

The mortgagee, however, is not to be deemed the owner of the ship, except in so far as may be necessary for making her a security for the mortgaged debt (sect. 34). This section was inserted for his protection against liability which might have attached to him by reason of his interest in the ship (see *Dickinson* v. *Kitchen*, 8 E. & B. 789); and would have been quite unnecessary if the mortgage transferred no interest in the sense of ownership in her to him; or in other words if it created a mere charge on her in his favour.

Section 36 which protects registered mortgagees of ships from the operation of the reputed ownership clauses of the Bankruptcy Act[15] would also be unnecessary if a mortgagee had not such an interest in the ship as might render him her true owner within the meaning of those clauses.

Again, the right of the first registered mortgagee to take possession of the ship is too well settled to be capable of dispute; but the statute confers no such right in express terms, and it only exists by reason of the ownership transferred to the mortgagee by the mortgage itself; a mere charge would confer no such right. But as a mortgagee, unless in possession, would have no power of sale unless it were not expressly conferred on him, and as the mortgage contains no such power, the statute itself expressly confers it on registered mortgagees (sect. 35). But this affords no argument against the view that the mortgage itself confers on the mortgagee an interest in the sense of ownership in the ship herself.

The conclusion, then, to be drawn from the mortgage and the statute is that the mortgagee of a ship, like the mortgagee of any other property, acquires an ownership in the ship, viz., such ownership as the mortgagor has to give. A first mortgagee will thus acquire the whole ownership in the ship, but only of course as a security for his money. Second and other mortgagees will only acquire the interest left in the mortgagor, or in other words his right to redeem. That right will be legal or equitable, according as the time for paying off the first mortgage has not yet arrived or has passed.

As an incident of his mortgage and the ownership transferred thereunder, a first mortgagee has a right at common law to take possession of the mortgaged ship for the purpose of making his security available. A second and subsequent mortgagee is not entitled to take possession of the ship as against the first or any other prior mortgagee, but he nevertheless has as against all other persons the right to take possession which he can enforce by the appointment of a receiver. The right to enter into possession does not, however, arise until the mortgage debt is due or before then if the mortgagor is dealing with the mortgaged property in such a way as to impair the security.

Unless and until he exercises this right to enter into possession, the

---

14. By reason of section 2 of the Law Reform (Married Women and Tortfeasors) Act 1935 this is no longer a cause of automatic transfer of property.

15. Note: The doctrine of "reputed ownership" was abolished by the Insolvency Act 1985, section 235, Schedule 10, Part III.

mortgagee is not treated either according to general principles or under the Merchant Shipping Acts as the owner of the ship. Accordingly he is not to be considered as a co-owner and he does not have the rights of a co-owner, for example, to bring an action of restraint.[16]

MORTGAGE OF AN AIRCRAFT

Mortgages of aircraft are treated similarly to mortgages of ships. The general law relating to mortgages of chattels applies, save to the extent that it has been modified by statute. In the case of aircraft, the Mortgaging of Aircraft Order 1972[17] made under section 86 of the Civil Aviation Act 1982, provides registration provisions similar to, but not identical with, the regime under the Merchant Shipping Act 1894. These provisions will be considered in greater detail in this work, but it is important to note at this stage that, as regards the Bills of Sale Acts, unlike mortgages of ships which are wholly excluded by virtue of section 4 of the Bills of Sale Act 1878, by virtue of article 16(1) of the Mortgaging of Aircraft Order 1972, mortgages of aircraft are only excluded when registered and the provisions of the Bills of Sale Acts will apply to unregistered mortgages of aircraft. There is little case law on mortgages of aircraft, but there appears no reason why the principles to be distilled from the cases concerning mortgages of ships should not be applied, with any necessary modification, to mortgages of aircraft.

LEGAL AND EQUITABLE MORTGAGES

Mortgages may be legal or equitable. A legal mortgage of personalty is a conditional assignment to the mortgagee of the mortgagor's legal interest in the property. An equitable mortgage may according to general principles be created in two ways:

(i) Agreement

That is, by an agreement to make a legal mortgage, which, notwithstanding the lack of proper formality sufficient to create a legal mortgage, will be enforced in equity according to the maxim "equity treats as having been done that which ought to have been done".

The common method of creating an equitable mortgage of real property by the deposit of title deeds is not appropriate in the case of chattels, where there will rarely, if ever, be a document of title to deposit. In the case of registered ships, where it might otherwise be thought that the deposit of the registration

---

16. *The "Keroula"* (1886) 11 P.D. 92.
17. S.I. 1972 No. 1268.

certificate would be sufficient to create an equitable mortgage, section 15(1) of the Merchant Shipping Act 1894 rules this out, and any pledge of the certificate is null and void.[18]

However, in *Ex p. Hodgkin, re Softley*[19] the deposit of a builder's certificate of an unfinished ship was held to create an equitable mortgage. In *Lacon* v. *Liffen*[20] the deposit of a mortgage of a registered ship was held to amount to an equitable sub-mortgage.

(ii) The mortgage of an equitable interest

This needs little further elaboration, although it should be noted that second and subsequent mortgages will fall into this category of equitable mortgages, as after having disposed of the legal interest to the first mortgagee, the mortgagor has only an equitable interest (his equity of redemption) out of which to create subsequent mortgages. It should also be noted that section 53(1)(c) of the Law of Property Act 1925 provides:

a disposition of an equitable interest or trust subsisting at the time of the disposition, must be in writing signed by the person disposing of the same, or by his agent thereunto lawfully authorised in writing or by will.

---

18. *Wiley* v. *Crawford* (1861) 1 B. & S. 253.
19. (1875) L.R. 20 Eq. 746.
20. (1862) 4 Giff. 75.

2
OWNERSHIP

INTRODUCTION

Ships and aircraft are chattels and questions relating to their ownership are decided according to the principles applicable under the law of personal property, in particular the provisions as to passing of property and conveying of title contained in the Sale of Goods Act 1979. However, unlike other vehicles of transport such as the horse or the motor car, there is no market overt in ships or aircraft and title will not pass by delivery, nor will it be proven by possession.

The classic statement of this proposition in relation to a ship is to be found in the judgment of Turner L.J. in *Hooper* v. *Gumm*[1] where he said[2]:

> A ship is not like an ordinary personal chattel; it does not pass by delivery nor does the possession of it prove title to it. There is no market overt in ships . . . In the cases of ordinary purchases of property not purchased in market overt, the purchasers are bound to enquire into the title of the property purchased by them. They cannot shut their eyes and ears and claim the benefit of want of notice; if they think proper to buy without inquiring into the title of the person from whom they buy, they must be held to be affected with notice of what would have appeared if the inquiry had been made.

It is submitted that the statement may be applied with equal force to an aircraft.

SHIPS

What is a "ship"?

"Ship" is defined by section 742 of the Merchant Shipping Act 1894: " 'Ship' includes every description of vessel used in navigation not propelled by oars." "Vessel" is in turn defined by the same section: " 'Vessel' includes any ship or boat, or other description of vessel used in navigation." An examination of the authorities does not reveal a particularly consistent approach in the construction of this statutory definition of a ship. It is helpful to consider the various parts of the definition separately.

1. (1867) L.R. 2 Ch.App. 282.
2. *Ibid.* at p. 290.

8

"includes"

It is clear that the use of the word "includes" predicates an "extensive", rather than an "exclusive" or "exhaustive" definition.

"propelled by oars"

An object which would otherwise be considered as falling within the term "ship" does not cease to be a ship if it is sometimes propelled by oars. In *Ex p. Ferguson and Hutchinson*[3] a fishing coble was held to be a "ship" even though fitted with oars which were used to take her out of harbour to enable her sails to be hoisted. However, in *Everard* v. *Kendall*[4] barges propelled by oars only were held to be outside the definition of a ship.

"used in navigation"

It is a question of fact whether a vessel is "used in navigation" and particular regard is to be had to what use she has been, and is now, put. In *European and Australasian Royal Mail* v. *P. & O.*[5] a vessel which had formerly been registered, but which had had all masts, spars and rigging removed except for her lower masts and standing rigging and was moored fore and aft with two anchors and which had been used for the past four years as a coal hulk was held no longer to be a "ship" but to have become a mere chattel, a floating coal hulk.

In *Southport Corporation* v. *Morris*[6] an electric passenger launch used exclusively on a small artificial lake was held not to be "used in navigation" and thus not to be a ship. However, that case was distinguished in *Weeks* v. *Ross*[7] where a motor boat used exclusively in the River Exe between Exeter and a lock, beyond which a canal connected via further locks with a tidal estuary, was held to be a ship.

A fairly liberal approach to the interpretation of the phrase "used in navigation" can be seen in a number of cases concerned with towed barges:

In *St. John Pilot Commissioners* v. *Cumberland Ry & Coal Co.*[8] the following were held to be ships: barges which had two small sails used to steady the vessels and to assist in strong breezes, which could run before the wind, but which could not otherwise be safely navigated as sailing vessels in the usual way and were intended to be towed from port to port, which had a captain and crew, steering gear and anchors. If they had been fully rigged they would have been capable of being navigated as ordinary steamers.

3. (1871) L.R. 6 Q.B. 280.
4. (1870) L.R. 5 C.P. 428.
5. (1866) 14 L.T. 704.
6. [1893] 1 Q.B. 359.
7. [1913] 2 K.B. 229.
8. [1910] A.C. 208.

In *The "Mac"*,[9] *The "Mudlark"*,[10] *The "Harlow"*[11] and *The "Champion"*,[12] hopper barges lacking any means of propulsion and which were towed from place to place were held to be ships.

What is not a "ship"

The following have been held not to be ships: a landing stage[13]; a gas float moored as a beacon[14]; a newbuilding which was launched unfinished without engines or boilers[15]; a pontoon crane[16]; a flying boat[17]; a seaplane.[18]

It should also be noted that by section 1(1) of the Merchant Shipping Act 1921:

the expression "ship" [includes] every description of lighter, barge, or like vessel used in navigation in Great Britain, however propelled:

Provided that a lighter, barge or like vessel used exclusively in non-tidal waters, other than harbours, shall not for the purposes of this Act, be deemed to be used in navigation.

"British ship"

In order for a ship to be considered as a British ship for the purposes of the Merchant Shipping Acts she must fall within one or other of the classes of British ships defined by section 2 of the Merchant Shipping Act 1988 which provides:

British ships

2.—(1) A ship shall be a British ship for the purposes of the Merchant Shipping Acts if—

    (a) the ship is registered in the United Kingdom under any of the following enactments, namely—

        (i) Part I of the 1894 Act or section 5 of the Merchant Shipping Act 1983 (registration of small ships), or

        (ii) Part II of this Act (registration of British fishing vessels); or

    (b) the ship is registered in the United Kingdom in pursuance of an Order in Council under section 80 of the Merchant Shipping Act 1906 (Government ships); or

    (c) the ship is a fishing vessel within the meaning of Part II of this Act which is eligible to be registered under that Part of this Act by virtue of section 14 below, but—

        (i) is excluded from registration under that Part of this Act by regulations made under section 13 below, and

        (ii) is not registered under the law of any country outside the United Kingdom; or

---

9. (1882) 6 P.D. 126 (C.A.).
10. [1911] P. 116.
11. [1922] P. 175.
12. [1934] P. 1.
13. *The "Craighall"* [1910] P. 207 (C.A.).
14. *The Gas Float Whitton No. 2* [1897] A.C. 357 (H.L.).
15. *The "Andalusian"* (1878) 3 P.D. 182.
16. *Merchants' Marine Insurance* v. *North of England P & I Assoc.* (1926) 26 Ll.L.Rep. 201 (C.A.).
17. *Polpen Shipping* v. *Commercial Union* [1943] K.B. 161.
18. *Watson* v. *RCA Victor* (1934) 50 Ll.L.Rep. 77.

(d) the ship is registered under the law of a relevant overseas territory; or

(e) the ship is less than 24 metres in length and—

(i) is not a fishing vessel within the meaning of Part II of this Act, and

(ii) is not registered in the United Kingdom under an enactment falling within paragraph (a)(i) above or under the law of any country outside the United Kingdom, but

(iii) is wholly owned by one or more persons qualified to be owners of British ships by virtue of section 3(1) below.

(2) This section shall have effect in relation to any time before the end of the period referred to in section 13(3)(b) below as if the enactments falling within subsection (1)(a)(i) included Part IV of the 1894 Act (registration of British fishing boats).

Registration

Before considering in detail the provisions of the Merchant Shipping Acts as to registration, it should be noted that the register does not, nor is it intended to provide a comprehensive scheme of registration of interests in ships in the way that the Land Registration Acts are intended to provide such a scheme in relation to registered land. The register provides only *prima facie* evidence of title. In *Baumvoll Manufactur Von Karl Scheibler* v. *Furness*[19] Lord Herschell L.C. said[20]:

Although the legislature has now taken greater security to see that the person registered as owner is properly registered than it had done before, all it has done is to make the register *prima facie* evidence of ownership. In fact it assumes that anybody may displace altogether the statutory effect which has been given to it by proving what the facts really are.

Moreover, section 56 of the Merchant Shipping Act 1894 expressly provides that: "No notice of any trust, express, implied, or constructive shall be entered in the register or be receivable by the registrar, . . . " Nevertheless, such interests are not abolished by the Act as is made clear by section 57 which provides:

The expression "beneficial interest", where used in this part of this Act, includes interests arising under contract and other equitable interests; and the intention of this Act is, that without prejudice to the provisions of this Act for preventing notice of trusts from being entered in the register or received by the registrar, and without prejudice to the powers of disposition and giving receipts conferred by this Act on registered owners and mortgagees, and without prejudice to the provisions of this Act relating to the exclusion of unqualified persons from the ownership of British ships, interests arising under contract or other equitable interests may be enforced by or against owners and mortgagees of ships in respect of their interest therein in the same manner as in respect of any other personal property.

Thus in *The "Venture"*[21] a resulting trust in favour of a person who had advanced part of the purchase money for a ship was enforced by the court according to the usual equitable principles.

Section 57[22] was necessitated by the decision in *Liverpool Borough Bank* v.

---

19. [1893] A.C. 8.
20. *Ibid.* at p. 20.
21. [1908] P. 218 (C.A.).
22. Originally enacted as section 3 of the Merchant Shipping Act 1862.

Turner[23] which decided that under the former statutory provisions the court had no power to enforce equities where the formality provisions of the 1854 Act had not been complied with. Although the actual decision in that case has been reversed by section 57, in the course of his judgment Wood V.-C. summarised the purposes behind the statutory scheme of registration of ships in the following words[24]:

There are two points of public policy which may be suggested in these Acts relating to shipping: the one policy regarding the interests of the nation at large, relating to the question who shall be entitled to the privileges of the British flag—a question of deep import to the nation, involving the question whether or not the whole country may be exposed to the calamities of war in respect of the protection which at all times must be afforded to the British flag; the other policy being similar to that which gave rise to the Acts for registration of titles to land—the object being to determine what should be a proper evidence of title in those who deal with the property in question.

The first (chauvinistic) policy reason advanced by Wood V.-C. has a rather hollow ring to it in the 1980s when the "privileges" of the British flag may involve compliance with manning and safety regulations not required by some other flags, and the "protection" which must at all times be afforded to the British flag has recently been put to the test in the Persian Gulf. Nevertheless, historically, it was the primary reason for registration.

A separate register of British fishing vessels is provided for by Part II of the Merchant Shipping Act 1988.

Entitlement to registration

Section 3 of the Merchant Shipping Act 1988 sets out the categories of persons who are qualified to be owners of British ships, following the divisions of British nationality introduced by the British Nationality Act 1981, and also including the category of British Nationals (Overseas) arising out of the return of Hong Kong. It also includes citizens of the Republic of Ireland and U.K. companies. It should be noted that the rights as regards the entitlement of these various categories of qualified persons to have their ships registered are not the same and section 4 of the Act differentiates in determining the circumstances in which a ship is entitled to be registered as a British ship under Part I of the Merchant Shipping Act 1894 according to which category of qualified persons owns a majority interest in the ship.[25] A person not qualified to own a British ship may nevertheless be one of her owners, provided a majority interest[26] is owned by

23. (1861) 2 De G.F. & J. 502.

24. *Ibid.* at p. 830.

25. It should be noted that these sections, together with sections 2 and 5 to 8 of the 1988 Act repeal and replace sections 1, 2 and 3 of the 1894 Act which provided for compulsory registration of British ships and that Part II of the 1988 Act provides for a separate register for fishing vessels which henceforth may not be registered under Part I of the 1894 Act.

26. Which is defined as legal title to 33 or more of the 64 shares.

qualified persons and the ship is registered accordingly. Sections 3 and 4 of the 1988 Act provide:

Persons qualified to be owners of British ships

3.—(1) For the purposes of Part I of the 1894 Act the following persons are persons qualified to be owners of British ships, namely—

(a) British citizens;

(b) British Dependent Territories citizens;

(c) British Overseas citizens;

(d) persons who under the British Nationality Act 1981 are British subjects;

(e) persons who under the Hong Kong (British Nationality) Order 1986 are British Nationals (Overseas);

(f) bodies corporate incorporated in the United Kingdom or in any relevant overseas territory and having their principal place of business in the United Kingdom or in any such territory; and

(g) citizens of the Republic of Ireland.

(2) Subject to subsection (3) below, references (however phrased) in any statutory provision to persons who are, for the purposes of Part I of the 1894 Act, qualified to be owners of British ships shall be construed in accordance with subsection (1) above.

(3) For the purposes of section 5 of the Merchant Shipping Act 1983 the following persons are persons qualified to be owners of British ships, namely—

(a) persons falling within paragraphs (a) to (e) and (g) of subsection (1) above; and

(b) Commonwealth citizens not falling within those paragraphs.

(4) It is hereby declared that a person who is not qualified under subsection (1) above to be an owner of a British ship may nevertheless be one of the owners of such a ship if—

(a) a majority interest in the ship (within the meaning of section 4 below) is owned by persons who are qualified to be owners of British ships; and

(b) the ship is registered, in accordance with the provisions of that section, under Part I of the 1894 Act.

Registration under Part I of 1894 Act

Entitlement to registration under Part I of 1894 Act

4.—(1) Subject to sections 6 and 7 below, this section has effect for the purpose of determining whether a ship is entitled to be registered under Part I of the 1894 Act in the United Kingdom.

(2) Subject to subsection (3), a ship shall be entitled to be registered if a majority interest in the ship is owned by one or more persons qualified to be owners of British ships by virtue of section 3(1)(a), (b), (e) or (f) above.

(3) Where—

(a) a ship falling within subsection (2) is 24 metres or more in length, and

(b) the person, or (as the case may be) each of the persons, by whom the majority interest in the ship is owned is not resident in the United Kingdom,

the ship shall only be entitled to be registered if a representative person is appointed in relation to the ship.

(4) Where a majority interest in a ship is owned by one or more persons qualified to be owners of British ships by virtue of section 3(1)(c), (d) or (g) above, the ship shall be entitled to be registered—

   (a) if that person, or (as the case may be) any of those persons, is resident in the United Kingdom, or

   (b) (where that condition is not satisfied) if the Secretary of State furnishes him or them with a declaration that he consents to the ship being registered, and, in addition, a representative person is appointed in relation to the ship.

  (5) Where a majority interest in a ship is owned by the following persons, namely—

   (a) one or more persons qualified to be owners of British ships by virtue of section 3(1)(a), (b), (e) or (f), and

   (b) one or more persons so qualified by virtue of section 3(1)(c), (d) or (g),

the ship shall be entitled to be registered—

   (i) if any of those persons is resident in the United Kingdom, or

   (ii) (where that condition is not satisfied) if a representative person is appointed in relation to the ship.

  (6) A ship shall, in accordance with section 13(2)(a) below, not be entitled to be registered if it is a fishing vessel within the meaning of Part II.

  (7) For the purposes of this section—

   (a) one or more persons shall be treated as owning a majority interest in a ship if there is vested in that person or in those persons, taken together, the legal title to 33 or more of the 64 shares into which the property in the ship is divided for the purposes of registration, in accordance with section 5 of the 1894 Act (there being left out of account for this purpose any share in which any beneficial interest is owned by a person who is not qualified to be an owner of a British ship); and

   (b) a body corporate shall be treated as resident in the United Kingdom if it is incorporated in the United Kingdom and has its principal place of business there.

  (8) Nothing in this section applies to a ship to which section 80 of the Merchant Shipping Act 1906 applies (Government ships).

It should be observed that the scheme of the Act provides that where the majority interest is not resident in the United Kingdom, a representative person has to be appointed in relation to the ship. The representative person must either be a United Kingdom resident or a United Kingdom company having its principal place of business in the United Kingdom. Section 5 of the 1988 Act which deals with representative persons provides as follows:

Representative persons

  5.—(1) Where the entitlement of any ship to be registered is, by virtue of any provision of section 4, conditional on the appointment of a representative person in relation to the ship, the owner of the ship shall—

   (a) before applying for the ship to be registered, appoint an individual or body corporate satisfying the prescribed requirements to be the representative person in relation to the ship, and

   (b) secure that, so long as the ship remains registered, an individual or body corporate satisfying those requirements is so appointed.

  (2) For the purposes of subsection (1) the prescribed requirements are—

   (a) that the representative person is either—

    (i) an individual resident in the United Kingdom, or

    (ii) a body corporate incorporated in the United Kingdom and having its principal place of business there; and

   (b) such other requirements as the Secretary of State may by regulations prescribe.

(3) Where subsection (1) applies to a ship, any person who is registered under section 59(2) of the 1894 Act (registration of ship's manager) in relation to the ship shall, if that person is such an individual or body corporate as is mentioned in subsection (2)(a)(i) or (ii) above, be treated for the purposes of this Part of this Act as the representative person for the time being appointed in relation to the ship.

(4) The owner of any ship in relation to which any representative person is for the time being appointed shall—

    (a) on applying for the ship to be registered, notify the registrar to whom the application is made of the name and address of the representative person; and

    (b) in the event of any change in the identity, or in the address, of the representative person so appointed, notify the registrar of the ship's port of registry of the name and address of the new representative person, or (as the case may be) of the new address, as soon as practicable after the change occurs;

and the registrar in question shall record any particulars notified to him in pursuance of this section in the register kept by him under Part I of the 1894 Act.

(5) Any document required or authorised, by virtue of any statutory provision, to be served for the purpose of the institution of, or otherwise in connection with, proceedings for an offence under the Merchant Shipping Acts, or under any instrument in force under those Acts, shall, where the person to be served is the owner of a registered ship, be treated as duly served on him if—

    (a) delivered to any representative person for the time being appointed in relation to the ship, or

    (b) sent to any such person by post at the address notified (or, as the case may be, last notified) to the registrar under subsection (4) in relation to that person, or

    (c) left for any such person at that address.

(6) Any person who contravenes subsection (1)(b) or (4)(b) above shall be guilty of an offence and liable on summary conviction to a fine not exceeding the third level on the standard scale.

Section 6 of the 1988 Act gives the Secretary of State power to refuse registration in circumstances where he is not satisfied that the ship is entitled to be registered and also where, although the ship is entitled to be registered, he is satisfied that it would be inappropriate for the ship to be registered having regard to her condition or the welfare of persons employed or engaged on board her. Section 6 of the 1988 Act provides as follows:

Refusal of registration

6.—(1) If for any reason it appears to the Secretary of State that a ship in respect of which an application for registration has been made may not be entitled to be registered, he may by notice served on—

    (a) the applicant, or

    (b) any representative person for the time being appointed in relation to the ship,

require that person to furnish him with such information as he thinks necessary for the purpose of determining whether the ship is entitled to be registered.

(2) Where the Secretary of State has served a notice under subsection (1) with respect to any ship, then, unless he has become satisfied that the ship is entitled to be registered, he shall, as soon as practicable after the end of the period of 30 days beginning with the date of service of that notice, give to registrars of British ships generally a direction requiring them not to register the ship.

(3) Notwithstanding that any ship in respect of which an application for registration has been made is entitled to be registered, the Secretary of State may give to registrars of

British ships generally a direction requiring them not to register the ship if he is satisfied that, having regard—

   (a) to the condition of the ship so far as relevant to its safety or to any risk of pollution, or

   (b) to the safety, health and welfare of persons employed or engaged in any capacity on board the ship,

it would be inappropriate for the ship to be registered.

Similarly the Secretary of State is given power by section 7 of the 1988 Act to direct the removal of a ship from the register in certain circumstances. Section 7 of the 1988 Act provides as follows:

Power of Secretary of State to direct removal from the register

7.—(1) If for any reason it appears to the Secretary of State that a registered ship may no longer be entitled to be registered, he may by notice served on—

   (a) the owner of the ship, or

   (b) any representative person for the time being appointed in relation to the ship,

require that person to furnish him with such information as he thinks necessary for the purpose of determining whether the ship is entitled to be registered.

(2) Where the Secretary of State has served a notice under subsection (1) with respect to any ship, then, unless he has become satisfied that the ship is entitled to be registered, he shall, as soon as practicable after the end of the period of 30 days beginning with the date of service of that notice, serve a notice under subsection (4) on the owner or on any representative person for the time being appointed in relation to the ship.

(3) Where the Secretary of State is satisfied—

   (a) that, having regard to the matters mentioned in paragraph (a) or (b) of section 6(3), it would be inappropriate for a registered ship to continue to be registered, or

   (b) that any penalty imposed on the owner of a registered ship in respect of a contravention of the Merchant Shipping Acts, or of any instrument in force under those Acts, has remained unpaid for a period of more than three months (and no appeal against the penalty is pending), or

   (c) that any summons for any such contravention has been duly served on the owner of a registered ship but the owner failed to appear at the time and place appointed for the trial of the information or complaint in question and a period of not less than three months has elapsed since that time,

the Secretary of State shall serve a notice under subsection (4) either on the owner or on any representative person for the time being appointed in relation to the ship.

(4) A notice under this subsection is a notice stating—

   (a) that the Secretary of State is not satisfied that the ship in question is entitled to be registered or (as the case may be) that he is satisfied as mentioned in paragraph (a),(b) or (c) of subsection (3); and

   (b) that he intends, after the end of the period of 30 days beginning with the date of service of the notice, to direct that the ship in question should cease to be registered unless he is satisfied that it would be inappropriate to do so by any representations made to him by or on behalf of the owner within that period.

(5) As soon as practicable after the end of that period the Secretary of State shall accordingly direct the registrar of the ship's port of registry to terminate the ship's registration unless he is satisfied that it would be inappropriate to do so by any such representations.

(6) Where the registration of any ship has terminated by virtue of this section, the

Secretary of State may subsequently, if he is satisfied that it would be appropriate to do so, direct the registrar of the ship's former port of registry to restore the ship's registration.

Corporations

Where a ship is owned by a British registered company, it is the company's "principal place of business" that determines whether the ship is entitled to be registered as a "British ship".[27] This is a question of fact to be answered according to the circumstances of the particular case. It is submitted that the considerations applicable to the determination of this issue are analogous to those applied in determining where a company is resident for taxation purposes. The test in such cases is said to depend upon "where its central control and management abide; where its real business is carried on": see *De Beers Consolidated Mines Ltd.* v. *Howe*[28] and *United Construction Co.* v. *Bullock*.[29]

The nationality of the individual shareholders or directors is or should be irrelevant for these purposes, the management and control of the company being carried on where the directors hold their meetings. However, it may be of some indirect relevance, particularly where there is a controlling shareholding.

In *The "Polzeath"*,[30] a case concerned with forfeiture under section 76 of the Merchant Shipping Act 1894, the chairman and majority shareholder of a British registered shipowning company resided in Hamburg and carried on the business of the company in Hamburg. It was accordingly held by the Court of Appeal that the "principal place of business" was in Hamburg, and the ship therefore forfeit to the Crown. Swinfen Eady L.J. said: "What one had to consider was what was the centre from which instructions were given and control exercised over the employees and business of the company." Similar considerations have been applied by the prize court in determining whether a ship is of enemy character.

In *The "St. Tudno"*[31] it was held that it was the duty of the prize court to look beyond the nominal ownership in order to ascertain who the real owners were. A ship owned by a British company with British directors, but in which a German corporation had a controlling shareholding and gave instructions to the directors who had to act upon such directions, was condemned as prize.[32]

However, it should be remembered that in principle a corporate body is a separate legal entity.[33] It is the legal and beneficial owner of its property and the shareholders of a company do not own that property. Thus shareholding in a company does not equate with shareholding in a ship belonging to the

---

27. See section 4(7)(b) of the 1988 Act.
28. [1906] A.C. 455 (H.L.).
29. [1960] A.C. 351 (H.L.).
30. [1916] P. 241 (C.A.).
31. [1916] P. 291.
32. Similarly in *The "Hamborn"* [1919] A.C. 993.
33. *Saloman* v. *Saloman & Co. Ltd.* [1897] A.C. 22.

company, even if the only asset of the company is the ship and the object of the company is restricted to the ownership and operation of the ship.[34]

In *Union Bank of London* v. *Lenanton*[35] a ship built in England to be delivered to a foreign purchaser at a foreign port was held not to be a British ship so as to require[36] registration whilst remaining undelivered and the property of a British subject.

Failure to register

By section 72 of the 1894 Act[37] it is provided:

Liabilities of unregistered ships

72.—(1) Where a ship—
    (a) is 24 metres or more in length, and
    (b) is wholly owned by one or more persons qualified to be owners of British ships, but
    (c) is neither registered under this Part of this Act nor registered under the law of any country outside the United Kingdom,
then (notwithstanding that the ship is not entitled to any benefits, privileges, advantages or protection usually enjoyed by a British ship) the ship shall, for the purposes mentioned in subsection (2) of this section, be dealt with in the same manner in all respects as if the ship were a British ship.
    (2) Those purposes are—
    (a) the payment of dues, fees or other charges;
    (b) liability to fines and forfeiture; and
    (c) the punishment of offences committed on board the ship, or by any persons belonging to the ship.
    (3) In this section "length", in relation to a ship, has the same meaning as in the tonnage regulations of this Act.

The mechanics of registration

Registrars

Registration is carried out by "registrars" of British ships. Registrars are defined under section 4 of the 1894 Act,[38] which provides:

    (1) The Registrar of British ships at any port in the United Kingdom approved by the Commissioners of Customs and Excise for the registry of ships shall be any officer (whether at that port or elsewhere) appointed for the purpose by the Commissioners.
    (2) [Repealed.]

---

34. *The "Evpo Agnic"* [1988] 2 Lloyd's Rep. 411; [1988] 1 W.L.R. 1090.
35. (1878) 3 C.P.D. 243.
36. Registration was compulsory under the former provisions of the 1894 Act.
37. As amended by Schedule 1 to the 1988 Act.
38. As amended by Schedule 1 to the 1988 Act.

(3) A registrar shall not be liable to damages or otherwise for any loss accruing to any person by reason of any act done or default made by him in his character of registrar, unless the same has happened through his neglect or wilful act.

Register

Each registrar is obliged to keep a "register" in which to make entries concerning the registration of British ships. Section 5 of the 1894 Act[39] provides:

5. Every registrar of British ships shall keep a register of such ships (referred to in this Part of this Act as "the register" and entries in the register shall be made in accordance with the following provisions:—
   (i) The property in a ship shall be divided into sixty-four shares:
   (ii) Subject to the provisions of this Act with respect to joint owners or owners by transmission, not more than sixty-four individuals shall be entitled to be registered at the same time as owners of any one ship; but this rule shall not affect the beneficial title of any number of persons or of any company represented by or claiming under or through any registered owner or joint owner:
   (iii) A person shall not be entitled to be registered as owner of a fractional part of a share in a ship; but any number of persons not exceeding five may be registered as joint owners of a ship or of any share or shares therein:
   (iv) Joint owners shall be considered as constituting one person only as regards the persons entitled to be registered, and shall not be entitled to dispose in severalty of any interest in a ship, or in any share therein in respect of which they are registered:
   (v) A corporation may be registered as owner by its corporate name.

The particulars required to be entered by the registrar in his register are prescribed by section 11 of the 1894 Act[40] which provides:

11. As soon as the requirements of this Act preliminary to registry have been complied with the registrar shall enter in the register the following particulars respecting the ship:—
   (a) the name of the ship and the name of the port to which she belongs:
   (b) the details comprised in the surveyor's certificate:
   (c) the particulars respecting her origin stated in the declaration of ownership: and
   (d) the name and description of her registered owner or owners, and if there are more owners than one, the proportions in which they are interested in her.

Under section 12 of the Act, the registrar is obliged to retain in his possession certain of the documents produced to him for the purposes of registration. Section 12 of the 1894 Act provides:

12. On the registry of a ship the registrar shall retain in his possession the following documents: namely, the surveyor's certificate, the builder's certificate, any bill of sale of the ship previously made, the copy of the condemnation (if any), and all declarations of ownership.

---

39. As amended by Schedule 1 to the 1988 Act.
40. As amended by Schedule 1 to the 1988 Act.

Survey and measurement

In order to complete the necessary details in the register it is necessary for the ship to be surveyed and measured prior to registration by a surveyor of ships who produces a tonnage certificate, and section 6 of the 1894 Act,[41] therefore, provides:

6. Every ship shall before registry be surveyed by a surveyor of ships and her tonnage ascertained in accordance with the tonnage regulations of this Act, and the surveyor shall grant his certificate specifying the ship's tonnage and build, and such other particulars descriptive of the identity of the ship as may for the time being be required by the [Department of Transport], and such certificate shall be delivered to the registrar before registry.

Marking of ship

The ship also requires to be marked in accordance with the provisions of section 7 of the 1894 Act[42] which provides:

7.—(1) Every ship shall before registry be marked permanently and conspicuously to the satisfaction of the [Department of Transport] as follows:—
  (a) Her name shall be marked on each of her bows, and her name and the name of her port of registry must be marked on her stern, on a dark ground in white or yellow letters, or on a light ground in black letters, such letters to be of a length not less than four inches, and of proportionate breadth;
  (b) Her official number and the number denoting her registered tonnage shall be cut in on her main beam;
  (c) A scale of feet denoting her draught of water shall be marked on each side of her stem and of her stern post in Roman capital letters or in figures, not less than six inches in length, the lower line of such letters or figures to coincide with the draught line denoted thereby, and those letters or figures must be marked by being cut in and painted white or yellow on a dark ground, or in such other way as the [Department of Transport] approve.
  (2) [Repealed.]
  (3) If the scale of feet showing the ship's draught of water is in any respect inaccurate, so as to be likely to mislead, the owner of the ship shall be liable to a fine not exceeding one hundred pounds.
  (4) The marks required by this section shall be permanently continued, and no alteration shall be made therein, except in the event of any of the particulars thereby denoted being altered in the manner provided by this Act.
  (5) If an owner or master of a registered ship neglects to keep his ship marked as required by this section or if any person conceals, removes, alters, defaces, or obliterates, or suffers any person under his control to conceal, remove, alter, deface, or obliterate any of the said marks, except in the event aforesaid, or except for the purpose of escaping capture by an enemy, that owner, master, or person shall for each offence be liable to a fine not exceeding one hundred pounds, and on a certificate from a surveyor of ships, or [Department of Transport]Inspector under this Act, that a ship is insufficiently or inac-

41. As amended by Schedule 1 to the 1988 Act.
42. As amended by Schedule 1 to the 1988 Act.

curately marked the ship may be detained until the insufficiency or inaccuracy has been remedied.

Application for registry

Section 8 of the 1894 Act provides:

8. An application for registry of a ship shall be made in the case of individuals by the person requiring to be registered as owner, or by some one or more of the persons so requiring if more than one, or by his or their agent, and in the case of corporations by their agent, and the authority of the agent shall be testified by writing, if appointed by individuals, under the hands of the appointers, and, if appointed by a corporation, under the common seal of that corporation.

Declaration of ownership

An important prerequisite to registration as a British ship under the Act is that the applicant for registry has to make a declaration of his ownership and the entitlement of the ship to be registered as a British ship. Section 9 of the 1894 Act[43] provides:

9. A person shall not be entitled to be registered as owner of a ship or of a share therein until he, or in the case of a corporation the person authorised by this Act to make declarations on behalf of the corporation, has made and signed a declaration of ownership, referring to the ship as described in the certificate of the surveyor, and containing the following particulars:—

   (i) A statement of his qualification to own a British ship, or in the case of a corporation, of such circumstances of the constitution and business thereof as prove it to be qualified to own a British ship:

  (ii) A statement of the time when and the place where the ship was built, or, if the ship is foreign built, and the time and place of building unknown, a statement that she is foreign built, and that the declarant does not know the time or place of her building; and, in addition thereto, in the case of a foreign ship, a statement of her foreign name, or, in the case of a ship condemned, a statement of the time, place, and court at and by which she was condemned:

 (iii) [Repealed.]

 (iv) A statement of the number of shares in the ship the legal title to which is vested in him or (as the case may be) the corporation, whether alone or jointly with another person or persons

  (v) A declaration that, to the best of his knowledge and belief, a majority interest in the ship is owned by persons qualified to be owners of British ships, and the ship is otherwise entitled to be registered; and

 (vi) In the case of a ship which is for the time being registered under the law of any country outside the United Kingdom, a declaration that, if the ship is still so registered at the time when it becomes registered under this Part of this Act, he will take all reasonable steps to secure the termination of the ship's registration under the law of that country.

In the application of this section to a ship which is not wholly owned by persons qualified to be owners of British ships, paragraph (i) above shall have effect only in relation to persons who are so qualified.

43. As amended by Schedule 1 to the 1988 Act.

Evidence on first registry

Under section 10 of the 1894 Act certain specified documents are required to be produced to the registrar on the first registry of the ship. Section 10 provides:

10.—(1) On the first registry of a ship the following evidence shall be produced in addition to the declaration of ownership:—

(a) in the case of a British-built ship, a builder's certificate, that is to say, a certificate signed by the builder of the ship, and containing a true account of the proper denomination and of the tonnage of the ship, as estimated by him, and of the time when and the place where she was built, and of the name of the person (if any) on whose account the ship was built, and if there has been any sale, the bill of sale under which the ship, or a share therein, has become vested in the applicant for registry:

(b) in the case of a foreign-built ship, the same evidence as in the case of a British-built ship, unless the declarant who makes the declaration of ownership declares that the time and place of her building are unknown to him, or that the builder's certificate cannot be procured, in which case there shall be required only the bill of sale under which the ship, or a share therein, became vested in the applicant for registry:

(c) in the case of a ship condemned by any competent court, an official copy of the condemnation.

(2) The builder shall grant the certificate required by this section, and such person as the Commissioners of Customs recognise as carrying on the business of the builder of a ship, shall be included, for the purposes of this section, in the expression "builder of the ship."

(3) If the person granting a builder's certificate under this section wilfully makes a false statement in that certificate he shall for each offence be liable to a fine not exceeding one hundred pounds.

Certificate of registry

Upon completion of registry, the registrar grants a certificate of registry comprising the particulars respecting the ships which have been entered in the register. Section 14 of the 1894 Act[44] provides: "On completion of the registry of a ship, the registrar shall grant a certificate of registry comprising the particulars respecting her entered in the register in pursuance of section 11 of this Act."

The certificate is in the form prescribed in Part II of Schedule 1 to the 1894 Act (see section 65). By section 64 of that Act, a certificate of registry is admissible in evidence and by section 695 it is evidence of the matters stated in it. A fee is payable upon registration under the Act.

Prima facie evidence of nationality

The certificate of registry is *prima facie* evidence that the ship in respect of which it is issued is a British ship, but this presumption can be rebutted by evi-

---

44. As amended by Schedule 1 to the 1988 Act.

dence that the vessel is in fact owned by a person not qualified to own a British ship: *R.* v. *Bjornsen.*[45]

Not a document of title

The certificate of registry is an important document, and although it is evidence of title, it is not a document of title. In this respect it is of course different from a land certificate issued to an owner of registered land. It is by section 15(1) of the 1894 Act to be used: "only for the lawful navigation of the ship, and shall not be subject to detention by reason of any title, lien, charge, or interest whatever had or claimed by any owner, mortgagee, or other person to, on, or in the ship."

Under section 15(2) a person who refuses without reasonable cause to deliver up the certificate of registry to the person entitled to custody of it on request is liable to be summoned before a court to explain himself and may be subject to a fine if he has no sufficient explanation for his behaviour. That section provides:

If any person, whether interested in the ship or not, refuses on request to deliver up the certificate of registry when in his possession or under his control to the person entitled to the custody thereof for the purposes of the lawful navigation of the ship, or to any registrar, officer of customs, or other person entitled by law to require such delivery, any justice by warrant under his hand and seal, or any court capable of taking cognizance of the matter, may summon the person so refusing to appear before the justice or court, and to be examined touching such refusal, and unless it is proved to the satisfaction of such justice or court that there was reasonable cause for such refusal, the offender shall be liable to a fine . . . but if it is shown to the justice or the court that the certificate is lost, the person summoned shall be discharged, and the justice or the court shall certify that the certificate of registry is lost.

The High Court in the exercise of its jurisdiction under section 20(2)(a) of the Supreme Court Act 1981 also has jurisdiction to order the delivery up of a certificate of registry to the owners of a ship or to the court itself.

Thus in *Wiley* v. *Crawford & Fenwick*[46] the plaintiff was the owner and master of the ship *Pacific* which was about to sail to Spain and the defendant, who had a claim in respect of another ship, threatened to arrest. The plaintiff agreed to deposit the certificate of registry for five days in order to secure the ship not sailing. Before the five days had elapsed the plaintiff demanded the return of the certificate of registry, which the defendant refused. In an action by the plaintiff for its return, the court held that as a certificate of registry may not be pledged or used for any purpose other than the navigation of the ship, the deposit was illegal and void and the defendant was not therefore entitled to detain the certificate.

Similarly, in *The "Barbara"*[47] a person who was detaining the certificate of registry was ordered to deliver it up to the court which was selling the ship in a

---

45. (1865) 10 Cox C.C. 74.
46. (1861) 1 B. & S. 253.
47. (1802) 4 C.Rob. 2.

bottomry action. In *The "Frances"*[48] it was held that the court will not interfere in order to give possession of the certificate of registry to a person whose title to be considered as the registered owner is subject to doubt.

In *Gibson* v. *Ingo*[49] it was held that a master who was dismissed had no lien on the certificate of registry for wages or disbursements (although he would of course have a maritime lien on the ship herself). This is the case whether or not the master is also a co-owner.[50]

Neither does a shipbroker have a lien on the certificate of registry for advances to the owner.[51]

A vendor of a ship with a covenant for title retains after sale such interest in the certificate of registry as will enable him to sustain a suit for delivery against a party unlawfully detaining it, in order to fulfil his contract and defend himself in an action brought against him on the covenant.[52]

In *Arkle* v. *Henzell*[53] the majority owner of shares in a ship had management of her and required the master, who was also a part-owner, to give up the certificate of registry of the ship. He gave no reason and the ship was at that time lying in the port of discharge without having completed discharging. It was held that in refusing to give up the certificate of registry the master had reasonable cause as he had not been told he was to be dismissed and while he continued to be master he was the proper person to have custody of it.

New certificates

A new certificate may be granted by the registrar in the following circumstances:

(1) Upon delivery up of the old certificate—section 17 of the 1894 Act provides: "The registrar of the port of registry of a ship may, with the approval of the Commissioners of Customs [and Excise], and on the delivery up to him of the certificate of registry of a ship, grant a new certificate in lieu thereof."

(2) Where the certificate has been mislaid, lost or destroyed. Section 18 of the 1894 Act[54] provides:

18.—(1) In the event of the certificate of registry of a ship being mislaid, lost, or destroyed, the registrar of her port of registry shall grant a new certificate of registry in lieu of her original certificate.

(2) If—

(a) the port where the ship is at the time of the event (or, as the case may be, where it first arrives thereafter) is a port in a country outside the British Islands, and

---

48. (1820) 2 Dods. 420.
49. (1847) 6 Hare 112.
50. See *The "St. Olaf"* (1876) 3 Asp.M.L.C. 268.
51. See *Gibson* v. *Ingo* (*supra*).
52. See *Gibson* v. *Ingo* (*supra*).
53. (1858) 8 El.& Bl. 828.
54. As amended by Schedule 1 to the 1988 Act.

    (b) the master of the ship, or some other person having knowledge of the facts of the case, makes a declaration before the appropriate person stating—
        (i) the facts of the case, and
        (ii) the names and descriptions of the registered owners of the ship to the best of the declarant's knowledge and belief,
the appropriate person may thereupon grant a provisional certificate containing a statement of the circumstances under which it is granted.

    (3) The provisional certificate shall within ten days after the first subsequent arrival of the ship at her port of discharge in the United Kingdom, where she is registered in the United Kingdom, or in the British possession in which she is registered, or where she is registered at a port of registry established by Order in Council under this Act at that port, be delivered up to the registrar of her port of registry, and the registrar shall thereupon grant the new certificate of registry; and if the master without reasonable cause fails to deliver up the provisional certificate within the ten days aforesaid, he shall be liable to a fine not exceeding fifty pounds.

    (4) In this section "the appropriate person", in relation to a port in a country outside the British Islands, means—
    (a) any British consular officer within whose consular district the port lies, or
    (b) where Her Majesty's Government in the United Kingdom is represented in that country by a High Commissioner, any member of the High Commissioner's official staff nominated by him for the purposes of this Part of this Act, or
    (c) where that country is a colony, the Governor of the colony or any person appointed by him for those purposes;
and in this subsection "High Commissioner" includes an acting High Commissioner and "Governor" includes an acting Governor.

The certificate is required to be given up to the registrar where the ship is either actually or constructively[55] lost, taken by the enemy, burnt, or broken up or ceases to be a British ship. Section 21 of the 1894 Act [56] provides:

21.—(1) In the event of a registered ship being actually or constructively lost, taken by the enemy, burnt, or broken up, or
    (a) ceasing to be entitled to be registered (whether because a majority interest in the ship is no longer owned by persons qualified to be owners of British ships or for any other reason), or
    (b) becoming registered, otherwise than under this Part of this Act, in the United Kingdom,
every registered owner of the ship or any share in the ship shall, immediately on obtaining knowledge of the event, if no notice thereof has already been given to the registrar, give notice thereof to the registrar at her port of registry, and that registrar shall make an entry thereof in the register and the registry of the ship shall terminate forthwith.

    (2) Except where the ship's certificate of registry is lost or destroyed, the master of the ship shall, as soon as practicable after the event, deliver up the certificate—
    (a) to the registrar of the ship's port of registry, or
    (b) if the port where the ship is at the time of the event (or, as the case may be, where it first arrives thereafter) is a port in a country outside the British Islands, to the appropriate person (as defined by section 18(4) of this Act);
and any person receiving a certificate in pursuance of paragraph (b) above shall forthwith forward it to the registrar of the ship's port of registry.

55. The word has the same meaning as in section 60 of the Marine Insurance Act 1906, *per* Swinfen Eady L.J. in *Manchester Ship Canal Co.* v. *Horlock* [1914] 2 Ch. 199 (C.A.) at p. 208.
56. As amended by Schedule 1 to the 1988 Act.

(3) If any such owner or master fails, without reasonable cause, to comply with this section, he shall for each offence be liable to a fine not exceeding [one hundred pounds].

(4) The registry of a registered ship shall also terminate if—

    (a) the owner of the ship gives notice to the registrar of the ship's port of registry that he desires to terminate the ship's registry, and

    (b) the registrar records the giving of that notice in the register.

(5) Where the registry of a ship terminates by reason of—

    (a) any notice given in pursuance of subsection (4) of this section, or

    (b) any direction given by the Secretary of State under section 7(5) of the Merchant Shipping Act 1988 (power to direct removal from register in certain cases),

subsections (2) and (3) of this section shall have effect in relation to the delivering up and forwarding of the ship's certificate of registry as if the giving of that notice or direction were the event referred to in subsection (2).

(6) Where the registry of a ship terminates—

    (a) under subsection (1) or (4) of this section, or

    (b) as mentioned in subsection (5)(b) of this section,

the termination of its registry shall not affect any entry made in the register so far as relating to any undischarged registered mortgage, or any existing certificate of mortgage, of that ship or of any share in it.

(7) Subsection (6) of this section shall not apply to an entry in the register in a case where—

    (a) the mortgage in question becomes registered under Part II of the Merchant Shipping Act 1988, or

    (b) the registrar is satisfied that every person appearing on the register to be interested as a mortgagee under the mortgage in question has consented to the entry ceasing to have effect.

Provisional certificates

Where a ship becomes a British ship abroad, there is provision for a provisional certificate to be issued which lasts for three months or until the ship arrives at a port where there is a registrar, whichever first occurs. Section 22 of the 1894 Act[57] provides:

Provisional certificate for ship becoming entitled to be registered while abroad

22.—(1) If a ship becomes entitled to be registered while at a port in a country outside the British Islands, then (subject to the following provisions of this section) the appropriate person (as defined by section 18(4) of this Act) may, on the application of the master of the ship, grant to him a provisional certificate stating the matters specified in subsection (2) of this section, and shall forward a copy of the certificate at the first convenient opportunity to the Registrar-General of Shipping and Seamen.

(2) Those matters are—

    (a) the name of the ship;

    (b) the time and place of the purchase of the ship and the names of the purchasers; and

    (c) the best particulars respecting the tonnage, build and description of the ship which the person granting the certificate is able to obtain.

---

57. As amended by Schedule 1 to the 1988 Act.

(3) No provisional certificate shall be granted by any person under this section unless he is satisfied that an application under section 8 of this Act for registry of the ship has been made or is intended.

(4) A provisional certificate shall have the effect of a certificate of registry until—

(a) the expiration of three months from its date, or

(b) the ship's arrival at a port where there is a registrar,

whichever happens first, and shall then cease to be of any effect.

(5) Where a provisional certificate has been granted for a ship under this section, no further provisional certificate shall be so granted for the ship within one year from the date of that certificate except with the consent of the Secretary of State.

Fishing vessels

A separate scheme for the registration of fishing vessels is provided by Part II of the Merchant Shipping Act 1988.

The provisions of this Part of the 1988 Act are quite different from the provisions of Part I of the Act concerning registration under Part I of the Merchant Shipping Act 1894.

Whereas registration under Part I of the 1894 Act has, by the new provisions in Part I of the 1988 Act, been made voluntary, more open and less restrictive as to the ships entitled to be registered as British ships, the provisions for registration of fishing vessels are very restrictive and are compulsory where the vessel fishes for profit. In particular, not only does the beneficial interest in the fishing vessel have to be considered, and in the case of corporate ownership, the beneficial ownership of the shares in the company and the identity of its directors, but the managers and operators and charterers must be qualified persons and the vessel must be managed and its operations directed and controlled from within the United Kingdom. There is even power in the Secretary of State to order an investigation by an inspector as to the eligibility of a vessel to be registered as a British fishing vessel.

The two schemes of registration are mutually exclusive, and a fishing vessel may no longer be registered under Part I of the 1894 Act.

"Fishing vessel" is defined by section 12(1) as meaning: "a vessel for the time being used (or, in the context of an application for registration, intended to be used) for or in connection with fishing for sea fish, other than a vessel used (or intended to be used) for fishing otherwise than for profit."

In order to clear up one difficulty of construction that had arisen elsewhere in the Merchant Shipping Acts concerning such a definition of a fishing vessel, section 12(2) of the 1988 Act declares that: "a vessel for the time being used (or intended to be used) wholly for the purpose of conveying persons wishing to fish for pleasure is not a fishing vessel for the purposes of [Part II of the 1988 Act]."

A wide definition of beneficial ownership is provided by section 12(4) which states:

For the purpose of this Part the beneficial ownership of a fishing vessel shall be determined by reference to every beneficial interest in that vessel, however arising (whether held by a trustee or nominee or arising under a contract or otherwise), other than an interest held by any person as mortgagee.[58]

Eligibility for registration

The restrictive provisions for the eligibility of a fishing vessel to be registered as a British fishing vessel are set out in sections 14 and 15 of the 1988 Act which provide as follows:

Eligibility for registration as British fishing vessel

14.—(1) Subject to subsections (3) and (4), a fishing vessel shall only be eligible to be registered as a British fishing vessel if—
  (a) the vessel is British-owned;
  (b) the vessel is managed, and its operations are directed and controlled, from within the United Kingdom; and
  (c) any charterer, manager or operator of the vessel is a qualified person or company.
  (2) For the purposes of subsection (1)(a) a fishing vessel is British-owned if—
  (a) the legal title to the vessel is vested wholly in one or more qualified persons or companies; and
  (b) the vessel is beneficially owned—
    (i) as to not less than the relevant percentage of the property in the vessel, by one or more qualified persons, or
    (ii) wholly by a qualified company or companies, or
    (iii) by one or more qualified companies and, as to not less than the relevant percentage of the remainder of the property in the vessel, by one or more qualified persons.
  (3) The Secretary of State may by regulations specify further requirements which must be satisfied in order for a fishing vessel to be eligible to be registered as a British fishing vessel, being requirements imposed—
  (a) in connection with the implementation of any of the requirements specified in subsection (1)(a) to (c), or
  (b) in addition to the requirements so specified,
and appearing to the Secretary of State to be appropriate for securing that such a vessel has a genuine and substantial connection with the United Kingdom.
  (4) Where, in the case of any fishing vessel, the Secretary of State is satisfied that—
  (a) the vessel would be eligible to be registered as a British fishing vessel but for the fact that any particular individual, or (as the case may be) each of a number of particular individuals, is not a British citizen (and is accordingly not a qualified person), and
  (b) it would be appropriate to dispense with the requirement of British citizenship in the case of that individual or those individuals, in view of the length of time he has or they have resided in the United Kingdom and been involved in the fishing industry of the United Kingdom,
the Secretary of State may determine that that requirement should be so dispensed with; and, if he does so, the vessel shall, so long as paragraph (a) above applies to it and any

---

58. This may be compared with the definition applicable to Part I of the 1894 Act by section 57 of that Act, which provides: "The expression 'beneficial interest', where used in this Part of this Act, includes interests arising under contract and other equitable interests."

such determination remains in force, be treated for the purposes of this Part as eligible to be registered as a British fishing vessel.

(5) Where any share in a vessel is beneficially owned jointly by persons not all of whom are qualified persons or companies, then, for the purposes of this section, the whole of that share shall be treated as beneficially owned by persons who are not qualified persons or companies.

(6) For the purpose of determining whether a fishing vessel is eligible to be registered as a British fishing vessel, the Secretary of State may, if he thinks fit, appoint a person—

    (a) to investigate the eligibility of the vessel to be so registered, and

    (b) to make a report of his conclusions to the Secretary of State;

and any person so appointed shall, for the purpose of conducting the investigation, have the powers conferred on an inspector by the provisions of section 27 of the Merchant Shipping Act 1979 (other than paragraphs (d) to (h) of subsection (1) of that section).

(7) In this section—

"qualified company" means a company which satisfies the following conditions, namely—

    (a) it is incorporated in the United Kingdom and has its principal place of business there;

    (b) at least the relevant percentage of its shares (taken as a whole), and of each class of its shares, is legally and beneficially owned by one or more qualified persons or companies; and

    (c) at least the relevant percentage of its directors are qualified persons;

"qualified person" means—

    (a) a person who is a British citizen resident and domiciled in the United Kingdom, or

    (b) a local authority in the United Kingdom; and

"the relevant percentage" means 75 per cent. or such greater percentage (which may be 100 per cent.) as may for the time being be prescribed.

Grant or refusal of applications for registration of fishing vessels

15.—(1) If, on an application for the registration of a fishing vessel made in accordance with regulations under section 13, the Secretary of State is satisfied—

    (a) that the vessel is eligible to be registered as a British fishing vessel, and

    (b) that any relevant requirements of any such regulations have been complied with in relation to the vessel,

he shall (subject to subsection (2)) cause the vessel to be registered as a British fishing vessel.

(2) Notwithstanding that the Secretary of State is so satisfied, he may refuse any such application if he is satisfied that there is not in force in respect of the vessel any certificate required to be so in force by virtue of section 4 of the Fishing Vessels (Safety Provisions) Act 1970 (prohibition on going to sea without appropriate certificates).

(3) If, on any such application, the Secretary of State is not satisfied as mentioned in subsection (1), he shall refuse the application.

There is provision in the 1988 Act for termination of registration by the Secretary of State after notice served on the owner, charterer, manager or operator in connection with her eligibility or certification. Where registration is so terminated the vessel cannot be registered again unless the earlier default was due to inadvertence or the vessel has been sold at arm's length or the Secretary of State consents.

Sections 16 and 17 of the 1988 Act provide as follows:

Termination of registration where vessel is not eligible for registration or is not certificated

16.—(1) If for any reason it appears to the Secretary of State that a registered vessel may no longer be eligible to be registered as a British fishing vessel, he may by notice served on—

(a) the owner of the vessel, or

(b) any charterer, manager or operator of the vessel,

require that person, at such time or times as may be specified in the notice—

(i) to produce to the Secretary of State such documents or descriptions of documents specified in the notice, and

(ii) to furnish to him, in such form as may be specified in the notice, such accounts, estimates, returns or other information (of whatever nature) specified in the notice,

as the Secretary of State thinks necessary for the purpose of determining whether the vessel is eligible to be so registered.

(2) In a case where the owner of a registered vessel is a company, subsection (1) shall apply to any person holding any shares in the company as it applies to the company.

(3) Where the Secretary of State has served a notice under subsection (1) with respect to any vessel, then, unless he has become satisfied that the vessel is eligible to be registered as a British fishing vessel—

(a) he shall, as soon as practicable after the end of the period of 30 days beginning with the date of service of that notice, serve a notice under subsection (6) on the owner of the vessel, and

(b) the vessel's registration shall terminate by virtue of this subsection at the relevant time.

(4) Where it appears to the Secretary of State that there is not in force in respect of any registered vessel any such certificate as is mentioned in section 15(2), he may by notice served on the owner of the vessel require the vessel to be presented for a survey under the fishing vessel survey rules within the period of 30 days beginning with the date of service of the notice.

(5) If the vessel is not presented for such a survey within that period—

(a) the Secretary of State shall serve a notice under subsection (6) on the owner of the vessel, and

(b) the vessel's registration shall terminate by virtue of this subsection at the relevant time.

(6) A notice under this subsection is a notice stating—

(a) that the Secretary of State is not satisfied that the vessel in question is eligible to be registered as a British fishing vessel, or

(b) that the vessel has not been presented for a survey as required by a notice under subsection (4),

as the case may be, and that the vessel's registration will accordingly terminate at the relevant time by virtue of subsection (3) or (5).

(7) In this section "the relevant time", in relation to a notice under subsection (6), means the end of the period of 14 days beginning with the date of service of that notice.

Consequences of termination of registration by virtue of s. 16

17.—(1) Where the registration of any vessel has terminated by virtue of section 16(3) or (5), then, without prejudice to the operation of any other provision of this Part of this Act or of regulations under section 13, the vessel shall not again be registered as a British fishing vessel unless—

(a) the Secretary of State is satisfied that the earlier failure of the vessel to be eligible to be so registered or (as the case may be) to be presented for a survey was due to inadvertence, and (in the latter case) that the vessel has since been presented for a survey, or

(b) the Secretary of State consents to the vessel being so registered, or

(c) in the case of a vessel whose registration terminated by virtue of section 16(3), the Secretary of State is satisfied that the vessel has been disposed of by its former registered owner by means of a transaction at arm's length and that no person who for the time being is a relevant owner of the vessel was a relevant owner of it at the time when its registration terminated.

(2) In subsection (1)(a) "survey" means a survey under the fishing vessel survey rules.

(3) For the purposes of subsection (1)(c) a person is a relevant owner of a vessel at any time if at that time—

(a) the legal title to the vessel or any share in it is vested in that person, or

(b) the vessel or any share in it is beneficially owned by that person, or

(c) any shares in a company falling within paragraph (a) or (b) above are legally or beneficially owned by that person,

whether vested in, or (as the case may be) owned by, that person alone or together with any other person or persons.

Transfer of ownership

It is necessary in considering the question of the transfer of ownership in ships to distinguish between registered ships and unregistered ships. Whereas no special form is necessary to transfer ownership in an unregistered ship, a registered ship has to be transferred by bill of sale which has itself to be registered. As stated above, a ship is "goods" within the meaning of the sale of goods legislation, and it is, therefore, necessary to see how the provisions of the Sale of Goods Act 1979 relating to the transfer of property and title apply to the sale of a ship, before turning to consider the further requirements of the Merchant Shipping Acts.

The Sale of Goods Act 1979

UNREGISTERED SHIPS

Property in an unregistered ship is transferred by any legal means of transferring property in a chattel. A transfer or assignment of any ship or vessel or share therein is not a bill of sale within the meaning of the Bills of Sale Acts 1878 and 1882, and, therefore, does not have to be registered under those Acts.[59]

An agreement to sell a vessel may be enforced by specific performance in an appropriate case.[60]

REGISTERED SHIPS

Where the ship is a registered vessel, although it is possible that property in the ship may pass under section 18(1) of the Sale of Goods Act 1979 upon signing a

---

59. *Union Bank of London* v. *Lenanton* (1878) L.R. 3 C.P.D. 243 (C.A.).
60. See *Behnke* v. *Bede Shipping Co.* [1927] 1 K.B. 649 and *Lloyd del Pacifico* v. *Board of Trade* (1930) 35 Ll.L.Rep. 217.

memorandum of agreement and payment of the deposit, before formal title is transferred by execution of the bill of sale, the normal rule is that the parties intend property to pass upon execution of the bill of sale, payment of the balance of the price and physical delivery of the ship.

In *Naamlooze Vennootschap Stoomvaart Maatschappij Vredobert* v. *European Shipping Co.*[61] the House of Lords held that where five British ships were being sold to foreigners, no property passed to the purchasers upon execution of the contract, property being intended to pass when the ships had been taken off the British register and put on to the register of the foreign flag and the fact that the contract stated the purchasers "to buy now" did not indicate that the contract was a "sale" as opposed to an "agreement to sell" within the meaning of the Sale of Goods Act.

That decision was followed and applied to a Norwegian Saleform contract by the High Court of Kenya in *The "Despina Pontikos."*[62]

NEWBUILDINGS

The governing rule in relation to newbuildings, as much as to ships already built, is that property passes when it is intended to pass: see section 17 of the Sale of Goods Act 1979.

As far as the ship herself is concerned, although the general rule is that property will remain in the builder until the ship has been completed,[63] nevertheless, it will often be the case that property will be intended to pass before completion when the construction has reached a particular stage.

In each case it will be a question of fact whether the stage of completion has been reached at which the parties intended property to pass. Thus in *Wood* v. *Bell*[64] property was held to have passed where the purchaser's name was stamped on a plate on the keel but in *Laing* v. *Barclay, Curle & Co. Ltd.*[65] it was held that a provision in the contract, that delivery was not considered completed until trials, prevented property from passing.

In *Seath* v. *Moore*[66] Lord Watson said[67]:

. . . where it appears to be the intention, or in other words the agreement, of the parties to a contract for building a ship, that at a particular stage of its construction, the vessel, so far as then finished, shall be appropriated to the contract of sale, the property of the vessel as soon as it has reached that stage of completion will pass to the purchaser, and subsequent additions made to the chattel thus vested in the purchaser will, *accessione*, become his property.

61. (1926) 25 Ll.L.Rep. 210 (H.L.).
62. [1974] 3 A.L.R.Comm. 329 (Sheridan J.).
63. See *Clarke* v. *Spence* (1836) 4 A. & E. 448.
64. (1856) 6 E. & B. 355.
65. [1908] A.C. 35.
66. (1886) 11 App.Cas. 350.
67. *Ibid.* at p. 380.

He went on to consider some of the authorities[68] and continued[69]:

It appears to me to be the result of these decisions that such an intention or agreement ought, in the absence of any circumstances pointing to a different conclusion, to be inferred from a provision in the contract to the effect that an instalment of the price shall be paid at a particular stage, coupled with the fact that the instalment has been duly paid and that until the vessel reached that stage the execution of the work was regularly inspected by the purchaser, or someone on his behalf. I do not think it is indispensable in order to sustain that inference that there shall be a stipulation for payment of an instalment in the original contract, or that the stipulated payment shall have been actually paid. The absence of these considerations, which are in themselves of great importance, might in my opinion, be supplied by other circumstances.

Later he said[70]:

There is another principle which appears to me to be deducible from these authorities and to be in itself sound, and that is, that materials provided by the builder and portions of the fabric, whether wholly or partly finished, although intended to be used in the execution of the contract, cannot be regarded as appropriated to the contract, or as "sold", unless they had been affixed to or in a reasonable sense made part of the corpus.

In *Re Blyth Shipbuilding & Dry Docks Co. Ltd.*[71] a question arose as to whether material in a yard which had been approved by a surveyor, but not yet incorporated into the ship, had passed to the purchaser. In holding that it had not, Sargant L.J. said[72]:

For appropriation I think there must be some definite act, such as the affixing of the property to the vessel itself, or some definite agreement between the parties which amounts to an assent to the property in the materials passing from the builders to the purchasers.

Similarly in *Reid* v. *MacBeth & Gray*[73] where a contract provided that materials were to become the property of the purchaser when brought into the shipyard, it was held that although certain material had been designated by Lloyd's inspection certificates as intended for a particular ship, property in them did not pass to the purchaser as they had not yet entered the yard.

The Merchant Shipping Acts

TRANSFER BY BILL OF SALE

Where a ship is registered under Part I of the Merchant Shipping Act 1894, a transfer of the ship or any share therein (when disposed of to a person qualified to own a British ship) must be by bill of sale.

Section 24 of the 1894 Act[74] provides as follows:

68. *Woods* v. *Russell* (1822) 5 B. & Ald. 942; *Clarke* v. *Spence* (1836) 4 A. & E. 448; *Laidler* v. *Burlinson* (1837) 2 M. & W. 602; *Wood* v. *Bell* (1856) 6 E. & B. 355.
69. *Ibid.* at p. 380.
70. *Ibid.* at p. 381.
71. [1926] Ch. 494.
72. *Ibid.* at p. 518.
73. [1904] A.C. 223.
74. As amended by Schedule 1 to the 1988 Act.

24.—(1) Any transfer of—
   (a) a registered ship, or
   (b) a share in any such ship,
shall be effected by a bill of sale, unless the transfer will result in a majority interest in the ship no longer being owned by persons qualified to be owners of British ships.

(2) The bill of sale shall contain such description of the ship as is contained in the surveyor's certificate, or some other description sufficient to identify the ship to the satisfaction of the registrar, and shall be executed by the transferor in the presence of, and be attested by, a witness or witnesses.

A vessel which has been "constructively lost" within the meaning of section 21 and whose registry is therefore considered closed may be transferred without a bill of sale.[75]

DECLARATION OF TRANSFER

The transferee of a vessel registered under Part I of the 1894 Act is not entitled to be registered as the owner until he has made a declaration of transfer stating his qualification to own a British ship, and that to the best of his knowledge and belief, a majority interest in the ship is owned by persons qualified to own a British ship and the ship is otherwise entitled to be registered.

Section 25 of the 1894 Act[76] provides as follows:

25. Where a registered ship or a share therein is transferred in accordance with section 24(1) of this Act, the transferee shall not be entitled to be registered as owner thereof until he, or, in the case of a corporation, the person authorised by this Act to make declarations on behalf of the corporation, has made and signed a declaration (in this Act called a declaration of transfer) referring to the ship and containing—
   (a) a statement of the qualification of the transferee to own a British ship, or if the transferee is a corporation, of such circumstances of the constitution and business thereof as prove it to be qualified to own a British ship; and
   (b) a declaration that, to the best of his knowledge and belief, a majority interest in the ship is owned by persons qualified to be owners of British ships, and the ship is otherwise entitled to be registered.

In the application of this section to a ship which is not wholly owned by persons qualified to be owners of British ships, paragraph (a) above shall have effect only in relation to persons who are so qualified.

Such a declaration should be made in the prescribed form[77] and before a registrar of British ships, a justice of the peace, a commissioner for oaths or a British consular officer.[78]

PRODUCTION TO THE REGISTRAR

The bill of sale and the declaration of transfer have to be produced to the registrar at the port of registry in order that the transfer may be entered in the regis-

---

75. See *Manchester Ship Canal Co.* v. *Horlock* [1914] 2 Ch. 199 (C.A.).
76. As amended by Schedule 1 to the 1988 Act.
77. See section 65 and Part II of Schedule 1.
78. Section 61.

ter by the registrar who also endorses on the bill of sale the date and time of the entry in the register. It is important to observe that bills of sale are entered in the register in the order in which they are produced to the registrar.

Section 26 of the 1894 Act[79] provides as follows:

26.—(1) Every bill of sale for the transfer of a registered ship or of a share therein, when duly executed, shall be produced to the registrar of her port of registry, with the declaration of transfer, and the registrar shall thereupon enter in the register the name of the transferee as owner of the ship or share, and shall endorse on the bill of sale the fact of that entry having been made, with the day and hour thereof.

(2) Bills of sale of a ship or of a share therein shall be entered in the register in the order of their production to the registrar.

The registrar has power under section 60 of the 1894 Act, with the consent of the Commissioner of Customs and Excise, to dispense with the declaration or other evidence required subject to such terms as he thinks fit.

Transfer by operation of law

Property in a ship can of course pass by operation of law in the same way as any personalty. This will usually be upon the death or insolvency of the registered owner, and will be subject to the general law relating to inheritance and bankruptcy.

DECLARATION OF TRANSFER

Where property in a British ship or share therein passes by operation of law other than transfer as above (for example on the death or insolvency of the registered owner) a declaration of transmission has to be made. This should be in the same form (or as near as circumstances permit) to a declaration of transfer, but in addition containing a statement of the manner in which the property has been transmitted. In the case of transfer upon insolvency the declaration should be accompanied by proof of title of the claimant under the insolvency and, in the case of transfer on death, the instrument of representation. Upon receipt of the appropriate documents, the registrar makes an entry in the register accordingly.

Section 27 of the 1894 Act[80] provides as follows:

27.—(1) Where the property in a registered ship or share therein is transmitted to [any person by any lawful means other than a transfer under section 24 of this Act and a majority interest in the ship remains in the ownership of persons qualified to be owners of British ships]

(a) That person shall authenticate the transmission by making and signing a declaration (in this Act called a declaration of transmission) identifying the ship and

---

79. As amended by Schedule 1 to the 1988 Act.
80. As amended by Schedule 1 to the 1988 Act.

containing the several statements hereinbefore required to be contained in a declaration of transfer, or as near thereto as circumstances admit, and also a statement of the manner in which and the person to whom the property has been
transmitted.

(b) [Repealed.]

(c) If the transmission is consequent on bankruptcy, the declaration of transmission
shall be accompanied by such evidence as is for the time being receivable in courts
of justice as proof of the title of persons claiming under a bankruptcy.

(d) If the transmission is consequent on death, the declaration of transmission shall
be accompanied by the instrument of representation, or an official extract therefrom.

(2) The registrar, on receipt of the declaration of transmission so accompanied, shall
enter in the register the name of the person entitled under the transmission as owner of
the ship or share the property in which has been transmitted, and, where there is more
than one such person, shall enter the names of all those persons, but those persons, however numerous, shall, for the purpose of the provision of this Act with respect to the
number of persons entitled to be registered as owners, be considered as one person.

SALE BY THE COURT

Where a ship or any share therein is sold by the court, the order of the court
shall contain a declaration vesting in some person named by the court (usually
the Admiralty Marshal) the right to transfer the ship or share who is thereby
entitled to transfer the ship as if he were the registered owner. Every registrar is
obliged to register transfers from that person as if he were the registered owner.

Section 29 of the 1894 Act provides as follows:

29. Where any court, whether under the preceding sections of this Act or otherwise,
order the sale of any ship or share therein, the order of the court shall contain a declaration vesting in some person named by the court the right to transfer that ship or share,
and that person shall thereupon be entitled to transfer the ship or share in the manner
and to the same extent as if he were the registered owner thereof; and every registrar
shall obey the requisition of the person so named in resect of any such transfer to the
same extent as if such person were the registered owner.

Failure or irregularity of registration

It is to be observed that the Act requires both the transfer to be by way of bill of
sale and for the transfer to be registered. Full legal title to a registered ship will
not pass to the transferee unless and until both of these requirements have been
satisfied. Nevertheless, as between the transferor and the transferee, it is the
execution of the instrument of transfer that operates to pass property in the
ship.

The distinction was discussed by Dr Lushington in The *"Spirit Of The
Ocean"* [81] in which he said:

81. (1865) B. & L. 336.

The duty to register the transfer of ownership rests with the vendee, the bill of sale entirely divests title of the vendor. Immediately upon execution of the bill of sale, the vendee becomes entitled to all the benefits of ownership and takes with him all concurrent liabilities. Registration is a record of a fact done—a record of the sale and not the sale itself.

Thus in *Stapleton v. Haymen*,[82] where the assigneee in bankruptcy of the vendor sought to retake possession of a ship from the purchaser who had been refused registration being an infant, it was held that, as between the vendor and his assignees and the vendee, property in a ship passes by bill of sale. Although the transfer is not registered, equitable title passes.

Similarly, in *Sutton v. Buck*[83] it was held that possession of a ship under a transfer which was void for non-registration was sufficient title to maintain an action in trover against a stranger.

Such title, being only equitable, is liable to be defeated by a *bona fide* purchaser for value taking a legal title by registration of a subsequent transfer or mortgage from the registered owner.

Thus in *The "Horlock"*[84] although the vendor had obtained his title by fraud, the purchaser from him (who had registered his title) had no notice of any fraud and the court refused to look behind the register for the purposes of dispossessing the innocent purchaser of his registered title.

Similarly in *The "Eastern Belle"*[85] a shipowner sold certain shares in a ship, but the purchaser neglected to register the sale. The shipowner subsequently mortgaged the whole ship to a third party who had no knowledge of the previous sale of the shares. The mortgage was to secure a balance in excess of the value of the ship. When the purchaser of the sharers came to register them he discovered the mortgage and commenced an action against his co-owner seeking an account and a sale of the ship. The mortgagee intervened and sought release of the ship. The court held that he was entitled to release of the ship.

The equitable title will also be subject to any prior equities affecting the title of the vendor. Thus in *The "Venture"*[86] a resulting trust in favour of a person who had advanced part of the purchase money for a ship was enforced.

On the other hand, where the registration of a vessel has been made or procured by fraud, the court can look behind the register in order to ascertain the true facts.

This is illustrated in three Canadian cases[87] decided under the provisions of the English Merchant Shipping Acts which applied in Canada at the time they were decided.

---

82. (1864) 2 H. & C. 918.
83. (1810) 2 Taunt. 302.
84. (1877) 2 P.D. 243.
85. (1875) 3 Asp.M.L.C. 19.
86. [1908] P. 218 (C.A.).
87. Referred to in Buchan, *Mortgages of Ships—Marine Security in Canada* (Butterworths, 1986).

In *McLean* v. *Grant*,[88] an unregistered vessel was sold by her builder but, because part of the consideration could not be performed, the sale was cancelled and the transfer documents destroyed by agreement between the vendor and the purchaser. However, the purchaser, who had remained in possession of the vessel, proceeded to register her. The court held that the registry having been obtained by fraud was null and void and title remained in the builder.

In *Gibson* v. *Gill*,[89] there was a sale and mortgage back to the vendor of an unregistered steam ferry. The purchaser partially rebuilt the vessel and then registered her without mention of the mortgage. The court held that title in the vessel at the time of registration was in the mortgagee and that the registration was, therefore, fraudulent and void as against him.

In *Robillard* v. *The St. Roch and Charland*,[90] the court went one stage further and held that a purchaser who had been registered as owner but who had knowledge that the vendor, although himself registered as owner, in fact held the vessel for another and had no right to sell her, was not the owner of the vessel, having obtained his title by fraud.

It is not only in cases of fraud that the court will look behind the register in order to ascertain the true position.

In *The "Bineta"*,[91] although a vessel had been sold and the purchaser duly registered as owner, possession was retained by the vendor pending payment of the purchase price. When the purchaser failed to pay the purchase price, the vendor in the exercise of his unpaid seller's lien sold the vessel to a third party. It was held that the third party was entitled to be registered as the owner and the register was ordered to be corrected accordingly.

Similarly, although a person may continue to be named on the register as registered owner, this alone will not be sufficient to make him liable to third parties as owner, where a transfer has in fact taken place.

In *Young* v. *Brander & Dunbar*,[92] owing to the delay of the vendees in producing the necessary documents to the registrar, the legal title remained in the vendors for a period of one month after the sale, during which time repairs to the ship had been ordered by the master under the direction of the vendee. It was held that the vendors were not liable for the repairs, the vendees being strangers to the legal owners with no authority express or implied to bind them.

Again in *M'Iver* v. *Humble, Holland & Williams*[93] a partner defectively conveyed his share in a ship and as a consequence his name remained on the register. Nevertheless, the court held that he was not a partner in fact and was not liable for goods sold and delivered to the ship.

Where the first purchaser fails to register the bill of sale pursuant to section

88. (1840) 3 N.B.R. 50 (C.A.).
89. (1880) 19 N.B.R. 565 (C.A.).
90. (1922) 62 D.L.R. 145.
91. [1966] 2 Lloyd's Rep. 419.
92. (1806) 8 East. 10.
93. (1812) 16 East. 169.

26, nevertheless this failure will not defeat the title of a *bona fide* purchaser from him.[94]

Transmission to unqualified persons

Where a transmission other than by transfer under section 24 of the 1894 Act results in a majority interest no longer being held by persons qualified to be owners of a British ship, the court may order a sale of the ship.

Section 28 of the 1894 Act[95] provides as follows:

28.—(1) Where the property in a registered ship or share therein is transmitted to any person by any lawful means other than a transfer under section 24 of this Act, but as a result a majority interest in the ship no longer remains in the ownership of persons qualified to be owners of British ships, then—

    (a) if the ship is registered in England and Wales or in Northern Ireland, the High Court, or

    (b) if the ship is registered in Scotland, the Court of Session,

may, on an application by or on behalf of that person, order a sale of the property so transmitted and direct that the proceeds of sale, after deducting the expenses of the sale, shall be paid to that person or otherwise as the court direct.

(2) The court may require any evidence in support of the application they think requisite, and may make the order on any terms and conditions they think just, or may refuse to make the order, and generally may act in the case as the justice of the case requires.

(3) Every such application for sale must be made within four weeks after the occurrence of the event on which the transmission has taken place, or within such further time (not exceeding in the whole one year from the date of the occurrence) as the court allow.

(4) If such an application is not made within the time aforesaid, or if the court refuse an order for sale, the ship or share transmitted shall thereupon be subject to forfeiture under this Act.

Power of court to prohibit transfer

An interested person may apply to the court for an order prohibiting for a period of time any dealing with a ship or share and the court has power to grant such an order if it thinks fit and upon such terms as it thinks just.

Section 30 of the 1894 Act[96] provides as follows:

30. Each of the following courts, namely:—

    (a) in England and Wales or in Northern Ireland, the High Court; and

    (b) in Scotland, the Court of Session,

may, if the court think fit (without prejudice to the exercise of any other power of the court), on the application of any interested person make an order prohibiting for a time specified any dealing with a ship or any share therein, and the court may make the order on any terms or conditions they think just, or may refuse to make the order, or may discharge the order when made, with or without costs, and generally may act in the case as the justice of the case requires; and every registrar, without being made a party to the

---

94. See *The "Australia"* (1859) 13 Moo.P.C. 132.
95. As amended by Schedule 1 to the 1988 Act.
96. As amended by Schedule 1 to the 1988 Act.

proceeding, shall on being served with the order or an official copy thereof obey the same.

Registered fishing vessels

Similar provisions apply to the transfer of registered fishing vessels which must be transferred by bill of sale.

Section 19 of the 1988 Act provides as follows:

Transfer of vessel or share by bill of sale

19.—(1) Any transfer of—
  (a) a registered vessel (not being a vessel registered in pursuance of paragraph 2(c) of Schedule 2), or
  (b) a share in any such vessel,
shall be effected by a bill of sale satisfying the requirements specified in subsection (2), unless the transfer will result in the vessel ceasing to be British-owned for the purposes of section 14(1)(a).
  (2) Those requirements are that the bill of sale—
  (a) is in such form as may be prescribed or approved by the Secretary of State; and
  (b) contains a description of the vessel sufficient to identify the vessel to the satisfaction of the Secretary of State.
  (3) Where any such vessel or share has been transferred in accordance with subsection (1), the transferee shall not be registered as owner of the vessel or share unless—
  (a) he has made an application for the purpose in accordance with regulations under section 13 and has produced to the Secretary of State the bill of sale by which the vesssel or share has been so transferred, and
  (b) the Secretary of State is satisfied as mentioned in section 15(1);
and section 15(2) and (3) shall apply in relation to an application under this subsection as they apply in relation to an application for the registration of a fishing vessel.
  (4) If an application under subsection (3) is granted by the Secretary of State, the Secretary of State shall—
  (a) register the bill of sale referred to in paragraph (a) of the subsection by causing the applicant's name to be entered in the register as owner of the vessel or share in question, and
  (b) endorse on the bill of sale the fact that entry has been made, together with the date and time when it was made.
  (5) Bills of sale shall be registered under subsection (4) in the order in which they are produced to the Secretary of State for the purposes of registration.
  (6) If on an application under subsection (3) the Secretary of State is not satisfied that the vessel with respect to which the application is made is eligible to be registered as a British fishing vessel—
  (a) the Secretary of State shall serve a notice under subsection (7) on the owner of the vessel; and
  (b) the vessel's registration shall terminate by virtue of this subsection at the end of the period of 14 days beginning with the date of service of that notice.
  (7) A notice under this subsection is a notice stating—
  (a) that the Secretary of State is not satisfied that the vessel in question is eligible to be registered as a British fishing vessel; and
  (b) that the vessel's registration will accordingly terminate by virtue of subsection (6) at the end of the period referred to in that subsection.

Where a registered fishing vessel or any share therein is transmitted otherwise than by transfer pursuant to section 19 of the 1988 Act, the new owner has to make an application for registry to the Secretary of State.

Section 20 of the 1988 Act provides as follows:

Transmission of property in vessel or share other than under s.19

20.—(1) Where a registered vessel, or a share in a registered vessel, is transmitted to any person by any lawful means other than by a transfer under section 19, that person shall not be registered as owner of the vessel or share unless—

(a) he has made an application for the purpose in accordance with regulations under section 13 and has produced to the Secretary of State such evidence of the transmission as may be prescribed; and

(b) the Secretary of State is satisfied as mentioned in section 15(1);

and section 15(2) and (3) shall apply in relation to an application under this subsection as they apply in relation to an application for the registration of a fishing vessel.

(2) If an application under subsection (1) is granted by the Secretary of State, he shall cause the applicant's name to be entered in the register as owner of the vessel or share.

(3) The preceding provisions of this section shall apply in relation to transmission of the interest of a joint owner in a registered vessel or in a share in any such vessel as they apply in relation to the transmission of any such vessel or share, except that anything required to be done by virtue of subsection (1)(a) shall be done by both or all of the joint owners of the vessel or share.

(4) If on an application under subsection (1) the Secretary of State is not satisfied that the vessel with respect to which the application is made is eligible to be registered as a British fishing vessel—

(a) the Secretary of State shall serve a notice under subsection (5) on the owner of the vessel; and

(b) the vessel's registration shall terminate by virtue of this subsection at the end of the period of 14 days beginning with the date of service of that notice.

(5) A notice under this subsection is a notice stating—

(a) that the Secretary of State is not satisfied that the vessel in question is eligible to be registered as a British fishing vessel; and

(b) that the vessel's registration will accordingly terminate by virtue of subsection (4) at the end of the period referred to in that subsection.

FAILURE TO REGISTER A FISHING VESSEL

The consequences of failing to register a fishing vessel eligible for registration as a British fishing vessel (unless it is registered in some other country) are that it is an offence to fish with the vessel for profit. In addition, although not being entitled to any of the benefits of being a British ship, it is nevertheless subject to liabilities as if it were a British ship.

Section 22 of the 1988 Act provides as follows:

Offences relating to, and liabilities of, unregistered fishing vessels

22.—(1) If any fishing vessel to which this subsection applies fishes for profit—

(a) the skipper, the owner and any charterer of the vessel shall each be guilty of an offence; and

(b) the vessel shall be liable to forfeiture.

(2) Subsection (1) applies to any fishing vessel which is either—
    (a) eligible to be registered under this Part, or
    (b) wholly owned by one or more persons qualified to be owners of British ships for the purposes of Part I of the 1894 Act,
but is neither registered under this Part nor excluded from registration by regulations under section 13 nor registered under the law of any country outside the United Kingdom.

(3) Subsection (1) also applies to any fishing vessel which (notwithstanding that it is not entitled to be so registered) is for the time being registered in the United Kingdom under Part I of the 1894 Act or section 5 of the Merchant Shipping Act 1983 (registration of small ships).

(4) Subject to subsection (8), if any prescribed marks are displayed on a fishing vessel which is not a registered vessel, the skipper, the owner and any charterer of the vessel shall each be guilty of an offence.

(5) If the skipper or owner of a fishing vessel which is not a registered vessel does anything, or permits anything to be done, for the purpose of causing the vessel to appear to be a registered vessel, then (subject to subsection (8))—
    (a) the skipper, the owner and any charterer of the vessel shall each be guilty of an offence; and
    (b) the vessel shall be liable to forfeiture.

(6) Where a fishing vessel is not a British ship and is not registered under the law of any country outside the United Kingdom, but—
    (a) it is eligible to be registered under this Part, or
    (b) it is wholly owned by one or more such persons as are mentioned in subsection (2)(b), or
    (c) (subject to subsection (8)) any prescribed marks are displayed on it,
then (notwithstanding that the vessel is not entitled to any benefits, privileges, advantages or protection usually enjoyed by a British ship) the vessel shall, for the purposes mentioned in subsection (7), be dealt with in the same manner in all respects as if the vessel were a British ship.

(7) Those purposes are—
    (a) the payment of dues, fees or other charges;
    (b) liability to fines and forfeiture; and
    (c) the punishment of offences committed on board the vessel, or by any persons belonging to it.

(8) Where the registration of any vessel has terminated by virtue of any provision of this Part, any prescribed marks displayed on the vessel within the period of 14 days beginning with the date of termination of that registration shall be disregarded for the purposes of subsections (4) to (6).

(9) Subsections (1), (4) and (5)(a) apply to offences falling within those provisions wherever committed.

(10) Section 76 of the 1894 Act (proceedings on forfeiture of ship) shall apply to any vessel liable to forfeiture under this section as it applies to any such ship as is mentioned in subsection (1) of that section.

AIRCRAFT

What is an "aircraft"?

The Paris Convention of 1919 defined aircraft as: "Any machine that can derive support in the atmosphere from the reactions of the air", which is suggested by

Shawcross and Beaumont[97] as now forming part of international cutomary law. There is no statutory definition contained in the Civil Aviation Act 1982 or the Air Navigation Order 1985, although the definition contained in the Air Navigation Orders of 1949 and 1954 as including "all balloons (whether captive or free), kites, gliders, airships and flying machines" is retained by way of the table of general classification in Schedule 1.

Registration

Section 60(3)(a) of the Civil Aviation Act 1982 empowers Her Majesty in Council to make provision as to the registration of aircraft in the United Kingdom. That power has been exercised in the Air Navigation Order 1985 which provides, in Part I, for registration and marking of aircraft.

The provisions regarding the registration of aircraft have more far-reaching implications than the corresponding provisions relating to ships. In particular, subject to certain limited exceptions, an aircraft shall not fly in or over the United Kingdom unless it is registered in some part of the Commonwealth or in a Chicago Convention country or in some other country with a bilateral agreement with the United Kingdom permitting such flight.

Article 3 of the Air Navigation Order 1985 provides as follows:

3.—(1) An aircraft shall not fly in or over the United Kingdom unless it is registered in:

    (a) some part of the Commonwealth; or

    (b) a Contracting State; or

    (c) some other country in relation to which there is in force an agreement between Her Majesty's Government in the United Kingdom and the Government of that country which makes provision for the flight over the United Kingdom of aircraft registered in that country:

Provided that:

    (i) a glider may fly unregistered, and shall be deemed to be registered in the United Kingdom for the purposes of articles 13, 14, 19 and 32 of this Order, on any flight which—

        (a) begins and ends in the United Kingdom without passing over any other country, and

        (b) is not for the purpose of public transport or aerial work;

    (ii) any aircraft may fly unregistered on any flight which:

        (a) begins and ends in the United Kingdom without passing over any other country, and

        (b) is in accordance with the "B Conditions" set forth in Schedule 2 to this Order;

    (iii) this paragraph shall not apply to any kite or captive balloon.

(2) If an aircraft flies over the United Kingdom in contravention of paragraph (1) of this article in such manner or circumstances that if the aircraft had been registered in the United Kingdom an offence against this Order or any regulations made thereunder would have been committed, the like offence shall be deemed to have been committed in respect of that aircraft.

---

97. *Air Law* (4th ed., Butterworths, 1977).

The Civil Aviation Authority maintains a register of United Kingdom aircraft in which it records the name and address of every person entitled as owner to a legal interest in the aircraft or any share therein, the make and type of aircraft and its serial number. Also recorded is the assigned registration mark of four capital letters, which have to be displayed on the aircraft prefixed with the nationality mark "G"[98] and a hyphen, and the number of the registration certificate. Where the aircraft is chartered by demise, the name and address of the demise charterer is also recorded in the register.

In order to obtain registration an application has to be made in writing to the Civil Aviation Authority giving particulars and evidence of the aircraft's details and ownership.

The categories of persons qualified to hold a legal or beneficial interest by way of ownership in an aircraft registered in the United Kingdom or a share therein are similar to the categories provided by the Merchant Shipping Act 1988. Where an unqualified person holds a legal or beneficial interest by way of ownership the Civil Aviation Authority may nevertheless register the aircraft if he resides in the United Kingdom, but the aircraft may not then be used for air transport or aerial work.

Where a qualified person is demise charterer of the aircraft he may apply for its registration notwithstanding that an unqualified person is entitled as owner to a legal or beneficial interest therein.

If an unqualified person becomes entitled as owner to a legal or beneficial interest by way of ownership in the aircraft or any share therein, the registration becomes void and the certificate of registration has to be returned to the Civil Aviation Authority by the registered owner except where there is an undischarged mortgage entered in the register of aircraft mortgages.

There is an overriding power not to cancel the registration if the Civil Aviation Authority considers cancellation would be inexpedient in the public interest.

Articles 4 and 5 of the Air Navigation Order 1985 provide as follows:

4.—(1) The Authority shall be the authority for the registration of aircraft in the United Kingdom and shall keep the register on its premises and may record therein the particulars specified in paragraph (7) of this article in a legible or a non legible form so long as the recording is capable of being reproduced in a legible form.

(2) Subject to the provisions of this article, an aircraft shall not be registered or continue to be registered in the United Kingdom if it appears to the Authority that:

    (a) the aircraft is registered outside the United Kingdom and that such registration does not cease by operation of law upon the aircraft being registered in the United Kingdom; or

    (b) an unqualified person holds any legal or beneficial interest by way of ownership in the aircraft or any share therein; or

    (c) the aircraft could more suitably be registered in some other part of the Commonwealth; or

---

98. The designated mark for United Kingdom aircraft.

(d) it would be inexpedient in the public interest for the aircraft to be or to continue to be registered in the United Kingdom.

(3) The following persons and no others shall be qualified to hold a legal or beneficial interest by way of ownership in an aircraft registered in the United Kingdom or a share therein—

(a) the Crown in right of Her Majesty's Government in the United Kingdom;
(b) Commonwealth citizens;
(c) citizens of the Republic of Ireland;
(d) British protected persons;
(e) bodies incorporated in some part of the Commonwealth and having their principal place of business in any part of the Commonwealth;
(f) firms carrying on business in Scotland.

In this sub-paragraph "firm" has the same meaning as in the Partnership Act 1890.

(4) If an unqualified person residing or having a place of business in the United Kingdom holds a legal or beneficial interest by way of ownership in an aircraft, or a share therein, the Authority, upon being satisfied that the aircraft may otherwise be properly so registered, may register the aircraft in the United Kingdom. The person aforesaid shall not cause or permit the aircraft, while it is registered in pursuance of this paragraph, to be used for the purpose of public transport or aerial work.

(5) If an aircraft is chartered by demise to a person qualified as aforesaid the Authority may, whether or not an unqualified person is entitled as owner to a legal or beneficial interest therein, register the aircraft in the United Kingdom in the name of the charterer upon being satisfied that the aircraft may otherwise be properly so registered, and subject to the provisions of this article the aircraft may remain so registered during the continuation of the charter.

(6) Application for the registration of an aircraft in the United Kingdom shall be made in writing to the Authority, and shall include or be accompanied by such particulars and evidence relating to the aircraft and the ownership and chartering thereof as it may require to enable it to determine whether the aircraft may properly be registered in the United Kingdom and to issue the certificate referred to in paragraph (8) of this Article. In particular, the application shall include the proper description of the aircraft according to column 4 of the "General Classification of Aircraft" set forth in Part A of Schedule 1 to this Order.

(7) Upon receiving an application for the registration of an aircraft in the United Kingdom and being satisfied that the aircraft may properly be so registered, the Authority shall register the aircraft, wherever it may be, and shall include in the register the following particulars:

(a) the number of the certificate;
(b) the nationality mark of the aircraft, and the registration mark assigned to it by the Authority;
(c) the name of the constructor of the aircraft and its designation;
(d) the serial number of the aircraft;
(e) (i) the name and address of every person who is entitled as owner to a legal interest in the aircraft or a share therein,, or, in the case of an aircraft which is the subject of a charter by demise, the name and address of the charterer by demise; and
(ii) in the case of an aircraft registered in pursuance of paragraph (4) or (5) of this article, an indication that it is so registered.

(8) The Authority shall furnish to the person in whose name the aircraft is registered (hereinafter in this article referred to as "the registered owner") a certificate of registration, which shall include the foregoing particulars and the date on which the certificate was issued:

Provided that the Authority shall not be required to furnish a certificate of registration if the registered owner is the holder of an aircraft dealer's certificate granted under this Order who has made to the Authority and has not withdrawn a statement of his intention that the aircraft is to fly only in accordance with the conditions set forth in Part C of Schedule 1 to this Order, and in that case the aircraft shall fly only in accordance with those conditions.

(9) The Authority may grant to any person qualified as aforesaid an aircraft dealer's certificate if it is satisfied that he has a place of business in the United Kingdom for buying and selling aircraft.

(10) Subject to paragraphs (4) and (5) of this article, if at any time after an aircraft has been registered in the United Kingdom an unqualified person becomes entitled to a legal or beneficial interest by way of ownership in the aircraft or a share therein, the registration of the aircraft shall thereupon become void and the certificate of registration shall forthwith be returned by the registered owner to the Authority.

(11) Any person who is the registered owner of an aircraft registered in the United Kingdom shall forthwith inform the Authority in writing of:

(a) any change in the particulars which were furnished to the Authority upon application being made for the registration of the aircraft;

(b) the destruction of the aircraft, or its permanent withdrawal from use;

(c) in the case of an aircraft registered in pursuance of paragraph (5) of this article, the termination of the demise charter.

(12) Any person who becomes the owner of an aircraft registered in the United Kingdom shall within 28 days inform the Authority in writing to that effect.

(13) The Authority may, whenever it appears to it necessary or appropriate to do so for giving effect to this Part of this Order or for bringing up to date or otherwise correcting the particulars entered on the register, amend the register or, if it thinks fit, may cancel the registration of the aircraft, and shall cancel that registration if it is satisfied that there has been a change in the ownership of the aircraft.

(14) The Secretary of State may, by regulations, adapt or modify the foregoing provisions of this article as he deems necessary or expedient for the purpose of providing for the temporary transfer of aircraft to or from the United Kingdom register, either generally or in relation to a particular case or class of cases.

(15) In this article references to an interest in an aircraft do not include references to an interest in an aircraft to which a person is entitled only by virtue of his membership of a flying club and the reference in paragraph (11) of this article to the registered owner of an aircraft includes in the case of a deceased person, his legal personal representative, and in the case of a body corporate which has been dissolved, its successor.

(16) Nothing in this article shall require the Authority to cancel the registration of an aircraft if in its opinion it would be inexpedient in the public interest to do so.

(17) The registration of an aircraft which is the subject of an undischarged mortgage entered in the Register of Aircraft Mortgages kept by the Authority pursuant to an Order in Council made under section 86 of the Civil Aviation Act 1982 shall not become void by virtue of paragraph (10) of this article, nor shall the Authority cancel the registration of such an aircraft pursuant to this article unless all persons shown in the Register of Aircraft Mortgages as mortgagees of that aircraft have consented to the cancellation.

5.—(1) An aircraft (other than an aircraft permitted by or under this Order to fly without being registered) shall not fly unless it bears painted thereon or affixed thereto, in the manner required by the law of the country in which it is registered, the nationality and registration marks required by that law.

(2) The marks to be borne by aircraft registered in the United Kingdom shall comply with Part B of Schedule 1 to this Order.

(3) An aircraft shall not bear any marks which purport to indicate:
  (a) that the aircraft is registered in a country in which it is not in fact registered; or
  (b) that the aircraft is a State aircraft of a particular country if it is not in fact such an aircraft, unless the appropriate authority of that country has sanctioned the bearing of such marks.

3

CREATION, SCOPE, TRANSFER AND DISCHARGE OF MORTGAGES

CREATION

Ships

The requirements of the Merchant Shipping Acts

Just as in Chapter 2 it was observed that the Merchant Shipping Acts provide for a scheme for registration of ownership, so, too, do they provide for a scheme for registration of limited proprietary interest by way of mortgage or charge. Where a registered ship or share therein is mortgaged or charged, in order that the mortgagee may acquire a legal interest and the protection afforded by the 1894 Act, such mortgage or charge must be in the form prescribed by the Act and it must, furthermore, be registered in accordance with the provisions of the Act. Outside the scheme of the Act, however, a British ship may be mortgaged or charged (just as it may be sold) by any method recognised by the law of personal property as effective for such purpose.

It should also be observed, that in the same way as the register of ownership provides only *prima facie* evidence of title, so, too, the register of mortgages is not conclusive as to the existence or validity of the mortgage and the court will, where necessary look behind the register in order to establish the true state of affairs.

In *The "Innisfallen"*[1] an action for restraint was brought by the plaintiff claiming to be a co-owner. The court held that he was in fact a mortgagee and refused to grant the order. Dr Lushington said[2]:

The Plaintiff swears that the arrangement was that, until payment, the vessel should continue the absolute property of his firm, and that the arrangement was insisted upon in lieu of a mortgage, in order that the Plaintiff should, as actual part-owner, exercise control over the movements of the vessel, to which, as mortgagee, he would not be entitled. The result of the Plaintiff's contention would be, that he was not exactly an absolute owner, not exactly a mortgagee, but that for some purposes he was an absolute owner, and for others a mortgagee. Now without going to the length of saying that the Court would in no case recognise such an agreement, so involved, as it were, wheel within

1. (1866) L.R. 1 A. & E. 72.
2. *Ibid.* at p. 76.

wheel, I shall hold that the Court will not recognise it unless it is clearly proved, and definite, and complete in all its parts.

So, too, in *The "Keroula"*[3] shares in a ship were transferred as security for a loan and upon the loan not being repaid, the holders of the shares applied for an order of restraint claiming to be co-owners. The court held that it was entitled to look behind the register to the true nature of the transaction, which it held to be a mortgage or shares and accordingly refused to grant the order.

In *Burgis* v. *Constantine*[4] a mortgage had been executed in blank by the registered owners and then subsequently completed by the mortgagees who had registered it. The court held that the document was a nullity and the registration was therefore void.

The opposite situation arose in a Canadian case,[5] *Grady* v. *White*,[6] where one of two joint purchasers of a vessel was not entitled to be registered as the owner of a British ship (being an American citizen) and he, therefore, registered a mortgage of 32/64th shares. In an action upon the mortgage the court held that the true nature of the transaction was not a mortgage but a joint purchase and ordered the transfer of 32/64th shares instead notwithstanding that this could lead to an action by the Crown for forfeiture.

Registered ships

Section 31(1) of the 1894 Act[7] provides a straightforward scheme as follows:

A registered ship or a share in any such ship, may be made a security for the repayment of a loan or the discharge of any other obligation and on the production of the instrument creating the security (referred to in this Act as a mortgage) the registrar of the ship's port of registry shall record it in the register.

The registrar is not required to register instruments not in the prescribed form. Section 65(2) of the 1894 Act provides:

A registrar shall not be required without the special direction of the Commissioners of Customs and Excise to receive and enter in the register any bill of sale, mortgage or other instrument for the disposal or transfer of any ship or share, or any interest therein which is made in any form other than for the time being required under this part of this Act, or which contains particulars other than those contained in such form . . .

However, although the formal mortgage document must be in the prescribed form for the purposes of registration under the Act, it is standard practice for the detailed stipulations concerning the mortgage to be set out in a separate collateral deed of covenants.[8]

3. (1886) 11 P.D. 92.
4. [1908] 2 K.B. 484 (C.A.).
5. Decided under the English Merchant Shipping Acts which were applicable in Canada at that time.
6. [1930] 1 D.L.R. 838.
7. As amended by Schedule 1 to the 1988 Act.
8. The contents of the deed of covenants are considered further in Chapter 4.

In *The "Benwell Tower"*[9] the question arose as to the validity of this approach. In the course of giving judgment Bruce J. said:

It has consequently been the practice for a long series of years, in cases where ships have been mortgaged, for the detailed stipulations of the mortgage to be contained in a separate instrument . . . I cannot regard the circumstance that the terms regulating the advances were contained in a collateral agreement as unusual in transactions of this kind, or as invalidating the stipulations contained in the collateral agreement. It is true that the directions in the printed note of the form of mortgage issued by the Board of Trade have not been followed, and possibly the Registrar of Shipping might on that ground have refused to register the mortgage, but I cannot treat the mortgage as invalid. I must treat it as a mortgage to secure the account referred to in the registered instrument, and in order to ascertain what items may be properly included in that account, I must have regard to the terms of the letter constituting the collateral agreement.

In spite of the fact that the court permitted reference to the terms of the collateral deed in *The "Benwell Tower"* notwithstanding that no reference thereto was noted in the registered mortgage instrument, it is preferable so as to avoid a court holding that a person dealing with the mortgagor had no notice of the terms of the collateral deed for express reference to be made in the registered mortgage to the collateral deed.

Mortgages are recorded in the register in the order in time in which they are produced to the registrar. Section 31(2) provides:

Mortgages shall be recorded by the registrar in the order in time in which they are produced to him for that purpose, and the registrar shall by memorandum under his hand notify on each mortgage that it has been recorded by him, stating the day and hour of that record.

MISTAKES AS TO NAME OR DESCRIPTION

Notwithstanding the provision of section 47 that "A ship shall not be described by any name other than that by which she is for the time being registered", provided the identity of the ship is ascertained, it is not fatal that the name or description of the ship contained in the mortgage deed does not correspond exactly with the registered name.

In *Bell* v. *Bank of London*[10] the owner and builder of an unfinished ship executed a mortgage in the name of *The City of Bruxelles* whereby 64/64th shares were mortgaged to the bank. Upon completion of the ship she was registered in the name of *The City of Brussels* and on the following day the mortgage was registered. The owner subsequently became bankrupt. In an action by his assignees against the bank, it was held that if prior to registration an owner executes an instrument which if it were executed after registration would pass an interest, then it is sufficient that it is in fact registered. Furthermore, as the mortgage deed was prior to registration the name of the ship in it was irrelevant because her identity was not in dispute.

9. (1895) 8 Asp.M.L.C. 13.
10. (1858) 3 H. & N. 730.

FAILURE TO REGISTER

Where the formal requirements of registration have not been complied with, nevertheless as between the mortgagor and the mortgagee the instrument will be effective. As against third parties, however, the instrument will not provide the mortgagee with the priority afforded by the Act to registered mortgages.

EFFECTIVE DATE OF THE MORTGAGE

A mortgage is valid from the date that it is granted not from the date of registration which only determines priority in relation to other mortgages.[11]

MORTGAGE FROM AN UNREGISTERED OWNER
OF A REGISTERED SHIP

Where, although the ship is registered, the mortgagor is the beneficial owner, but not the registered owner, the mortgage cannot be registered even though it is in the prescribed form.[12]

Unregistered ships

A mortgage of an unregistered ship cannot be registered under the Merchant Shipping Acts and need not be registered under the Bills of Sale Acts. It need not therefore be in any particular form.

Corporations

Mortgages of ships require registration under section 395 of the Companies Act 1985 which provides as follows:

(1) . . . a charge[13] created by a company registered in England and Wales and being a charge to which this section applies[14] is, so far as any security on the company's property or undertaking is conferred by the charge, void against the liquidator and any creditor of the company, unless the prescribed particulars of the charge together with the instrument (if any) by which the charge is created or evidenced, are delivered to or received by the registrar of companies for registration in manner required by this Chapter within 21 days after the date of the charge's creation.

Fishing vessels

The 1988 Act makes provision for the mortgaging of registered fishing vessels. These provisions largely mirror the provisions considered above in relation to

11. See *Keith* v. *Burrows* (1876) 1 C.P.D. 722, affd. (1877) 2 App.Cas. 636 and *Barclays Bank* v. *Poole* [1907] 2 Ch. 284.
12. *Chasteauneuf* v. *Capeyron* (1882) 7 App.Cas. 127.
13. By section 396(4) of the Act "charge" includes "mortgage".
14. By section 396 of the Act the section applies to "a charge on a ship or aircraft or any share in a ship".

ships registered under Part I of the 1894 Act. However, they do introduce a system of registration of intended mortgages along the lines of that applying to aircraft mortgages.[15]

Paragraphs 1, 2 and 4 of Schedule 3 to the 1988 Act provide as follows:

1. In this Schedule—
> "mortgage" shall be construed in accordance with paragraph 2(2) below;
> "registered mortgage" means a mortgage registered in pursuance of paragraph 2(3) below; and
> "registered vessel" means a vessel registered otherwise than in pursuance of paragraph 2(c) of Schedule 2.

Mortgages of registered vessels

2.—(1) Any registered vessel or share in a registered vessel may be made a security for the repayment of a loan or the discharge of any other obligation.

(2) The instrument creating any such security (referred to in this Schedule as a mortgage) shall be in such form as is prescribed or approved by the Secretary of State.

(3) Where a mortgage executed in accordance with sub-paragraph (2) is produced to the Secretary of State, he shall—
> (a) register the mortgage by causing it to be recorded in the register, and
> (b) endorse on it the fact that it has been recorded, together with the date and time when it was recorded.

(4) Mortgages shall be registered under sub-paragraph (3) in the order in which they are produced to the Secretary of State for the purposes of registration.

4.—(1) Where any person who is an intending mortgagee under a proposed mortgage of—
> (a) a registered vessel, or
> (b) a share in a registered vessel,

notifies the Secretary of State in writing of the interest which it is intended that he should have under the proposed mortgage, the Secretary of State shall cause that interest to be recorded in the register.

(2) Where any person who is an intending mortgagee under a proposed mortgage of—
> (a) a fishing vessel which is not for the time being a registered vessel, or
> (b) a share in any such vessel,

notifies the Secretary of State in writing of the interest which it is intended that he should have under the proposed mortgage and furnishes him with such particulars of that vessel as may be prescribed, the Secretary of State—
> (i) shall cause that interest to be recorded in the register, and
> (ii) if the vessel is subsequently registered (otherwise than in pursuance of paragraph 2(c) of Schedule 2), shall cause the vessel to be registered subject to that interest or, if the mortgage has by then been executed in accordance with paragraph 2(2) and produced to the Secretary of State, subject to that mortgage.

(3) In a case where—
> (a) paragraph 3 operates to determine the priority between two or more mortgagees, and

---

15. See below page 54.

(b) any of these mortgagees gave a notification under sub-paragraph (1) or (2) above with respect to his mortgage,

paragraph 3 shall have effect in relation to that mortgage as if it had been registered at the time when the relevant entry was made in the register under sub-paragraph (1) or (2) above.

(4) Any notification given by a person under sub-paragraph (1) or (2) (and anything done as a result of it) shall cease to have effect—

(a) if the notification is withdrawn, or
(b) at the end of the period of 30 days beginning with the date of the notification, unless the notification is renewed in accordance with sub-paragraph (5).

(5) The person by whom any such notification is given may renew or further renew the notification, on each occasion for a period of 30 days, by notice in writing given to the Secretary of State—

(a) before the end of the period mentioned in sub-paragraph (4)(b), or
(b) before the end of the current period of renewal,

as the case may be.

(6) Any notification notice purporting to be given under this paragraph (and anything done as a result of it) shall not have effect if the Secretary of State determines that it was not validly given.

Aircraft

Provision has been made for registered aircraft to be mortgaged and for such mortgages to be registered. The mechanism for so doing is provided for in the Mortgaging of Aircraft Order 1972.

Article 3 of the Order provides: "An aircraft registered in the United Kingdom nationality register[16] or such an aircraft together with any store of spare parts for that aircraft may be made security for a loan or other valuable consideration."

The words "mortgage of an aircraft" are defined in Article 2 of the Order as including "a mortgage which extends to any store of spare parts for that aircraft but does not otherwise include a mortgage created as a floating charge".

Article 4 of the Order provides:

(1) Any mortgage of an aircraft[17] registered in the United Kingdom nationality register may be entered in the Register of Aircraft Mortgages kept by the [Civil Aviation] Authority.

(2) Applications to enter a mortgage in the Register shall be made to the [Civil Aviation] Authority by or on behalf of the mortgagee in the form set out in Part I of Schedule I hereto,[18] and shall be accompanied by a copy of the mortgage, which the applicant shall certify to be a true copy, and the appropriate charge.[19]

16. This is defined by article 2(2) as meaning "the register of aircraft maintained by the [Civil Aviation] Authority in pursuance of an Order in Council under section 8 of the Civil Aviation Act 1949 (now section 60 of the Civil Aviation Act 1982)".

17. Which is defined by article 2(2) as including "a mortgage which extends to any store of spare parts for that aircraft but does not otherwise include a mortgage created as a floating charge".

18. See Appendix 5.

19. Defined by article 2(2) as meaning "the charge payable under section 9 of the Civil Aviation Act 1971".

The 1972 Order provides for a scheme of registration of priority notices in respect of intended mortgages. Article 5 of the Order provides:

(1) A notice of intention to make an application to enter a contemplated mortgage of an aircraft in the Register (hereinafter referred to as a "priority notice") may also be entered in the Register.

(2) Application to enter a priority notice in the Register shall be made to the [Civil Aviation] Authority by or on behalf of the prospective mortgagee in the form set out in Part II of Schedule I hereto,[20] and shall be accompanied by the appropriate charge.[21]

Article 6 of the Order provides:

(1) Where two or more aircraft are the subject of one mortgage or where the same aircraft is the subject of two or more mortgages, separate applications shall be made in respect of each aircraft or of each mortgage as the case may be.

(2) Where a mortgage is in a language other than English, the application to enter the mortgage in the Register shall be accompanied not only by a copy of that mortgage but also by a translation thereof, which the applicant shall certify as being, to the best of his knowledge and belief, a true translation.

Article 7 of the Order provides:

(1) When an application to enter a mortgage or priority notice in the Register is duly made the [Civil Aviation] Authority shall enter the mortgage or the priority notice, as the case may be, in the Register by placing the application form therein and by noting on it the date and time of the entry.

(2) Applications duly made shall be entered in the Register in order of their receipt by the [Civil Aviation] Authority.

(3) The [Civil Aviation] Authority shall by notice in its Official Record specify the days on which and the hours during which its office is open for registering mortgages and priority notices. Any application delivered when the office is closed for that purpose shall be treated as having been received immediately after the office is next opened.

(4) The [Civil Aviation] Authority shall notify the applicant of the date and time of the entry of the mortgage or priority notice, as the case may be, in the Register and of the register number of the entry and shall send a copy of the notification to the mortgagor and the owner.

Article 10 of the Order provides:

Any of the following courts, that is to say the High Court of Justice in England, the Court of Session in Scotland and the High Court of Justice in Northern Ireland may order such amendments to be made to the Register as may appear to the Court to be necessary or expedient for correcting any error therein. On being served with the Order the [Civil Aviation] Authority shall make the necessary amendment to the Register.

Corporations

Mortgages of aircraft require registration under section 395 of the Companies Act 1985.[22]

---

20. See Appendix 5.
21. Defined by article 2(2) as meaning "the charge payable under section 9 of the Civil Aviation Act 1971".
22. See above page 51.

SCOPE

Ships

"Ship"

The scope of the mortgage in statutory form was considered in *Coltman* v. *Chamberlain*[23] where it was held that a mortgage of a ship passed to the mortgagee under the word "ship":

"all articles necessary to the navigation of the ship or to the prosecution of the adventure, and without which no prudent person would sail, which were on board at the date of the mortgage and articles brought on board in substitution for them subsequently to the mortgage."

In order to be covered by the mortgage the articles must have been specifically appropriated to the ship.[24]

"Appurtenances"

In *The "Humorous", The "Mabel Vera"*[25] there was a mortgage of two fishing vessels and "their appurtenances". At the time of the mortgage, one fishing vessel had nets appropriated to it, but the other fishing vessel had not. It was held in an action by the mortgagee who had entered into possession, that the nets on board the latter vessel at the time when he entered into possession did not pass under the mortgage as no nets had been appropriated to her at the time of the mortgage.

The word "appurtenances" was considered in *The "Dundee"*[26] where it was held to include anything belonging to the owner which is on board the ship for the accomplishment of the voyage and adventure on which she is engaged.

In *The Hull Ropes Company* v. *Adams*[27] a trawl warp was purchased by the mortgagor after the date of the mortgage on hire-purchase and put on board the ship. Subsequently the mortgagee entered into possession. It was held that the trawl warp was covered by the mortgage and that property in it had passed to the mortgagee, notwithstanding the hire-purchase agreement. Under section 9 of the Factors Act the mortgagor was a "buyer in possession" and the addition of the warp to the equipment of the mortgaged ship was held to constitute sufficient "disposition" under the Act, being a delivery or transfer under the mortgage, so as to pass property to the mortgagee.

---

23. (1890) 25 Q.B.D. 328.
24. See *In re Salmon & Woods, ex. p. Gould* (1885) 2 Mor. Bky. Cas. 137 and *Armstrong* v. *McGregor* (1875) 12 S.C. 339.
25. [1933] P. 109.
26. (1823) 1 Hagg. 109.
27. (1895) 65 L.J.Q.B. 114.

Other articles on board

It should be noted that where an article is not covered under the mortgage of the "ship" and "appurtenances" under the principle considered above, if it is intended to form part of the security for the transaction it will require to be mortgaged by separate instrument. Given that *ex hypothesi* such a mortgage cannot fall within the exception relating to "ships" under the Bills of Sale Acts, the form of such instrument will have to be in the form prescribed by those Acts and it will have to be registered in accordance with those Acts.

Cargo

The cargo carried on board a ship is not covered by a mortgage of a ship even where it is actually owned by the mortgagor. Nor is it an appurtenance.[28]

Freight

Freight is not covered by a mortgage of a ship without more. The basic rule is that, in the absence of a separate assignment of freight, unless and until a mortgagee enters into possession he has no right to freight earned.

Aircraft

Apart from the physical body of the aircraft and the engines fitted for the time being, as seen above, the Mortgaging of Aircraft Order 1972 expressly provides that any store of spare parts for the aircraft may also be included in the mortgage. It would be usual in the drafting of an aircraft mortgage to provide that the mortgage extends to engines, parts and any replacements as well as to the aircraft documents.

TRANSFER

Generally

The transfer of a mortgage may take place by agreement or by operation of law. The scheme of the Merchant Shipping Act as to the registration of transfers of mortgages effectively mirrors the scheme provided for registration of transfers of ownership.

In outline, the provisions for transfer of ownership by registration of a bill of sale in prescribed form contained in sections 24 and 26, are reflected in section 37 which provides for registration of an instrument of transfer in prescribed form. Similarly, the provisions relating to registration of transfer of ownership by operation of law contained in section 27 are reflected in section 38. The Mortgaging of Aircraft Order 1972 makes no specific provision regarding transfer of

---

28. See *Langton* v. *Horton* (1842) 5 Beav. 9 and *Alexander* v. *Simms* (1854) 5 De G.M. & G. 57.

mortgages, although it does provide in article 8 for the amendment of entries in the register.

Ships

Transfer by agreement

Section 37 of the 1894 Act[29] provides:

A registered mortgage of a ship or any share may be transferred to any person, and on the production of the instrument effecting the transfer the registrar shall record it by entering in the register the name of the transferee as mortgagee of the ship or share, and shall by memorandum under his hand notify on the instrument of transfer that it has been recorded by him, stating the day and hour of the record.

Where the instrument of transfer is not registered it is nevertheless valid and effective as between the transferor and the transferee to pass all the rights under the mortgage.[30] Moreover, the court will enforce equities as between the owner of the ship and an unregistered transferee of the mortgage.[31] Under section 57 of the 1894 Act, the court can also enforce an agreement to transfer a mortgage, applying the maxim "equity treats as done that which ought to have been done".

Transfer by operation of law

Section 38 of the 1894 Act[32] provides as follows:

(1) Where the interest of a mortgagee in a ship or share is transmitted on death or bankruptcy, or by any lawful means other than a transfer under this Act, the transmission shall be authenticated by a declaration of the person to whom the interest is transmitted, containing a statement of the manner in which and the person to whom the property has been transmitted, and shall be accompanied by the like evidence as is by this Act required in case of a corresponding transmission of the ownership of a ship or share.

(2) The registrar on the receipt of the declaration, and the production of the evidence aforesaid, shall enter the name of the person entitled under the transmission in the register as mortgagee of the ship or share.

The words "or by any lawful means other than a transfer under this Act" were held in *Chasteauneuf* v. *Capeyron*[33] (as regards the same words appearing in the 1854 Act) to be restricted to transfers by operation of law unconnected with any direct act of the transferee, the Act making a clear distinction between "transfers" and "transmissions". It therefore appears that, if a transferee is unable to bring himself within section 38, he will be unable to obtain registration as mortgagee merely by his own declaration, and will need to obtain a

---

29. As amended by Schedule 1 to the 1988 Act.
30. *The "Two Ellens"* (1871) L.R. 3 A. & E. 345, 355.
31. *The "Cathcart"* (1867) L.R. 1 A. & E. 314.
32. As amended by Schedule 1 to the 1988 Act.
33. (1882) 7 App.Cas. 127.

transfer in the prescribed form so as to enable registration to be effected under section 37. This will require execution of the transfer by the transferor.

The alternative is to make an application to the Admiralty Court, preferably by means of an action *in rem*, or possibly by originating summons, for appropriate declaratory relief in the same manner as an application for a declaration of ownership.

Fishing vessels

Transfer by agreement

Paragraph 6 of Schedule 3 to the 1988 Act provides as follows:

(1) A registered mortgage may be transferred by an instrument made in such form as is prescribed or approved by the Secretary of State.

(2) Where any such instrument is produced to the Secretary of State, he shall—

    (a) cause the name of the transferee to be entered in the register as mortgagee of the vessel or share in question, and

    (b) endorse on the instrument the fact that that entry has been made, together with the date and time when it was made.

Transfer by operation of law

Paragraph 7 of Schedule 3 to the 1988 Act provides as follows:

Where the interest of a mortgagee in a registered mortgage is transmitted to any person by any lawful means other than by a transfer under paragraph 6, the Secretary of State shall, on production of such evidence of the transmission as may be prescribed, cause the name of that person to be entered in the register as mortgagee of the vessel or share in question.

Aircraft

Article 8 of the Mortgaging of Aircraft Order 1972 provides:

(1) Any change in the person appearing in the Register as mortgagee or as mortgagor or in the name or address of such person or in the description of the mortgaged property shall be notified to the [Civil Aviation] Authority by or on behalf of the mortgagee, in the form set out in Part III of Schedule 1 hereto.

(2) On receipt of the said form, duly completed and signed by or on behalf of the mortgagor and the mortgagee and on payment of the appropriate charge, the [Civil Aviation] Authority shall enter the notification in the Register and shall notify the mortgagor, the mortgagee and the owner that it has done so.

DISCHARGE

Generally

A mortgage may be discharged upon satisfaction of the mortgage debt. This may be achieved in three ways:

(i) upon redemption by the mortgagor or by any other person interested in the equity of redemption;

(ii) upon sale by the mortgagee or by the court, and the satisfaction of the mortgaged debt out of the proceeds of sale;

(iii) by foreclosure.

Ships

Section 32 of the 1894 Act[34] provides:

Where a registered mortgage is discharged, the registrar shall, on the production of the mortgage deed, with a receipt for the mortgage money endorsed thereon, duly signed and attested, make an entry in the register to the effect that the mortgage has been discharged, and on that entry being made the estate (if any) which passed to the mortgagee shall vest in the person in whom (having regard to intervening acts and circumstances, if any) it would have vested if the mortgage had not been made.

The obligation of the registrar upon discharge is thus to make an entry to that effect in the register. The registrar has no authority under the Act to erase the entry of a mortgage upon its being discharged.[35] However, in *The "Yolanda Barbara"*[36] Hewson J. granted a mortgagee who had redeemed by paying off the mortgage debt a declaration, *inter alia*, that he was entitled to have the entry of the mortgage removed and/or expunged from the register, and an order that the same be done. It is submitted that the relief sought in that case was probably incorrect to the extent that the order provided for the entry of the mortgage actually to be expunged as opposed to an entry being made to the effect that the mortgage had been discharged. Where a mortgagor is unable, for whatever reason, to produce the mortgage deed as required by section 32, it would be preferable for the sake of consistency with the overall scheme of the Act, for a court to make an order to the effect that a discharge be entered in the register rather than the entry be removed completely.

It is appropriate to order an entry in the register to be expunged where a mortgage has been registered by a person fraudulently representing himself to be a mortgagee;[37] or where the mortgage was not executed by the mortgagee.[38] These are obviously cases where no entry of a mortgage should ever have appeared in the register rather than the situation in *The "Yolanda Barbara"*[39] where the original entry of the mortgage was perfectly proper.

Where an entry of discharge has been made in the register by mistake, it has nevertheless been held to discharge the mortgage, and all subsequent entries

---

34. As amended by Schedule 1 to the 1988 Act.
35. *Chasteauneuf* v. *Capeyron* (1882) 7 App.Cas. 127.
36. [1961] 2 Lloyd's Rep. 337.
37. *Brond* v. *Broomhall* [1906] 1 K.B. 571.
38. *Burgis* v. *Constantine* [1908] 2 K.B. 484.
39. *Supra.*

relating to the mortgage were void. The mortgage could not be revived by a memorandum on the register that the discharge had been entered by mistake.[40]

On the other hand, where an entry of discharge was made by mistake and a bill of sale executed by a mortgagee, the court will direct registration of the purchaser as owner. In *The "Rose"*,[41] the mortgagor died intestate and insolvent and shortly afterwards the mortgagee sold the ship, executing a bill of sale and indorsing a discharge on the original mortgage believing this necessary to complete title. The mortgage indorsed with the discharge was produced to the registrar in error and he accordingly recorded it in the register. When the purchaser produced his bill of sale to the registrar he refused to register it as the mortgagee by whom it had been executed no longer had any title according to the register. The court nevertheless granted a declaration that he was the owner of the ship and was entitled to be registered as owner.[42]

The situation must in each case depend upon whether anyone relying upon the register will be prejudiced by the incorrect entry. If not the court may order the entry to be rectified, but it will not do so to the detriment of an innocent third party who has acted in reliance upon the entries in the register.

Fishing vessels

Paragraph 8 of Schedule 3 to the 1988 Act provides as follows:

Where a registered mortgage has been discharged, the Secretary of State shall, on production of the mortgage deed with such evidence of the discharge of the mortgage as is prescribed, cause an entry to be made in the register to the effect that the mortgage has been discharged.

Aircraft

The situation is similar, article 9 of the Mortgaging of Aircraft Order 1972 providing as follows:

(1) Where a registered mortgage is discharged the mortgagor shall notify the [Civil Aviation] Authority of the fact in the form set out in Part IV of Schedule 1 hereto.

(2) On receipt of the said form, duly completed and signed by or on behalf of the mortgagor and the mortgagee and a copy of the mortgage with a discharge or receipt for the mortgage money duly endorsed thereon, or of any other document which shows, to the satisfaction of the [Civil Aviation] Authority, that the mortgage has been discharged and on payment of the appropriate charge, the [Civil Aviation] Authority shall enter the said form in the Register and mark the relevant entries in the Register "Discharged", and shall notify the mortgagee, the mortgagor and the owner that it has done so.

---

40. *Bell* v. *Blyth* (1868) L.R. 4 Ch.App. 136.
41. (1873) L.R. 4 A. & E. 6.
42. See also *Duthie* v. *Aiken* (1893) 20 Sess.Cas. (4th) 214 (Sc.).

4

DEED OF COVENANTS

INTRODUCTION

The basic structure of security for a straightforward ship or aircraft mortgage comprises four related elements:

   (i) a mortgage of the ship or aircraft herself;
  (ii) a mortgage or assignment of insurances;
 (iii) a mortgage or assignment of compensation payable in respect of requisition;
 (iv) an assignment of earnings.

These matters are often dealt with in a deed of covenants which in the case of a British ship will be collateral to the mortgage, but which in the case of other flags will constitute the mortgage. However, in some cases a separate assignment of earnings or insurances is taken.

Other security such as personal guarantees or a pledge of the shares in the owning company or cross-guarantees or mortgages on other vessels in the same fleet or owned by other companies within the same beneficial ownership may also be taken by way of additional security.

The content of the deed of covenants is of crucial importance as it enables the mortgagee to state expressly how he requires the mortgagor to behave in relation to the vessel, and what rights of enforcement he claims for himself, so as to avoid having to rely upon provisions of the general law relating to mortgages.

It is therefore necessary to consider in some detail the usual provisions to be found in a modern deed of covenants.

OUTLINE

Whether the mortgage relates to a ship or to an aircraft, one would expect that the deed of covenants would, after a preamble dealing with the date of the instrument, the parties thereto, the title of the mortgagor, the loan by the mortgagee upon the security of a mortgage, contain provisions dealing with the following matters:

1. *Definitions* of terms used in the instrument and principles of construction to be applied.
2. *Repayment* of the principal sum, together with *interest*.
3. Expression of *mortgage* and charge on the property.
4. Expression that mortgage is to be *continuing* and *additional security*.
5. Right of *consolidation*.
6. Exclusion of the rule in *Clayton's Case*.
7. *Mortgagor's positive covenants*:
   (a) to maintain flag and registration;
   (b) to maintain in good condition;
   (c) to keep insured;
   (d) to allow inspection by mortgagee;
   (e) to discharge all debts;
   (f) to provide information to mortgagee;
   (g) to notify mortgagee of perils, accidents, incidents etc.,
   (h) to pay all outgoings punctually;
   (i) to maintain copy of mortgage on board and to display notice that property mortgaged and that mortgagor has no authority to create liens;
   (j) to reimburse mortgagees' costs of protection or enforcement of security;
   (k) to pay mortgagees' legal costs and disbursements.
8. *Mortgagor's negative covenants*:
   (a) not to employ in illegal trades;
   (b) not (without consent) to encumber;
   (c) not (without consent) to sell;
   (d) not (without consent) to enter into certain charters;
   (e) not (without consent) to enter into earnings sharing agreement;
   (f) not (without consent) to put property into possession of repairer;
   (g) not (without consent) to appoint a manager;
   (h) not to pledge the credit of the mortgagee.
9. Mortgagee's liberty to protect security at mortgagor's expense.
10. *Events of default* whereby all outstanding indebtedness immediately becomes payable on demand:
    (a) failure by mortgagor to pay sum payable;
    (b) failure by mortgagor to perform or observe covenant;
    (c) death or insolvency of mortgagor;
    (d) total loss;
    (e) failure to pay earnings to mortgagee after demand;
    (f) impossibility or illegality of performance by mortgagor or mortgagee;
    (g) imperilling of security.
11. *Mortgagee's powers upon default*:
    (a) to take possession;
    (b) to take insurance documents and collect proceeds;

(c) to discharge claims and liens;

(d) to sell;

(e) to manage, insure, maintain, repair and employ pending sale and recover losses thereby incurred from mortgagor;

(f) to recover expenses incurred in exercise of powers from mortgagor.

12. Protection of purchasers.

13. Application of proceeds of sale, insurance monies, compensation and earnings.

14. *Delay and indulgence* not to constitute waiver by mortgagee.

15. Power of mortgagee to *delegate*.

16. Mortgagor to *indemnify* mortgagee.

17. Mortgagor's appointment of mortgagee as *attorney*.

18. *Further assurances*.

19. *Representation* and *notices*.

20. *Law*.

Whilst the above 20 points may be considered to constitute the basic framework of the majority of mortgages, they cannot be considered as comprehensive, and in each individual case some modification or adjustment may be required to reflect, for example:

(i) the particular requirements of the law of the flag or register;

(ii) the particular nature of the loan agreement or the circumstances in which the mortgage was created;

(iii) the specific characteristics of the ship or aircraft to be mortgaged.

In particular, in the case of aircraft mortgages, further express provision may be desirable to cover the more extensive statutory regulation of the maintenance and operation of aircraft compared to that governing the operation and maintenance of ships.

DETAILED CLAUSES

Having considered the content of the deed of covenants in outline, some typical provisions will be set out in detail following the 20-point outline.

Preamble

This will normally follow a form similar to the following:

THIS MORTGAGE is made the [date] of [month] [year]

BETWEEN:

(1) [name] of [address], hereinafter referred to as the "mortgagor" AND

(2) [name] of [address], hereinafter referred to as the "mortgagee" AND

(3) [name] of [address], hereinafter referred to as the "guarantor"[1]

---

1. Where there is a third party guarantor who is to be made a party to the mortgage for the purpose of additional security.

WHEREAS

(A) The mortgagor has represented to the mortgagee that he is the absolute owner of 64/64th shares of and in the ship [*or* the absolute owner of the aircraft] described in the First Schedule hereto.

(B) The mortgagor has requested the mortgagee and the mortgagee has agreed to lend to the mortgagor the sum of [amount] *or* by a loan agreement dated [date] a copy whereof appears in the Second Schedule hereto the mortgagee has agreed to make a loan to the mortgagor upon the terms and conditions therein contained.

(C) The mortgagor has agreed to provide security to the mortgagee by way of First Preferred Mortgage of the ship [or aircraft].

NOW THIS DEED WITNESSETH AS FOLLOWS:

1. Definitions and construction

Definitions

The content of this part of the deed of covenants will largely be dictated by the particular circumstances of the transaction. However, the following important definitions will usually be required in every case:

"*The outstanding indebtedness*" means the aggregate of all money from time to time owing by the mortgagor to the mortgagee.

"*The security period*" means the period commencing at the date hereof and terminating upon full and final settlement of the outstanding indebtedness.

"*The ship*" means the vessel described in the First Schedule and includes any share or interest therein, and the engines, machinery, boats, tackle, outfits, gear, instruments, parts, spare parts, fuel, consumable and other stores, belongings, appurtenances, accessories furnishings and all other equipment of whatever kind, whether on board or ashore or elsewhere, whether now belonging to the vessel or hereafter acquired, and all additions, improvements or replacements thereto.

"*The aircraft*" means the aircraft described in the First Schedule and includes any share or interest therein, and the engines, appliances, instruments, parts, spare parts, fuel, consumable and other stores, belongings, appurtenances, accessories, furnishings and all other equipment of whatever kind, whether on board or ashore or elsewhere, whether now belonging to the aircraft or hereafter acquired, and all additions, improvements or replacements thereto.

"*The engines*"[2] means the engines described in the First Schedule and any other engines from time to time installed on the aircraft which are or become the property of the mortgagor and any engines removed from the aircraft which remain the property of the mortgagor, together with all parts, spare parts and accessories belonging to any such engines.

"*Earnings*" means all freight, hire, passage monies, passenger fares, demurrage, despatch and detention monies, compensation payable in the event of requisition of the [ship or aircraft] for hire, remuneration for salvage or towage services and any other earnings whatsoever due or to become due to the mortgagor during the security period.

"*The Insurances*" means all contracts and policies of insurance from time to time effected or maintained in respect of the [ship or aircraft] and her earnings, or otherwise howsoever in connection with the [ship or aircraft] including all entries in any mutual assurance association of whatsoever nature.

"*Total Loss*" means:

    (i) actual, constructive, compromised or arranged total loss of the [ship or aircraft]

---

2. In the case of an aircraft mortgage.

    (ii) requisition of title or other compulsory acquisition of the [ship or aircraft]

    (iii) hijack, theft, capture, seizure, arrest, detention, condemnation, confiscation or loss of possession of the [ship or aircraft] unless the [ship or aircraft] be released and returned within 30 days

"*The mortgaged property*" means the [ship or aircraft and engines] and all other rights, assets, interests or property from time to time mortgaged, charged or assigned to the mortgagee pursuant to clause 3, including each and every part thereof.

"*The Acts*" means the Merchant Shipping Acts 1984 to 1988 [*or* the Civil Aviation Act 1982, the Air Navigation Order 1985] and the Regulations made thereunder or any addition, modification, re-enactment or consolidation of all or any of them from time to time.

"*The security documents*" means this deed, the mortgage [the assignment of earnings and insurances][3] and any other documents as may be executed to secure the outstanding indebtedness.

Construction

It is helpful to state express rules of construction such as the following:

In this mortgage and the Schedules hereto, unless the context otherwise requires:

    (a) references to the mortgagor and the mortgagee shall include their respective successors or assigns;

    (b) references to the singular shall include the plural and vice-versa;

    (c) references to the masculine shall include the feminine and neuter and vice-versa;

    (d) references to persons include any individual or body corporate or unincorporated, states, governmental and administrative entities, whether or not a separate legal entity;

    (e) references to schedules, clauses, sub-clauses, paragraphs, sub-paragraphs are to the schedules, clauses, sub-clauses, paragraphs, sub-paragraphs of this mortgage;

    (f) the index and marginal headings are for ease of reference only and are not to be used in the construction of this mortgage;

    (g) references to any statute, law, decree, or regulation shall be deemed to include references to any re-enactment, extension or amendment thereof from time to time;

    (h) references to any document including this mortgage shall be deemed to include references to any replacement, variation or supplement thereof from time to time.

2. Repayment and interest

In pursuance of the recited agreement and in consideration of the premises the MORTGAGOR hereby COVENANTS with the MORTGAGEE as follows:

(A) To repay to the mortgagee the principal sum [on demand] [*or* by the instalments and at the times specified in the loan agreement/Second Schedule hereto] provided however that the principal sum and the outstanding indebtedness shall become immediately due and payable on demand upon the happening of any of the events of default as hereinafter defined.

(B) To pay interest upon the principal sum at the rate of [rate or formula] such interest to accrue from day to day but to be payable at the time specified in the loan agreement/ Second Schedule hereto and to pay interest at the default rate upon the balance of the outstanding indebtedness from time to time.

---

3. If these are contained in a separate document or documents.

3. Mortgage and charge

As security for the payment of the outstanding indebtedness the MORTGAGOR hereby MORTGAGES AND CHARGES to and in favour of the MORTGAGEE all its rights title and interest present and future in the mortgaged property and GRANTS to the mortgagee a first preferred mortgage over the whole of the [ship or aircraft and engines] [up to the amount of ——][4] together with the right to register the same in the [state name of register] without any action on the part of the mortgagor and the mortgagor hereby ASSIGNS to the mortgagee (i) all the earnings of the ship [or aircraft] PROVIDED that if no default has been made hereunder the mortgagee may allow the mortgagor to collect the same and (ii) and all the insurances and all the benefits thereof including all claims of whatsoever nature and the return of premiums or calls.

In the case of aircraft it is necessary to include a provision along the following lines to cover the aircraft documents and maintenance contracts.

And GRANTS to the mortgagee a mortgage and/or fixed charge of:
  (i) the aircraft documents now existing and which may hereafter exist from time to time;
 (ii) in so far as, and to the extent that, they are capable of being charged or assigned, the rights of the mortgagor under all contracts, warranties and other agreements relating to or connected with the condition, use, repair, or operation of the aircraft now existing and which may hereafter arise from time to time.

4. Continuing security etc.

IT IS HEREBY AGREED AND DECLARED that the security created by the mortgage and by this deed shall be a continuing security in the hands of the mortgagee and shall not be satisfied by an intermediate payment or satisfaction of any part of the amount secured and that the security so created shall be in addition to and shall not in any way be prejudiced or affected by any collateral or other security now or hereafter held by the mortgagee, by whomsoever granted, for all or part of the amount secured and that every power and remedy given to the mortgagee hereunder shall be in addition to and not in limitation of any and every other power or remedy vested in the mortgagee and that all the powers and remedies so vested in the mortgagee may be exercised from time to time and as often as the mortgagee shall in its absolute discretion deem expedient.

5. Consolidation

The provisions of section 93 of the Law of Property Act 1925 and any re-enactment thereof shall not apply and the mortgagee shall have the right to consolidate.

6. Rule in Clayton's Case

Upon discovering that the mortgagor has encumbered or disposed of the mortgaged property or any part thereof or any interest therein the mortgagee shall be entitled to rule off the mortgagor's liabilities and to open a new account or accounts for the mortgagor and no amount credited to the mortgagor in any such new account shall be appropriated towards or have the effect of discharging any part of the liabilities due to the mortgagee incurred prior to such ruling off.

---

4. Some countries require a maximum sum to be stated.

7. Mortgagor's positive covenants

THE MORTGAGOR FURTHER COVENANTS with the MORTGAGEE and UNDERTAKES as follows:

(a) Registration

To keep the ship [or aircraft] at all times registered as a British[5] ship [or United Kingdom aircraft] and to do or to suffer to be done nothing whereby such registration may be forfeited or imperilled.

(b) Condition

To keep the ship [or aircraft and engines] at all times in a good and seaworthy [or airworthy] state of repair and in all respects in good operating condition, and to maintain, service, repair and overhaul the ship [or aircraft and engines] and make such alterations, modifications and improvements as may be required so as to maintain her present class and so as to comply with the provisions of the Acts and the Regulations made thereunder and all other regulations and requirements (statutory or otherwise) from time to time applicable to the ship [or aircraft] under English law or of any other jurisdiction into which the ship [or aircraft] may come and so as not to diminish the value of the ship [or aircraft and engines] other than in the normal course of operation.

In the case of an aircraft add:

and so as to comply with the maintenance schedules and mandatory operational modifications from time to time required by the manufacturers of the aircraft (including, but not restricted to) its airframe, avionics, mechanical parts and the engines.

Additional covenant in the case of aircraft:

to ensure that there are at all times throughout the currency of this agreement maintained in force a Certificate of Airworthiness issued by the Civil Aviation Authority[6] and all such certificates of maintenance review and certificates for release to service as are required from time to time under the Acts or by the Civil Aviation Authority or any other authority and that there are maintained on board all such logbooks and other documents as are required by law to be maintained on board.

Positive covenants continued

(c) Insurance

(i) To insure and keep the ship [or aircraft and engines] and her earnings insured at the mortgagor's expense with such underwriters or insurers and through such brokers as the mortgagee shall have approved in writing and for such sum or sums and against such risk of whatever nature and upon such terms as the mortgagee shall from time to time require.

(ii) To take steps to renew all such insurances on the due date at least 14 days before the expiry of cover and to procure that the brokers shall promptly confirm in writing to the mortgagee as and when such renewal is effected.

(iii) Punctually to pay all premiums, calls, contributions or other sums payable in

---

5. Or as applicable.
6. Or as the case may be according to nationality of registration.

respect of such insurances and, if so required by the mortgagee, to produce all receipts in respect thereof.

(iv) To arrange for the execution of such guarantees or other documents as may from time to time be required by any underwriters or insurers for or for the continuance of cover.

(v) To procure that the interest of the mortgagee and the loss payable clause set out below shall be duly indorsed upon all slips, cover notes, policies, certificates of entry or other instruments of insurance issued in connection with the insurances effected and that the said instruments be deposited with the approved brokers, or should the mortgagee so direct, with the mortgagee.

Loss payable clause

It is hereby noted that [name and address of the mortgagee] is interested in [name/ registration of ship or aircraft] as mortgagee under [date of mortgage] and in the event of payment of any monies due including laid-up returns or settlement of any claim arising under these insurances, no payments are to be made to the owners or according to their directions without the prior written consent of the mortgagee to whom all monies are payable under the mortgage. Provided however that any claim not exceeding [state sum] or its equivalent in any other currency may be made to the owners direct unless written instructions to the contrary have previously been received from the mortgagee. Underwriters will give 14 days' telegraphic notice before cancelling or varying this policy.

(vi) To procure that the protection and indemnity and/or war risk insurers shall (if so required by the mortgagee) provide to the mortgagee a letter or letters of undertaking in such form as may be required by the mortgagee.

(vii) Not to employ the ship [*or* aircraft] or suffer the ship [*or* aircraft] to be employed otherwise than in conformity with the terms of the instruments of insurance (including any express or implied warranties therein) nor do or fail to do anything in connection with the ship [*or* aircraft] whereby cover may be withdrawn, cancelled, imperilled or prejudiced in any way whatsoever unless the consent of the insurer has first been obtained and any requirements as to extra premium or otherwise as the insurers may require have been complied with.

(viii) To apply all such sums as are paid to the mortgagee in accordance with the provisions of the mortgage and of this deed for the purpose of making good the loss and fully repairing all damage in respect of which such sums have been received.

(d) Inspection

To permit the mortgagee or its servants or agents to board the ship [*or* aircraft] at all reasonable times for the purpose of inspecting the condition thereof or for satisfying themselves as regards proposed or executed repairs and to afford all necessary and proper facilities for such inspections.

(e) Debts etc.

Punctually to pay and discharge all debts, damages, and liabilities whatsoever which the mortgagor shall have been called upon to pay, discharge or secure which have given or may give rise to liens on or claims enforceable against the mortgaged property or any part thereof and in the event of the arrest or detention of the mortgaged property or any part thereof whether by legal process or in exercise or purported exercise of any such lien or claim to procure the release of the same forthwith upon receiving notice of such arrest or detention.

(f) Information

Promptly to furnish the mortgagee as and when requested with any information whatsoever regarding the mortgaged property or any part thereof as the mortgagee shall request.

(g) Notification

To notify the mortgagee forthwith of the following:
    (i) any accident to the ship [*or* aircraft] involving repairs the cost of which will or is likely to exceed [amount] or the equivalent in any other currency;
    (ii) any occurrence in consequence whereof the ship [*or* aircraft] has become or is likely to become a total loss;
    (iii) any requirement or recommendation made by any insurer, classification society or authority which is not complied with within any time limit specified therefor;
    (iv) any arrest or detention of the mortgaged property or any part thereof or the exercise or purported exercise of any lien thereon;
    (v) any petition or notice of any meeting to consider any resolution to wind up the mortgagor [*or* the guarantor] or any event analogous thereto in any jurisdiction whatsoever.

(h) Outgoings

Promptly to pay all tolls dues and other outgoings whatsoever in respect of the ship [*or* aircraft] and to keep proper books of account in respect of the ship [*or* aircraft] and the earnings thereof

In the case of a ship mortgage add:

and to furnish satisfactory evidence that the wages, allotments, insurance and pension contributions in respect of the master and crew, are being paid regularly and that they have no claims for wages beyond the ordinary arrears and that the master has no claim for disbursements other than those incurred by him in the ordinary course of trading on the voyage then in progress.

(i) Notice of mortgage

In the case of a ship:

To place and at all times during the security period to retain on board the vessel with the ship's papers a properly certified copy of this mortgage and to cause the same to be exhibited to all persons having business with the ship which might give rise to any lien on the ship and to place and keep the following notice in a prominent position in the chart room and in the master's cabin:

NOTICE OF MORTGAGE

This vessel is the subject of a first preferred ship mortgage in favour of [name of mortgagee]. Under the terms of the said mortgage neither the shipowners nor any charterer nor the master of this vessel nor any other person has any right power or authority to create incur or permit to be imposed upon this ship any lien whatsoever except in respect of crew's wages and salvage.

In the case of an aircraft:

To place and at all times during the security period to retain on board the aircraft with the aircraft documents a copy of this mortgage and to affix on the aircraft a notice in a location adjacent to and no less prominent than the certificate of airworthiness, and to affix on the engines a plate in a prominent place, stating as follows:

> "This Aircraft/Engine is subject to a mortgage in favour of [the name and address of the mortgagee] and may not be mortgaged, charged, leased or made the subject of any lien or encumbrance except with the prior written consent of [the name of the mortgagee]."

(j) Mortgagee's expenses in protecting security

To pay to the mortgagee on demand all monies whatsoever which the mortgagee shall expend, be put to or become liable for in or about the protection, maintenance or enforcement of the security hereby created or in or about the exercise by the mortgagee of any of the powers vested in it and to pay interest thereon from the date such expense or liability was incurred until the date of payment at the default rate before and after judgment.

(k) Mortgagee's legal expenses

To pay on demand all the mortgagee's legal costs, expenses and disbursements of whatsoever nature and any other charges incurred by the mortgagee in connection with the preparation, completion and registration of the security documents.

8. Mortgagor's negative covenants

(a) Illegal trades

Not to employ the ship [or aircraft] or suffer her [or its] employment in any part of the world or in any trade or business or for any purpose which is not covered by the insurances or which is forbidden by any applicable law or is otherwise illicit or in carrying illicit or prohibited goods or in any manner whatsoever as may render her [or it] or them liable to condemnation in a Prize Court or to destruction, seizure or confiscation or which is contrary to any insurance which is taken out in respect of her [or it] or them and in the event of hostilities in any part of the world (whether war be declared or not) not to employ the ship [or aircraft] or suffer her [or its] employment in carrying any contraband goods or to enter or remain in any area after it has been declared a war zone by any government or by the War Risk insurers unless the mortgagee has previously given its consent in writing and there is in force such special or additional insurance cover as the mortgagee may require.

(b) Not to encumber

Not without the prior written consent of the mortgagee to mortgage, charge or otherwise assign the mortgaged property or to suffer the creation of any such mortgage, charge or assignment to or in favour of any person other than the mortgagee.

(c) Not to sell

Not without the prior written consent of the mortgagee to sell, transfer or otherwise dispose of the mortgaged property or any part thereof or agree or purport to do any such thing.

(d) Not to enter into certain charters

Not without the prior written consent of the mortgagee to let the ship:
   (i) on demise charter for any period;
   (ii) by any time or consecutive voyage charter for a term which exceeds or by virtue of any optional extensions contained therein is likely to exceed [time period required];
   (iii) on terms whereby more than [number] months hire or equivalent is payable in advance;
   (iv) below the market rate then prevailing at the time of the fixture.

In the case of aircraft:

not without the prior written consent of the mortgagee to charter, lease or part with possession or control of the aircraft.

(e) Not to enter into earnings sharing agreement

Not without the prior written consent of the mortgagee to enter into any agreement or arrangement whereby the earnings of the ship [or aircraft] may be shared with any other person.

(f) Not to give possession to repairer

Not without the prior written consent of the mortgagee to put the ship [or aircraft] into the possession of any person for the purpose of work being carried out in an amount which exceeds or which is likely to exceed [state amount] unless such person shall have first provided to the mortgagee a written undertaking, in a form satisfactory to the mortgagee, not to exercise any lien in respect of such work.

(g) Not to appoint a manager

Not without the prior written consent of the mortgagee to appoint a manager of the ship [or a manager other than [name]].

(h) Not to pledge the credit of the mortgagee

Not to represent that the mortgagee is in any way concerned in the operation of the ship [or aircraft], the carriage of passengers or goods therein, or any other use to which the ship [or aircraft] may be put and not to pledge the credit of the mortgagee for any purpose whatsoever.

9. Mortgagee's liberty to protect security

(A) Without prejudice to any other rights or powers vested in it, the mortgagee shall be entitled (but not bound) at any time (whether before or after it has demanded payment of any of the outstanding indebtedness) and as often as it may deem necessary, to take such action as it shall in its absolute discretion think fit for the purpose of protecting the security created by the security documents and each and every expense, cost, payment, disbursement, loss, damage or liability incurred by the mortgagee in or about taking or attempting to take such action shall be repayable by the mortgagor on demand together with interest at the default rate from the date the same was incurred until payment before and after judgment.

(B) Without prejudice to the generality of the foregoing:
  (i) In the event of non-compliance with the provisions of clause 7(c) hereof,[7] or any
       part thereof, the mortgagee shall be at liberty to effect and thereafter to main-
       tain all such insurances as in its absolute discretion it shall think fit.
 (ii) In the event of non-compliance with any other provision the mortgagee shall be
       at liberty to make such payments or to arrange for the carrying out of such work
       or to take any such measures as it shall in its absolute discretion deem expedi-
       ent or necessary.

10. Events of default

Upon the happening of any of the following events the outstanding indebtedness shall
become immediately repayable to the mortgagee without further demand and the mortgagee shall be entitled without notice to the mortgagor to exercise all or any of the
powers vested in it.

(a) Failure to pay sum

The mortgagee fails to pay any sum of money payable under the security documents on
the date specified for payment thereof.

(b) Failure to perform or observe covenant

The mortgagee does not perform or observe any of the covenants or obligations contained in the security documents.

(c) Insolvency

A petition is filed or an order is made or an effective resolution is passed for the winding-
up of the mortgagor [or the guarantor] in any jurisdiction whatsoever (otherwise than for
the purpose of any reconstruction or amalgamation as shall have previously been
approved in writing by the mortgagee) or a Receiver is appointed over the undertaking
or property of the mortgagor [or guarantor] or the mortgagor suspends payment or
ceases to carry on its business or makes special arrangements or composition with its
creditors or an effective resolution is passed (except with the mortgagee's prior written
consent) for the reduction in the issued share capital of the mortgagor [or guarantor].

(d) Total loss

The ship [or aircraft] becomes a total loss.

(e) Failure to pay earnings

Any earnings are paid otherwise than in accordance with the directions of the mortgagee.

(f) Impossibility or illegality

If it becomes impossible or unlawful for the mortgagor to perform or observe any of the
covenants or obligations contained in the security documents or for the mortgagee to
exercise any of the rights or powers vested in it.

---

7. I.e. the covenant to insure, which it may often be more convenient to draft as an entirely separate clause.

(g) Imperilling of security

Anything is done or suffered to be done by the mortgagor, whether in connection with the mortgaged property or otherwise, which in the opinion of the mortgagee may imperil the security created by the security documents.

11. Mortgagee's powers upon default

Upon the happening of any of the events of default specified in clause 10 hereof, the mortgagee shall become entitled forthwith to exercise all or any of the powers vested in it and in particular:

(a) Possession

To take possession of the mortgaged property.

(b) Insurances

To require that all policies, contracts and all other documents whatsoever relating to the insurances or outstanding claims thereunder be forthwith delivered to the mortgagee or as he shall direct and to collect, recover, compromise and give a good discharge in respect of all claims outstanding or arising under the insurances and to take over or to institute (if necessary in the name of the mortgagee) all proceedings in connection therewith as the mortgagee shall in its absolute discretion think fit.

(c) Discharge claims etc.

To discharge, compound, release or compromise claims against the mortgagor in respect of the mortgaged property or any part thereof which have given or which may give rise to any charge or lien on the mortgaged property or which are or may be enforceable by proceedings against the mortgaged property or any part thereof.

(d) Sale

To sell the ship [or aircraft and engines] without prior notice to the mortgagor and with or without the benefit of any contract entered into in connection with the ship [or aircraft or engines] in such manner and for such consideration and upon such terms as the mortgagee in its absolute discretion shall think fit with power to postpone any such sale and without being answerable for any loss occasioned by such sale or resulting from the postponement thereof.

(e) To manage etc pending sale

Pending sale of the mortgaged property to manage, insure, maintain, repair, employ or lay up the ship [or aircraft] in such manner and for such period as the mortgagee shall in its absolute discretion think fit and to do all acts and things incidental or conducive thereto as if the mortgagee were the owner of the ship [or aircraft] without being responsible for any loss incurred thereby and to recover losses thereby incurred from the mortgagor upon demand together with interest thereon at the default rate from the date when such losses were incurred to the date of payment before and after judgment.

(f) Expenses incurred in exercise of powers

To recover from the mortgagor upon demand all expenses payments disbursements whatsoever incurred by the mortgagee in or about or incidental to the exercise of any of the powers vested in it together with interest thereon at the default rate from the date when the same were incurred until the date of payment before and after judgment PROVIDED ALWAYS that upon any sale of the mortgaged property or any part thereof the purchaser shall not be bound to see or enquire whether the power of sale has arisen and the sale shall be deemed to be within the power of the mortgagee and the mortgagee's receipt for the purchase money shall effectively discharge the purchaser who shall not be concerned with the manner of application of the proceeds of sale or be in any way answerable therefor.

12. Protection of purchasers

No person dealing with the mortgagee or with any Receiver appointed by the mortgagee hereunder shall be concerned to see or to enquire whether the power which the mortgagee or Receiver is purporting to exercise has arisen or has become exercisable or whether any money remains due on the security created hereby or otherwise as to the propriety or regularity of any sale or other dealing by the mortgagee or Receiver with the mortgaged property or any part thereof and all the protection afforded to purchasers by sections 104 and 107 of the Law of Property Act 1925 shall apply to any such person dealing with the mortgagee or such Receiver.

13. Application of proceeds of sale etc.

All monies arising from the sale or realisation of the mortgaged property and all monies received by the mortgagee or by any Receiver appointed hereunder shall be applied as follows:
FIRST in or towards payment of all costs and expenses and disbursements (including legal fees) of whatsoever nature incurred in connection with such sale or realisation.
SECONDLY in or towards payment of the balance of the outstanding indebtedness.
THIRDLY the balance (if any) to the mortgagor or other person entitled thereto.

14. Delay and indulgence

No delay or omission of the mortgagee to exercise any right or power vested in it shall impair such right or power to be construed as a waiver of or acquiescence in any default of the mortgagor and in the event of the mortgagee at any time agreeing to waive any such right or power such waiver shall be revocable by the mortgagee at any time and the right or power shall thenceforth be exercisable again as if there had never been such waiver.

15. Delegation

The mortgagee shall be entitled at any time and as often as it may in its absolute discretion deem expedient to delegate all or any of the powers and discretions vested in it in such manner and upon such terms and to such persons as it may in its absolute discretion think fit.

16. Indemnity

The mortgagor hereby agrees and undertakes to indemnify the mortgagee against all obligations and liabilities whatsoever arising which the mortgagee may incur in connection with the mortgaged property or otherwise howsoever in relation to or in connection with the mortgage and this agreement.

17. Power of attorney

The mortgagor hereby irrevocably appoints the mortgagee as its attorney for the duration of the security period for the purposes of doing in its name all acts which the mortgagor could do in relation to the mortgaged property PROVIDED that such power shall not be exercisable until the outstanding indebtedness becomes repayable. As regards any person dealing with the mortgagee, the exercise of the power by or on behalf of the mortgagee shall be conclusive evidence of its right to exercise the same and such person shall not be put on enquiry as to whether the outstanding indebtedness has become repayable nor shall any such person be affected by notice that the outstanding indebtedness has not become repayable.

18. Further assurances

The mortgagor hereby undertakes at its own expense to execute, sign, perfect, do and (if required) register every such further assurance, document, act, or thing as in the opinion of the mortgagee may be necessary or desirable for the purpose of more effectually mortgaging and charging the mortgaged property or perfecting the security created hereby.

19. Representation and notices

The mortgagor hereby appoints as its agent and representative [name and address] who is hereby authorised to accept service on behalf of the mortgagor of any notices or legal process.

Any notices, requests, demands or other communication to the parties hereto shall be deemed to have been given (i) in the case of telex, when sent; (ii) in the case of cable, when delivered to the cable company; (iii) in the case of letter, when posted; and (iv) in the case of facsimile transmission, when sent.

20. Law

The provisions of this agreement shall be governed by and construed in accordance with English law.

5

RIGHTS AND LIABILITIES OF THE MORTGAGOR AND THE MORTGAGEE

INTRODUCTION

The essence of the mortgage is that it is a transfer of property as security for a debt. A legal mortgage passes the mortgagor's interest in the mortgaged property to the mortgagee subject only to the mortgagor's right to redeem his property by paying off the mortgage debt in full, together with interest, at any time on or before the date specified in the mortgage as the date for repayment, or after that date provided always that the mortgage has not previously been foreclosed, or the property sold. The mortgagor's right to redeem after the date for repayment is referred to as his "equity of redemption".

The mortgage will remain as an encumbrance upon the property which is made security for the mortgage debt until it is discharged. A mortgage may be discharged upon satisfaction of the mortgage debt. This may be achieved in three ways:

 (i) upon redemption by the mortgagor or by any other person interested in the equity of redemption;
 (ii) upon sale by the mortgagee or by the court, and the satisfaction of the mortgaged debt out of the proceeds of sale;
 (iii) by foreclosure.

However, provided the mortgagor is not in default and does not in any way imperil the security of the mortgagee, he will be entitled to all the benefits of ownership and the use and profits of the ship or aircraft.

Although the common law and equitable principles which have evolved provide the general background against which the relationship of mortgagor and mortgagee must be examined, in the vast majority of cases the relationship will be regulated more specifically by the provisions of the deed of covenants.

The deed of covenants may, according to the circumstances surrounding the grant of the mortgage, make provision for collateral advantages in favour of the mortgagee. The rule as to their validity was summarised by Lord Parker in *Kreglinger* v. *New Patagonia Meat and Cold Storage Company*[1] where he said[2]:

1. [1914] A.C. 25.
2. At p. 61.

There is no rule in equity which precludes a mortgagee, whether the mortgage be made upon the occasion of a loan or otherwise, from stipulating for a collateral advantage provided such collateral advantage is neither (1) unfair and unconscionable or (2) in the nature of a penalty clogging the equity of redemption, or (3) inconsistent with or repugnant to the contractual or equitable right to redeem.

It is against this framework that the respective rights and liabilities of the mortgagor and the mortgagee are to be considered. Although it is necessary for the sake of convenience and clarity to treat the position of the mortgagor and the mortgagee separately, it should always be borne in mind that the position of each exists only in relation to the other.

THE MORTGAGOR

The right to redeem

The right of the mortgagor to repay the loan and redeem his property is central to the nature of a mortgage and, because of the possibility of a mortgagee exploiting his bargaining strength at the time the mortgage is entered into, the court will jealously guard the right of redemption. The equitable rule is that there must be "no clogs or fetters" on the equity of redemption.

The rule was described by Lord Bramwell in *Salt* v. *Marquess of Northampton*[3] as follows:

But there is a further equitable rule which seems to be this: that this right of redemption shall not even by bargain between the creditor and debtor be made more burdensome to the debtor than the original debt, except so far as additional interest and expenses consequent on the debt not having been paid at the time appointed, may have occurred or arisen; that any such agreement making such right of redemption more burdensome is void.

A provision attempting to exclude altogether the right to redeem is clearly an abuse and will not be enforceable. Similarly, where at the time the mortgage is entered into the mortgagor grants to the mortgagee an option to purchase the mortgaged property, thus effectively enabling the mortgagee to abrogate the mortgagor's right to redeem by the exercise of that option, this too will be held unenforceable.[4] However, where the option is granted after the execution of the mortgage, provided the two transactions are genuinely separate and independent, the option will be enforceable.[5] But not if in truth they are part and parcel of the same transaction.[6]

An alternative possibility is that the mortgage may provide for the exercise of the right to redeem to be postponed. In *Fairclough* v. *Swan Brewery*,[6a] the Privy Council held a postponement of the right to redeem to an extent which rendered the right illusory (in that case to very shortly before the expiry of the lease com-

3. (1892) App.Cas. 1.
4. *Samuel* v. *Jarrah* [1904] A.C. 323.
5. *Reeve* v. *Lisle* [1902] A.C. 461.
6. *Lewis* v. *Love* [1961] 1 W.L.R. 261.
6a. [1912] A.C. 562.

prising the mortgaged property) to be unenforceable. But a postponement which did not have that effect will not necessarily be struck down.[7]

Repayment

The deed of covenants will invariably contain an express covenant to repay the mortgage debt, but even if such a provision were to be missing, the covenant to repay will be implied.[8] The mortgagee will thus always have a right of action against the mortgagor on the covenant to repay, although such a right will only be *in personam*, and therefore of no particular value where the mortgagor is unable, as opposed to being merely unwilling, to repay the advance.

Interest

Likewise there will invariably be a covenant to pay interest upon the debt, such interest to continue to run after the date specified for repayment until repayment is actually made. A clause providing that the rate of interest is to be increased upon a failure to make repayment upon the due date will be struck down as a penalty.[9]

If there is no express provision for interest to be paid after the date for repayment has passed, nevertheless if the mortgagor fails to repay upon the due date, the mortgagee will be entitled to damages against the mortgagor for breach of his covenant to repay. Such damages will be assessed as interest at a commercial rate.

In some instances, interest will be expressed in the mortgage to be payable in advance. For example half-yearly or quarterly in advance on certain dates. In these circumstances, if repayment or recovery through enforcement of the security occurs after the date specified for the advance payment to be made, nevertheless the mortgagee is only entitled to interest that has actually accrued for the period of the delay in receiving repayment, and not to the whole amount of the advance payment provided for.

In *Banner* v. *Berridge*[10] interest was payable half-yearly in advance on certain dates. The mortgagee sold the ship and received the proceeds of sale three days after one of the half-yearly dates, and the court held that he was entitled to only three days' interest. It was held that the claim for six months' interest was inequitable and would not be allowed either as interest due under the mortgage or as six months' interest in lieu of notice to redeem. The court considered that a distinction was to be drawn between a case where the mortgagor seeks to redeem and the mortgage provides for six months' interest to be paid in lieu of

---

7. See for example *Knightsbridge Estates* v. *Byrne* [1939] Ch. 441.
8. *King* v. *King* (1735) 3 P.Wms. 358.
9. *Gregory* v. *Pilkington* (1856) 8 De G.M. & G. 616 and *Wallingford* v. *Mutual Society* (1880) 5 App. Cas. 685.
10. (1881) L.R. 18 Ch.D. 254.

notice, and a case where the vessel is sold by the mortgagee to realise his security.

Redemption

The right to redeem may be enforced by an action for redemption if tender of the mortgage debt is refused by the mortgagee.[11] The mortgagor is entitled to redeem the mortgaged property upon payment of the mortgage debt, together with any interest and the expenses incurred by the mortgagee in taking or holding possession or otherwise protecting his security.

In order to exercise the right to redeem, the mortgagor, or other person seeking to exercise the right, must tender the exact sum due either to the mortgagee, or to some other person duly authorised to receive payment.[12] Actual payment must be made, and it will not be sufficient for the mortgagor to aver a counterclaim against the mortgagee for an equal or greater amount.[13]

A cheque is not considered conditional payment of a secured debt sufficient to release the security,[14] nor is payment sent by registered post, which was stolen in transit, sufficient.[15]

The payment of a lesser sum than that due will operate as discharge *pro tanto* only in the absence of an agreement under seal, or some other consideration for the mortgagee's forbearance as regards the difference. This is the rule in *Foakes v. Beer*.[16]

However, payment of a lesser sum than the whole debt then outstanding if made at a different place or at an earlier date will be good consideration for discharge of the mortgage.[17] Similarly if payment is to be made by a different person[18] or in a different form.[19]

Composition with creditors is also good consideration for discharge of the whole debt by payment of a lesser sum.[20] Where it is no longer possible actually to redeem the mortgaged property, an action for redemption cannot lie, but the mortgagor may have an action for damages against the mortgagee if redemption has been prevented by the mortgagee's wrongful act or default.

In *Fletcher & Campbell* v. *City Marine Finance Ltd.*[21] the first plaintiff, as registered owner, mortgaged the vessel *Gay Tucan* to the defendants, a finance company, as security for a loan. The second defendant was the beneficial owner of the vessel. A default having been made in the payment of an instalment, the

---

11. *Wilkes* v. *Saunion* (1877) 7 Ch.D. 188.
12. *Re Defries* [1909] 2 Ch. 423.
13. *Samuel Keller (Holdings) Limited* v. *Martins Bank* [1971] 1 W.L.R. 43.
14. *Re Defries* [1909] 2 Ch. 423.
15. *Mitchell-Henry* v. *Norwich Union Life Insurance Society* [1918] 2 K.B. 67.
16. (1884) 9 App.Cas. 605.
17. *Smith* v. *Trowsdale* (1834) 3 E. & B. 83.
18. *Welby* v. *Drake* (1825) 1 Car. & P. 557.
19. *Goddard* v. *O'Brien* (1882) 9 Q.B.D. 37.
20. *Good* v. *Cheeseman* (1831) 2 B. & Ad. 328 and *Couldery* v. *Bartrum* (1881) 19 Ch.D. 394.
21. [1968] 2 Lloyd's Rep. 520.

defendants wrote to the first plaintiff advising that they were taking possession. The second plaintiff visited the defendants and tendered the debt, but the defendants refused to accept the tender on the ground that it should have been made by the first plaintiff. The defendants then sold the vessel and the first plaintiff claimed damages. Roskill J. held that the first plaintiff was entitled to damages on the grounds that a mortgagor had a right of action against his mortgagee if his right to redeem was prevented by the wrongful action of the mortgagee following *McLarty* v. *Middleton*.[22] After discussing that case he said[23]:

Accordingly, in my judgment, there is, as a matter of English law, a right in the mortgagor of a ship to recover damages against his mortgagee, if his right to redeem is prevented by the wrongful act of the mortgagee. I do not think it matters whether one makes the necessary implication into the collateral deed as a matter of law or whether one makes the implication therein as arising from the other express terms of the deed or whether one arrives at the same result by the application of basic principles of equity. Basically, as I have already said the ordinary principles of law relating to mortgages and their redemption apply and, as I read the cases, have always been applied to mortgages of ships during the 19th century . . . It would be strange if a mortgagor's only remedy in these circumstances were to bring a redemption action if he could do so timeously, particularly having regard to the system of registration of title now prescribed for ships by statute. It would obviously be difficult to deprive a bona fide purchaser for value of his title to a ship which he had already registered, even though he had acquired that title through default on the part of the mortgagee in the manner in which the latter had exercised his power of sale.

Joint mortgagors

The usual provision expressed in the deed of covenants where there is more than one mortgagor is that all the mortgagors are to be jointly and severally liable for the mortgage debt. Nevertheless, as between themselves, the position may be completely different. Only one may have had the benefit of the debt while the others were merely sureties. In this case, as between themselves, the sureties are entitled to be reimbursed by the principal debtor. Alternatively, they may have operated a joint account for a common adventure or may have apportioned the advance according to specific shares. In this situation they are liable, as between themselves, to contribute to the repayment of the debt according to their respective shares of their respective interests in the adventure as appropriate, or in the absence of some other arrangement, equally. The arrangements as among themselves will be of no concern to the mortgagee.

Joint mortgagees

Where mortgagees have advanced money jointly, payment to one is good discharge of the debt at law, but it does not discharge the security except to the

22. (1861) 4 L.T. 852.
23. *Ibid.* at p. 538 column 2.

extent of the payee's beneficial interest. In *Powell* v. *Broadhurst*,[24] the position was summarised by Farwell J. as follows:

If a mortgagor chooses to pay otherwise than in strict accordance with the terms of his contract he does so at his own risk. The proviso for redemption in a mortgage to several is never expressed to take effect on payment to the mortgagees or either of them, but to the mortgagees or the survivor of them; and if a mortgagor pays to one, although such payment may be a good discharge in law, yet the matter is at large when he comes into equity, and the Court takes into consideration all the facts of the case, and ascertains whether the payee was entitled to the whole or to a part only, or whether he was trustee with the other mortgagee and treats the payment as good in whole, or in part, or altogether bad accordingly, . . . [25]

Possession of the mortgaged property

Although by taking a mortgage the mortgagee becomes owner of the property, subject to the mortgagor's right of redemption, a mortgagee will not usually be interested in actually operating the ship or aircraft or in being the owner in the ordinary sense of the word. In the majority of cases such would defeat the entire purpose of the transaction. His only interest in taking ownership is as security for the repayment of the loan secured by the mortgage. The mortgagor will, therefore, remain in possession and continue to be the owner for all intents and purposes. He will operate the ship or aircraft, take the earnings and make the repayments under the loan agreement.

As far as registered mortgages of ships are concerned, this is reflected in section 34 of the Merchant Shipping Act 1894 which provides:

Except as far as may be necessary for making a mortgaged ship or share available as a security for the mortgaged debt, the mortgagee shall not by reason of the mortgage be deemed to be the owner of the ship or share, nor shall the mortgagor be deemed to have ceased to be the owner thereof.

Thus unless and until the mortgagee enters into possession, the mortgagor remains to all the world the owner of the ship, but that the mortgagee shall be deemed the owner for all purposes necessary to make the ship security for the mortgaged debt.

The position under the same provision int 1854 Act was considered in *Dickinson* v. *Kitchen*,[26] *per* Crompton J.:

The question in this case arose upon the mortgagee of the ship coming in under the interpleader process to claim the ship as owner against the execution creditor. By the ordinary incident of the conveyance to him by way of mortgage, he would be owner. The question therefore is, whether the conveyance by way of mortgage under . . . the statute, is an ordinary mortgage. If it is, the mortgagee is thereby, by reason of such mortgage, become the owner of the ship as against a subsequent execution at the suit of a creditor. I am of the opinion that the mortgage under the statute is an ordinary mortgage with ordinary incidents. It seems that none of these ordinary incidents are taken away by

24. [1901] 2 Ch. 160.
25. See also *Wallace* v. *Kelsall* (1840) 7 M. & W. 264; *Matson* v. *Dennis* (1864) 4 De G.J. & Sm. 345.
26. (1858) 8 El. & B. 789.

[the] section. That section was intended to protect a mortgagee taking possession of a mortgaged ship, in order to make it available as a security from certain liabilities which frequently attach an owner of a ship in possession.

It was further considered and its purpose explained by the Lord Chancellor, Lord Westbury, in *Collins* v. *Lamport*[27]:

Formerly, by reason of the earlier statutes, the mortgagee, the moment a mortgage was made and registered, became, in the eye of the law, the owner of the property; and the result was, that the law was in the habit of regarding the mortgagor as standing in the capacity of quasi agent to the mortgagee, and the mortgagee frequently found himself bound, either by the contracts of the mortgagor, or, at all events, by the necessary expenditure and outgoings of the vessel. That was a very serious injury and inconvenience to the mortgagees, and it interposed considerable difficulty in the way of the mortgagors getting money upon this species of security . . . The principle that was declared in opposition to the reason of those cases was, that the mortgagor should be deemed and regarded as the owner of the vessel. First there is a negative declaration that the mortgagee shall not, by reason of his mortgage, be deemed to be the owner; and then there is an affirmative declaration that the mortgagor shall not be deemed to have ceased to be the owner. The mortgagor therefore continues the owner; but it was necessary, . . . to add these words in declaring in what position the mortgagor shall stand, namely, he shall be owner save so far as may be necessary for making the ship or share available as a security for the mortgage debt.

Whilst out of possession, a mortgagee is entitled to take measures to protect either the title of the mortgagor or the mortgaged property. This includes intervening in any proceedings which affect his security and, if necessary, giving bail for the release of a ship in an admiralty action *in rem*.[28]

Mortgagor in possession

Introduction

While the mortgagor remains in possession of the mortgaged property, it is he and not the mortgagee who has to bear the expenses of operating the ship or aircraft and who has the right to the earnings therefrom.[29] It is the mortgagor and not the mortgagee who is responsible for compliance with the various duties and obligations laid upon an owner of a ship under the merchant shipping legislation or the Civil Aviation Acts.

Expenses

In the case of a ship, the authorities establish that, if he is not in possession, the mortgagee is not responsible for the wages and disbursements of the master[30];

27. (1864) 34 L.J.Ch. 196.
28. *The "Ringdove"* (1858) Swab. 310.
29. See Lord Mansfield in *Chinnery* v. *Blackman* (1784) 1 Hy.Bl. 117n.
30. See *Annett* v. *Carstairs* (1813) 3 Camp. 354.

nor for necessaries supplied to the ship.[31] It is submitted that the position as regards the mortgagee in possession of an aircraft is the same.

In *Castle* v. *Duke*[32] the question arose as to who was responsible as between the mortgagor and the mortgagee for the costs of repairs to the mortgaged ship in circumstances where the mortgagee, who was also the ship's broker, had ordered the repairs to be carried out. The court held that liability for the repairs depended upon the capacity in which the order had been given out.

In *The "Ripon City"* (*No. 2*),[33] minority shareholders in possession of the ship incurred liabilities including a claim for wages and disbursements by the master. The majority shareholders settled the claim, repaired the ship and had to pay a sum of money in order to cancel an unprofitable charter entered into by the minority shareholders. In distributing the proceeds of sale of the ship, the court held that the mortgagees of the minority shares were not liable to deduction of the costs and expenses of the majority shareholders in respect of the master's claim, the repairs and the cancellation charges as they were not in possession at the material time.

Freight

In the absence of any collateral assignment, the mortgagor is entitled to freight. The mortgagee is not entitled to freight until he enters into possession, and upon entering into possession he is not entitled by that act alone to recover the earnings of the ship received by the mortgagor before that time.[34]

It is submitted that the position as regards the earnings of an aircraft is the same.

The right to freight is considered further below in relation to the mortgagee and his right to receive freight and earnings.[35]

Insurance

The mortgagor is entitled to insure the ship or aircraft, and will usually be under an express obligation so to do under the deed of covenants. The mortgagee may prevent the ship sailing uninsured,[36] and by analogy prevent an aircraft from flying uninsured.

---

31. See *Jackson* v. *Vernon* (1879) 1 Hy.Bl. 114, *Baker* v. *Buckle* (1822) 7 Moore 349, *Twentyman* v. *Hart* (1816) 1 Stark 366, *The "Troubadour"* (1866) L.R. 1 A.& E. 302 and *The "Pickaninny"* [1960] 1 Lloyd's Rep. 533.
32. (1832) 5 Car. & P. 359.
33. [1898] P. 78.
34. See *Gardner* v. *Cazenove* (1856) 1 H. & N. 423; *Willis* v. *Palmer* (1860) 7 C.B.N.S. 340 and *Essarts* v. *Whinney* (1903) 9 Asp.M.L.C. 363.
35. See p. 164 et seq.
36. See the Scottish case of *Laming* v. *Seater* (1889) 16 Sess.Cas. 828.

The Marine Insurance Act 1906 provides that both the mortgagor and the mortgagee have an insurable interest. Section 14 provides[37]:

(1) Where the subject-matter insured is mortgaged, the mortgagor has an insurable interest in the full value thereof, and the mortgagee has an insurable interest in respect of any sum due or to become due under the mortgage.

(2) A mortgagee, consignee or other person having an interest in the subject-matter insured may insure on behalf and for the benefit of other persons interested as well as for his own benefit.

It was held in *Samuel* v. *Dumas*[38] that an equitable mortgagee had an insurable interest.

It should be noted that in the absence of an express provision, there is no general implied right on the part of a mortgagee to pay insurance premiums and add them to the mortgage debt. It may be, however, that there is an implied statutory right arising under section 108(1) and (2) of the Law of Property Act 1925 to insure against fire. See *The "Basildon"*.[39] In that case the question arose on a motion for judgment in default as to whether payments made for insurance were recoverable under the plaintiffs' first mortgage (which had no express provision) or under their second mortgage which did. The question was material owing to the existence of yet another mortgage ranking between the plaintiffs' first and second mortgages. Brandon J. dealt with this question of principle as follows:

The Plaintiffs claim that they had an implied right to make the payments and add them to the mortgage debt under the first mortgage on the ground that failure by the Defendants to continue the insurance of the vessel would impair the security of the first mortgage. I am not satisfied that the Plaintiffs had any such right under the first mortgage. It seems to me that there is an implied right to insure against fire under the Law of Property Act 1925[40] section 108(1) and (2). I say that because the definition of a mortgage contained in the definition section of the Law of Property Act 1925 is very wide and appears to cover the case of any chattel, including a ship. But this was a general insurance of a ship under an ordinary marine policy, either a full policy, or later a port policy, and it would seem to me quite artificial to decide that that policy was kept up even as regards the fire element of the risk under the provisions of the Law of Property Act which I have mentioned. It may well be that where a mortgagor fails to insure the mortgaged ship the mortgagee will be entitled to take possession of the vessel under the powers to take possession which always exist. If that sort of question arose, the question would be whether the failure to insure, either by itself or along with other activities of the mortgagor, constituted such an impairment of the security as would justify the mortgagee in taking possession.

. . . It seems to me that if a mortgagee did take possession in such circumstances, and properly took possession, he could then insure the ship and charge the insurance together with other outgoings against the freight which he received. But I am not satisfied that

37. See also the pre-Act cases of *Irving* v. *Richardson* (1831) 2 B. & Ad. 193; *Provincial Insurance Co. of Canada* v. *Leduc* (1874) L.R. 6 P.C. 224; and *Levy* v. *The Merchants' Marine Ins. Co.* (1885) Cab. & El. 474.
38. [1924] A.C. 431.
39. [1967] 2 Lloyd's Rep. 134.
40. Section 205(xvi) which provides: "'Mortgage' includes any charge or lien on any property for securing money or money's worth."

where the mortgagee does not take possession he is entitled to pay insurance premiums and add them to the mortgage debt.

In *The "Athenic"*[41] there was an agreement which provided:

I agree to execute, when called upon by you, a legal first mortgage on the steamship "Athenic" to secure all sums that may be owing by me to you, such mortgage to contain such provisions as you require . . . and to pay all expenses in connection with the preparation, execution, and registration of the mortgage . . . I also agree to insure the ship through you . . . and that you are to hold the policies.

Lord Merrivale P. held that upon its true construction the mortgage secured the payment from the mortgagor to the mortgagee of insurance premiums and solicitors' charges in connection with the preparation of the mortgage.

Although the mortgagee may have an insurable interest and be entitled to be listed on the policy as an assured, he may alternatively take an assignment of the policy as part of his security. In these circumstances he stands in the shoes of the mortgagor as regards the underwriters and will be in no better position than the mortgagor. In particular he will be without recourse if the policy is avoided by the underwriters on the grounds of breach of warranty, wilful misconduct or misrepresentation by the mortgagor. The mortgagee may be able to protect himself against such eventualities, at some expense, by taking out mortgagee's interest insurance.

Thus in *Graham Joint Stock Shipping Company* v. *Merchants' Marine Insurance Company*[42] a ship was scuttled by the master and crew with the connivance of the shipowner. The mortgagees brought an action on the policy. It was held by the House of Lords that they failed, not having proved that they were parties to the contract. On the facts of that case the court considered that the instructions of the mortgagee's attorney to the broker were to be construed as instructions to insure on behalf of the mortgagor, the mortgagee's interest being protected by an assignment of or charge on the policy and an irrevocable power of attorney to sue on the policy in the name of the mortgagor.

In *Swan & Cleveland's Graving Dock and Slipway Company* v. *Marine Insurance Company*[43] a ship was mortgaged "together with the policies of insurance effected thereon" and the mortgagee had possession of the policy. During the currency of the policy the ship suffered general and particular average losses. The mortgagor had the damage repaired and assigned to the repairers, as security for the cost of the repairs, the monies due under the policy and gave notice to both the underwriters and the mortgagees. The mortgagor subsequently became insolvent.

The court held that the mortgagee obtained the policy as security for his debt, and not merely as security for his security (viz. the ship) and was entitled to the monies under the policy to his own use and was not liable to apply it in payment of the costs of the repairs. It was further held that the mortgagor retained an

---

41. (1932) 42 Ll.L.Rep. 91.
42. [1924] A.C. 294.

43. (1906) 10 Asp.M.L.C. 450.

interest in the policy in the nature of an equity of redemption, and was entitled to sue upon it, or to require the mortgagee to sue upon it on his behalf in so far as he had an interest exceeding that of the mortgagee in the sum recovered. In the course of giving judgment Channell J. said:

> The rights between the mortgagor and the mortgagee must be determined by the mortgage deed so far as these have not been varied by subsequent agreement. If the money had been recovered from the underwriters before the ship had been repaired, it is quite clear that the money would belong to the mortgagee; and if the mortgagor claimed, as in substance he did claim in the present case, that the money should be applied in payment of the cost of repairs, he would have to get the authority or consent of the mortgagee so to apply it, or he would have to show that such consent had been given in the original contract.

Employment

He is entitled to enter into any contract with regard to the ship or aircraft which does not materially impair the security of the mortgage.

In *Collins* v. *Lamport*[44] it was held that contracts with respect to the ship entered into by the mortgagor, will be valid and effectual provided his dealings do not materially impair the security of the mortgage, and the mortgagee will be restrained by injunction from interfering with the due exercise of those contracts.

As long therefore as the dealings of the mortgagor with the ship are consistent with the sufficiency of the mortgagee's security, so long as those dealings do not materially prejudice or detract from or impair the sufficiency of the security of the vessel as comprised in the mortgage, so long is there parliamentary authority given to the mortgagor to act in all respects as owner of the vessel, and if he has authority to act as owner, he has, of necessity, authority to enter into all those contracts touching the disposition of the ship which may be necessary for enabling him to get the full value and the full benefit of his property. Whenever a mortgagee is in a position to show that the act of the mortgagor prejudices or injures his security, then the parliamentary declaration that the mortgagor shall be deemed to be owner ceases to have any binding effect as against the mortgagee and the mortgagee is in a position to claim and exercise the full benefit and rights given him by his mortgage; but subject to that qualification, every contract entered into by the mortgagor remaining in possession is a contract which derives validity from the declaration of his continuing to be the owner.

The difficult question of what contract will be considered materially to impair the security of the mortgagee is considered further below in the context of the mortgagee's right to enter into possession.

THE MORTGAGEE

The right of the mortgagee to take possession

The regulation of the right of the mortgagee to enter into possession is achieved primarily by the express provisions contained in the collateral deed of coven-

44. (1864) 34 L.J.Ch. 196.

ants. The contents of the deed of covenants has already been considered above in Chapter 4.

Nevertheless, the mortgagee has a right at common law, independently of contract, to enter into possession in two situations. First, where the mortgagor has made default either in the payment of interest under the mortgage or in the repayment of capital. Second, where even in the absence of any default, the mortgagor has allowed the security of the mortgage to have become impaired. In order to take full advantage of this first situation it is advisable to have a provision in the mortgage for the debt to be repayable upon demand.

However, it should be noted that where a provision for repayment on demand is included, the mortgagee must of course first make such a demand and, secondly, the mortgagee must thereafter allow the mortgagor a reasonable time in which to make repayment. What is a reasonable time will depend upon all the circumstances of the particular case.[45]

Although the mortgagee would be best advised to make an express demand for repayment, particularly having regard to the fact that he may be liable in damages to the mortgagor where he takes possession wrongfully,[46] in The "Halcyon Skies" (No. 2)[47] it was held on the facts and circumstances of that case that a demand for repayment was implicit in the dealings and communications between the parties.

However, unless and until either of these two situations arises, the mortgagee has no right to possession as against the mortgagor and if he enters into possession without being entitled to do so, the mortgagee may be liable to the mortgagor not only in respect of costs,[48] but also for substantial damages.[49]

In The "Blanche",[50] the mortgagee arrested the ship in an action for possession at a time before the mortgage monies had become due, and without any default on the part of the mortgagor. The ship was at that time under a charterparty not prejudicial to the security. The mortgagor applied for the release of the ship and the court ordered the vessel to be released as the mortgagor was not in default and the ship was not being dealt with so as to impair the security. In the course of his judgment Butt J. said:

I am prepared to hold that the mortgagee was not entitled to take possession before money secured by the mortgage is due. True the property in the ship is his, but the equities interfere and prevent his taking possession . . . I am quite satisfied that unless there was some attempt to impair the security, the plaintiff had no right to take possession.

In The "Innisfallen"[51] it was held that a mortgagee of shares not yet in possession had no right to restrain the co-owners from sending the ship on a voyage

45. See for example the decision of the Supreme Court of Canada in *Lister* v. *Dunlop Can. Ltd.* (1982) 135 D.L.R. (3d) 1.
46. See further below.
47. [1977] 1 Lloyd's Rep. 22.
48. See *The "Egerateria"* (1868) 38 L.J.Adm. 40.
49. See *The "Cathcart"* (1867) L.R. 1 A.& E. 314 and *The "Maxima"* (1878) 4 Asp.M.L.C. 21.
50. (1887) 6 Asp.M.L.C. 272.
51. (1866) L.R. 1 A.& E. 72.

under a charterparty not prejudicial to the security, even though the ship had been so let without his consent.

Where the mortgagor has, whilst in possession, entered into a charterparty, then unless that charterparty impairs the security created by the mortgage it will be binding upon the mortgagee, even if the mortgage debt has become due and so he would otherwise be entitled to enter into possession. The court will, if necessary, restrain the mortgagee from taking possession or allow him to do so only subject to his recognition of the charterparty.

Where however the charterparty impairs the security of the mortgagee he will be entitled to take possession and realise his security free of the charterparty.

If the mortgagee makes an application prematurely, in the sense that there has been no breach of covenant by the mortgagor and the court holds that the security is not imperilled, a subsequent application in the light of new circumstances will not be barred by the principle of *res judicata*.[52]

Impairment of security

It is not always easy to ascertain whether action taken by the mortgagor in relation to the ship will materially impair the security. The onus is upon the mortgagee to justify his taking possession by establishing that the security will otherwise be prejudiced, and consequently care must be taken before this right is exercised, as substantial damages may be awarded to the mortgagor where the mortgagee has taken possession without just cause.[53] Of course normally a properly worded provision in the deed of covenants will cover most likely situations where the mortgagee would wish to avail himself of his right to take possession.

The mere fact that the ship is about to put to sea on a foreign voyage is no ground upon which a mortgagee can base a claim for possession, even if the ship is to trade in places where enforcement of the mortgage security would be rendered more difficult. Thus in *The "Highlander"*[54] it was held that it was not possible for the mortgagee to arrest the ship to obtain bail merely because the ship was about to depart upon a foreign voyage.

In *The "Maxima"*,[55] shares in a ship were mortgaged, possession remaining in the mortgagor, and the managing owner, duly appointed by all the co-owners including the mortgagor, chartered the ship for a foreign voyage. The mortgagee arrested the ship after she had loaded and was about to proceed. The court held that even though the mortgagee had taken possession before the ship had sailed, but after the making of the charterparty, he could not arrest or demand bail in an action to enforce the mortgage debt provided the charter-

52. See the Nigerian case of *National Bank of Nigeria Ltd* v. *Okafor Lines Ltd (No. 2)* [1967] 2 A.L.R. Comm. 297 (High Court of Lagos State: Taylor C.J.).
53. See for example: *The "Cathcart"* (1867) L.R. 1 A. & E. 314; *The "Egerateria"* (1868) 38 L.J.Adm. 40.
54. (1843) 2 W.Rob. 109.
55. (1878) 4 Asp.M.L.C. 21.

party is not prejudicial to the security. If, on the other hand, the voyage was likely to be prejudicial to the plaintiffs' interest as mortgagee or was likely to lessen the sufficiency of the security, the court said it would have released only on terms satisfactory to the plaintiffs.

Similarly in *The "Fanchon"*,[56] 20/64th shares in a ship had been mortgaged to a bank and the ship was subsequently chartered for a voyage to carry cliff stone from Hull to Philadelphia. Immediately the mortgage debt became due, the mortgagees took possession by putting a man on board, commenced foreclosure proceedings, and had the ship arrested. The court held that in the absence of any evidence that the charterparty materially prejudiced their security, the mortgagees were bound by it and the ship would be released from arrest in order to perform the charterparty voyage.

Mortgagor in financial difficulties

However, where the mortgagor is in financial difficulties the courts have held that the mortgagee was justified in taking possession.

In a Scottish case, *Laming v. Seater*,[57] the mortgaged ship was put into a yard for repair by the mortgagors, but they were unable to pay for the repairs. The ship was due to proceed on a foreign voyage under a charterparty entered into by the mortgagors. The mortgagees paid part of the repair bill and the repairers took a second mortgage on the ship for the balance. The mortgagors agreed to take out and maintain a policy of insurance on the ship in the name of the mortgagees. The mortgagors failed to take out the insurance and the mortgagees took possession. The court held that they were entitled to do so and said:

It is plain enough that the mortgage was in jeopardy. The owners were in great pecuniary embarrassment and could not meet the costs of repairing the ship. Further, the owners had become bound to effect an insurance in the name of the mortgagees, which they did not do, and which, so far as I judge from the evidence, they were never in a position to do.

In *Johnston v. Royal Mail Steam Packet Company*[58] the mortgaged ship was let on a long-term charter for five years. The mortgagees were held to be entitled to take possession upon the liquidation of the mortgagor.

Maritime liens

It has been held that a subsequent bottomry bond does not necessarily impair the security[59] (a situation unlikely to arise today), although generally the fact that the mortgagor allows the ship to remain burdened with maritime liens will often amount to impairment of the security.

56. (1880) 5 P.D. 173.
57. 16 S.C. (4th series) 828.
58. (1867) L.R. 3 C.P. 38.
59. *The "Ripon City"* [1897] P. 226, 244 and *The "St.George"* [1926] P. 217.

In *The "Manor"*,[60] a mortgaged ship had been variously employed over a two-year period during the course of which maritime liens had been created in respect of wages and disbursements. She was also badly in need of repair. In these circumstances, the mortgagees entered into possession as she was about to embark upon two successive charters which were considered to be neither profitable nor proper. The court held that the mortgagees had been entitled to enter into possession in the circumstances which then existed. Lord Alverstone said:

> When we look at the broad facts of the case as they existed when this vessel came into Cardiff, I think it would be straining the rights of the mortgagor to excess if we were to hold that he was entitled to keep the management and chartering of this vessel in defiance of the rights of the mortgagee and prevent the mortgagee from taking possession . . . I think that the dealing with this ship by the mortgagor in the state of circumstances which then existed when she arrived in the port of Cardiff was such that, if she was left in the possession of the mortgagor the security of the mortgage would be seriously impaired.

Similarly Fletcher Moulton L.J. said:[61]

> It may well be that to allow a ship to become subject to a maritime lien may not be an infringement of the rights of the mortgagee, even though that maritime lien ranks above claims of the mortgagee. For example, it cannot be said to be a breach of the rights of the mortgagee, if a ship in distress accepts salvage assistance, though a maritime lien thereby arises. But there is an obvious difference between allowing a ship to become burthened with a maritime lien, and allowing her to remain burthened with such a lien, without the power to discharge it, for, to that extent, you have, as in this case, substantially diminished, that is to say, impaired the value of the mortgage security. Is a ship to be allowed to go on a long voyage incurring ruinous liabilities in the shape of maritime liens which count against her in priority to the mortgage? I am satisfied that equity would never interfere with a mortgagee taking possession under such circumstances as we find in this case, and, therefore, this action asking for a decree that the mortgagor was entitled to possession at the date of the writ cannot be maintained.

Quite

succintly

observed

Unusual or onerous charters

Where the mortgagor enters into a charterparty which is not in the usual form or contains onerous provisions or is on unprofitable terms, the mortgagee may be entitled to take possession free of the charterparty. The question is essentially one of degree.

In *The "Heather Bell"*,[62] the mortgagor of a ship entered into an agreement for the use of the ship with the plaintiff whereby the plaintiff was to have possession of the ship for about six weeks, the mortgagor was to insure her, the plaintiff was under no obligation to keep the ship in repair, and the profits were to be divided equally between the mortgagor and the plaintiff. The defendant mortgagee entered into possession of the ship upon default being made in one of the instalments due under the mortgage. The mortgagee was held liable in damages to

60. [1907] P. 339.
61. *Ibid.* at p. 361.
62. [1901] P. 272.

the plaintiff, the agreement being binding upon him as it was not prejudicial to the security created by the mortgage. In the course of his judgment, Lord Alverstone said:

I am not prepared to say that the agreement to run her on half profits must impair or does impair the security. No doubt it prevents the boat for a period of about 6 weeks from earning freight unless that freight is produced by the profits; but I cannot say that under the circumstances there might not be an honest expectation that there would be profits. Therefore, to undertake to run the boat at half profits seems to me not to be terms which must under the circumstances do any wrong to the rights of the mortgagee. I quite agree that the mortgagee has a right to prevent the vessel being run unless she is properly protected against perils of the sea; but it cannot be contended that if a charterparty is otherwise binding on the mortgagee the fact that he could have restrained her from running until properly insured would justify him setting aside a charterparty otherwise bona fide.

In *Law Guarantee & Trust Society* v. *Russian Bank for Foreign Trade*[63] mortgagors in possession entered into charterparties for the carriage of contraband to belligerent ports and the ships were not insured for war risks and in particular the risk of capture. The ships were liable to be seized as prize and the Court of Appeal held that the mortgagees were entitled to a declaration that they were not bound by the charterparties on the ground that they materially impaired the security of the mortgages.

Prior charterparties

Where, however, the ship has already been chartered at the time of the mortgage different considerations apply.

In *The "Celtic King"*,[64] the shipowner agreed with the defendants to provide a ship which was then being built to be run and operated by them in their line for a period of five years, upon such terms as they thought proper and for the account of and at the sole risk of the shipowner who was to divide the profits equally with the defendants. Subsequently, the shipowner mortgaged the ship to secure an account current and the mortgagees had no notice of any subsisting engagements with the defendants. The shipowner then gave a second mortgage to the plaintiffs who were aware of the existence of the agreement with the defendants and, although they were not aware of the precise terms, inferred that they were onerous. Upon the shipowner's death, the first mortgagees took possession of the vessel and sold her to the plaintiffs who at that time knew of the terms of the agreement with the defendants. Upon the defendants' application for an injunction restraining the plaintiffs from dealing with the ship contrary to the provisions of the agreement with the defendants, it was held that the injunction would be refused as the first mortgagees, who were unaware of the agreement with the defendants, were entitled to realise their security by selling the ship free of her engagements, and that the plaintiffs, although they had notice of

63. (1905) 10 Asp.M.L.C. 41.
64. [1894] P. 175.

the agreement with the defendants, were entitled to the same rights as were possessed by their vendor, the first mortgagees. Gorrell Barnes J. said[65]:

It is said upon the defendants' side that the contract would not have any depredatory effect upon the security of the mortgage. I cannot take that view. It seems to me that where there is a contract of this particular character it would be prejudicial to the security if the mortgagee were to be obliged to admit or forced to admit, that he could not sell the ship to realise his security in an open market without that restrictive covenant. It is not like an ordinary employment of a ship which is made from time to time as things are good and as things are bad; but it is a contract which binds the vessel for a very long period and has various clauses in it which might make it extremely difficult for anybody to purchase a ship of this kind if they were tied by its terms.

The dilemma which was presented to the court as a result of the conflicting claims of mortgagee and charterer was expressed by Gorrell Barnes J. in the following words:

I think myself that while on the one hand it is important that you should be able to charter vessels in the ordinary way without interference by mortgagees other than is necessary to protect their security, yet, on the other hand, a mortgagee who takes his rights without notice of any particular contract affecting the ship in this way, ought not to be prevented from realising his security.

The situation is otherwise where the mortgagee has actual notice of the charter at the time he takes his mortgage.

In *De Mattos* v. *Gibson*[66] the mortgaged ship was chartered to carry coals from the Tyne to Suez. After loading she put into Penzance for repairs, but the mortgagor was unable to pay for them. Accordingly the mortgagee took possession and undertook to pay for the repairs and then sought to sell the vessel. The charterer sought and obtained an interim injunction to prevent the mortgagee from interfering with the charterparty. Subsequently it was held by the Lord Chancellor, Lord Chelmsford, after a full trial that no injunction should be granted because the charterparty would not be able to be performed by the shipowner in any event owing to his financial position. However, both Knight-Bruce L.J., who granted the interlocutory injunction, and Lord Chelmsford L.C. stated that a mortgagor could be restrained by injunction from interfering with a charterparty existing at the time of the mortgage and of which he had notice.

The authority of *De Mattos* v. *Gibson* was more recently considered by Browne-Wilkinson J. in *Swiss Bank* v. *Lloyds Bank*[67] where he said[68]:

In my judgment that case is an authority binding on me that a person taking a charge on property which he knows to be subject to a contractual obligation can be restrained from exercising his rights under the charge in such a way as to interfere with the performance of that contractual obligation: in my judgment the *De Mattos* v. *Gibson* principle is merely

---

65. *Ibid.* at p. 188.
66. (1858) 4 De G. & J. 276.
67. [1979] Ch. 548 at pp. 569E to 575. The judgments of the Court of Appeal and the House of Lords reported in [1982] A.C. 584 do not consider this point.
68. *Ibid.* at page 573B.

the equitable counterpart of the tort. But two points must be emphasised about the decision in *De Mattos* v. *Gibson*: first, the ship was acquired with actual knowledge of the plaintiff's contractual rights; secondly, that no such injunction will be granted against the third party if it is clear that the original contracting party cannot in any event perform his contract.

It is also made clear by Browne-Wilkinson J. that constructive notice is not sufficient and that the doctrine will only apply where the mortgagee has actual notice of the charterparty when he takes the mortgage.

In *The "Lord Strathcona"*[69] a ship was chartered for 10 consecutive St. Lawrence seasons, with an option to the charterers for a further three or five seasons. During the currency of the charterparty, the shipowners mortgaged her to the plaintiffs who had notice of the charterparty. The shipowners became insolvent and made default in repayment under the mortgage. Accordingly the plaintiffs commenced and action *in rem* and obtained judgment and an order for sale. The charterers intervened to claim that the plaintiffs were not entitled to deal with the ship otherwise than in accordance with the charterparty. It was held that the shipowners were incapable of further performance of the charterparty by reason of their financial position and therefore the action of the mortgagees could not constitute interference with the charterparty.

Mode of taking possession

Two methods are possible: through the court by causing the ship to be arrested in an admiralty action *in rem* under section 21 of the Supreme Court Act 1981, or through self-help.

Where it is anticipated that there may be some resistance or opposition to the mortgagee taking possession it is advisable to invoke the assistance of the court through arrest in a mortgage action. The ship will be arrested by the Admiralty Marshal or his substitute, and any resistance or interference with that process would be a contempt of court.

Where the mortgagee elects to use the latter method, then he may take actual possession by putting his own representative on board, or where this is not possible he may take constructive possession by doing such act as clearly evidences an intention on his part to intervene, take possession and to assume the right of ownership. In *The "Benwell Tower"*[70] the ship was in France and although the mortgagees (who were also assignees of the freight under a separate assignment) sent their solicitor to take actual possession this was not possible under French law. The mortgagees arrested the ship, but not by way of asserting a claim to become mortgagees in possession. Accordingly the court held that they had not taken sufficient steps to indicate an intention to enter into possession of the ship as mortgagees in possession and to claim the freight as an incident of

69. [1925] P. 143.
70. (1895) 8 Asp.M.L.C. 13.

such possession. Their actions were ambiguous and equally consistent with their asserting a claim as assignees under the assignment.

If actual possession is possible, the mortgagee may dismiss the master and appoint his own master, or, alternatively, if the master is willing to continue to act, he may reappoint him in which case the master will henceforth be the agent of the mortgagee and not the agent of the mortgagor.

In *Benyon* v. *Godden*[71] it was held that where a mortgagee of shares had joined with the co-owners in appointing a new ship's husband he had taken constructive possession.

In *Rushden* v. *Pope*[72] it was held to be sufficient in order to obtain constructive possession for notice to be given by the mortgagee to the mortgagor, the charterer and all other persons interested: insurance brokers, underwriters and bill of lading holders.

Mortgagee in possession

Upon taking possession, the mortgagee will be entitled to the benefit of contracts relating to the enjoyment of the ship which have previously been entered into by the mortgagor, but he will be liable to pay the expenses incurred in the future operation and trading of the ship, as well as being under an obligation to ensure the performance of the shipowner's obligations. He will take the ship subject to the rights of holders of possessory liens.

In *Williams* v. *Allsupp*[73] the mortgagor delivered the mortgaged ship which had become in an unseaworthy condition to a repairer who duly repaired the ship, but whose account was not settled by the mortgagor. The mortgagees having recently become aware of the state of the ship and of the financial state of the mortgagor (which was not good) purported to take possession of the ship and demanded that she be handed over to them by the repairer, who refused to do so until his account was settled. The court held that as the repairer had a possessory lien in respect of the repairs he was entitled to exercise that possessory lien against the mortgagees' claim to possession.

Unless the lien holder has been guilty of unreasonable delay in enforcing his lien, the mortgagee will also take the ship subject to any maritime liens which have attached to the mortgaged property whilst in the possession of the mortgagor.[74]

However, the costs of discharging any liens in order actually to obtain possession of the ship may be recovered from the mortgagor.[75]

In *The "Orchis"*,[76] the mortgagees of 48/64th shares in a ship under arrest in an action paid off the plaintiff's claim in order to release the ship and to enable

71. (1878) L.R. 3 Ex.D. 263.
72. (1868) L.R. 3 Ex. 269.
73. (1861) 10 C.B.N.S. 417.
74. *The "Dowthorpe"* (1843) 2 Wm.Rob. 365 and *The "Royal Arch"* (1857) Swab. 269.
75. *Johnston* v. *Royal Mail* (1867) L.R. 3 C.P. 38 (wages paid to crew employed by the mortgagor).
76. (1890) 15 P.D. 38.

them to take possession under the mortgage. The court held that they were entitled to recover the sums so paid from the owners of the remaining shares.

Freight, earnings and expenses

As stated above,[77] the mortgagee is not entitled in the absence of a collateral assignment, to earnings of the vessel prior to entering into possession. The position was described by James L.J. in *Liverpool Marine Credit Company* v. *Wilson*[78] thus:

[the mortgagee] had no absolute right to the freight as an incident to his mortgage; he could not intercept the freight by giving notice to the charterer before payment; but if he took actual possession, or, . . . if he took constructive possession of the ship before the freight was actually earned, he thus became entitled to the freight as an incident of his legal possessory right . . .

As there stated, upon taking possession the situation alters. It was said in *Keith* v. *Burrows*:[79]

When a mortgagee takes possession he becomes the master or owner of the ship, and his position is simply this: from that time everything which represents the earnings of the ship which had not been paid before, must be paid to the person who then is the owner, who is in possession.

The mortgagee upon taking possession becomes entitled to any freight which is at that time in the course of being earned.[80] If the mortgagee has a lien for such freight, then the mortgagee upon taking possession succeeds to that lien.

In *Dean* v. *M'Ghie* Gaselee J. described the position thus[81]:

The mortgagee upon taking possession pays money the mortgagor ought to have paid (seamen's wages) and increases his debt by the amount of the payment. If he had received money which the mortgagor had title to receive he might fairly deduct the payment from the receipt, but the cases show the mortgagee has a right to freight.

The mortgagee is entitled to receive any freight due without deduction of any of the expenses of earning that freight incurred prior to the time when he took possession, as a mortgagee out of possession is not liable for the costs and expenses of operating the ship. In *Tanner* v. *Phillips*,[82] the charterparty provided for advances not exceeding £150 to be made by the charterers on account of freight. Advances in excess of £150 were duly made for ship's purposes before the mortgagees took possession. It was held that the mortgagees were entitled to receive the whole freight less the £150 authorised by the charterparty, but without any deduction for the advances in excess of £150 made prior to the mortgagees taking possession. "The advances in excess of the £150 were mere

77. See p. 83.
78. (1872) L.R. 7 Ch. 507 at p. 511.
79. (1877) 2 App.Cas. 636 at p. 646.
80. *Dean* v. *M'Ghie* (1826) 4 Bing. 45 and *Gumm* v. *Tyrie* (1865) 6 B. & S. 298.
81. At p. 49.
82. (1872) 1 Asp.M.L.C. 448.

personal loans, and had nothing to do with freight, and could not therefore be deducted out of it."[83]

The mortgagee is also entitled to receive all freight which actually becomes due after he has taken possession notwithstanding that it was actually earned prior to that time.

Thus in *Brown* v. *Tanner*,[84] after the ship had arrived at the port of discharge and was in the course of unloading her cargo, the mortgagee took possession and was held to be entitled to the freight earned on the voyage. Page-Wood L.J. said:

It is now settled beyond all dispute that the mortgagee of a ship becomes entitled to all the rights and liable to all the duties of an owner from the time of taking possession. Amongst the rights so accruing to him is that of receiving all freight remaining due when possession is taken.

Similarly in *Cato* v. *Irving*,[85] where the Vice-Chancellor said:

The authorities referred to in the argument establish that the mortgagee of a ship, who takes possession before the conclusion of the voyage, is entitled to the then accruing freight. It was contended by the Defendants that the present case does not come within this rule because the Plaintiffs did not take possession until the ship was in the docks, and the voyage therefore concluded. I consider that a mortgagee who takes possession at any time before the cargo is discharged comes within the rule. The right to freight does not accrue until the goods are not only conveyed to their destination but are also delivered; and a mortgagee who takes lawful possession of the ship while the goods are still on board, and is thereby entitled to deliver the goods and receive the freight, to the exclusion of the mortgagor, must be as much within the reason of the rule when the ship is in the docks as where she is only on the way to the docks at the time when possession is taken.

On the other hand, where freight becomes due before the mortgagee enters into possession, but nevertheless remains unpaid at the time he takes possession, the mortgagee is not entitled to that freight.[86]

In *Shillito* v. *Biggart*,[87] a dispute arose between the mortgagors and the mortgagees as to the entitlement to a sum in respect of freight earned on a voyage prior to the mortgagees' arrest of the ship, but which remained outstanding when the ship was arrested. The charterers interpleaded and the court held that notwithstanding the mortgagees' possession the freight was payable to the mortgagor as it had accrued due and was payable prior to the mortgagees taking possession.

Nor is the mortgagee entitled to recover freight which he has permitted the mortgagor to receive. In *Gardner* v. *Cazenove*,[88] the master received a sum of

---

83. *Per* Bacon V.-C. and see also The *"Salacia"* (1862) 32 L.J.Adm. 41 and The *"El Argentino"* [1909] P. 236.
84. (1868) L.R. 3 Ch.App. 597.
85. (1852) 5 De G. & Sm. 210.
86. *Anderson* v. *Butler's Wharf Co. Ltd.* (1879) 48 L.J.Ch. 824.
87. [1903] 1 K.B. 683.
88. (1856) 1 H. & N. 423.

money from the charterers on account of freight and, having no notice of the mortgage, remitted the same to the ship's husband. The court held that the mortgagees had no right to this sum.[89]

The entry into possession of the mortgaged property is essentially a right provided the mortgagee in order to realise his security, usually by exercising his power of sale. On the other hand, having entered into possession, the mortgagee is not obliged forthwith to exercise his power of sale. He may, subject to certain limitations, employ the ship on profitable trades, but in doing so he runs the risk that he will be held liable to account to the mortgagor should anything untoward happen to the mortgaged property.

In *Marriott* v. *The Anchor Reversionary Co.*[90] the mortgagee entered into possession and employed the mortgaged ship in a speculative trade during the course of which she was improperly managed and damaged while racing other vessels. As a result losses were incurred and the ship had to be sold for a greatly reduced price. The court held that the mortgagor was entitled to be credited with the value of the ship at the time the mortgagee had entered into possession. In the course of giving judgment, Lord Campbell said:[91]

I cannot concur in the unlimited right of the mortgagee to use the ship as the owner might do . . . Nor can I lay down the strict rule that the mortgagee can never lawfully employ the ship to earn freight, or that, after taking possession, he must allow her to lie idle till he may prudently sell her. He may take possession while she is prosecuting a voyage under a charter-party, and at the end of the voyage it is easy to conceive circumstances which would justify him in a temporary employment of the ship while waiting a favourable opportunity to sell her . . . But although there may be a great difficulty in defining the limits of the power of the mortgagee to use the ship, this, I think, may be laid down with perfect safety and confidence, that if the mortgagee does take possession he can only lawfully use the ship as a prudent man would use her, she being his own property.[92]

He cannot however be compelled by others to employ the ship rather than to exercise his power of sale.[93]

Expenses

By the act of entering into possession the mortgagee is asserting a claim to the ship as his own property and as such after such time as he takes possession he will be responsible for the expenses of her operation,[94] and the master will become his agent and under his instructions.[95]

However, although this must be so as regards carrying out the mortgagee's

89. *Willis* v. *Palmer* (1859) 7 C.B.N.S. 340 and *Essarts* v. *Whinney* (1903) 9 Asp.M.L.C. 363.
90. (1861) 30 L.J.Ch. 571.
91. *Ibid.* at pp. 572 to 573.
92. Similarly in *European & Australian Royal Mail Co. Ltd* v. *Royal Mail Steam Packet Co.* (1858) 4 K. & J. 676; *Haviland Routh & Co.* v. *Thompson* (1864) 3 Macph. 313 (Sc.).
93. *Samuel* v. *Jones* (1862) 7 L.T. 760.
94. *Re Litherland, ex p. Howden* (1842) 11 L.J.Bank. 19.
95. *The "Fairport"* (1884) 10 P.D. 13.

orders, as regards the employment and operation of the ship and as between the master on the one hand and the mortgagee on the other, the position may not necessarily be the same as regards third parties. The master may not have the same implied or ostensible authority from the mortgagee as he previously had from the mortgagor. In *The "Troubadour"*[96] it was held that there was no implication in law that the master was the agent of the mortgagee in possession as regards the ordering of necessaries supplied to the ship.

The appointment of a receiver[97]

There is normally express provision in the deed of covenants for the appointment by the mortgagee of a receiver who will be deemed to be the agent of the mortgagor, and who will accordingly be liable for any acts or defaults of such receiver.[98]

Whether or not the deed of covenants expressly provides for the appointment of a receiver, the mortgagee may in any event apply to the court for the appointment of a receiver where the mortgagor is in breach or the mortgagee's security is threatened. The function of a receiver is to collect the profits from the mortgaged property (freight etc.) and to pay any necessary expenses pending the realisation of the security by the mortgagee or by the court.

Where it is necessary either for the property to be disposed of, or it is in the interests of all parties concerned, the court may appoint a receiver and manager with wider powers actually to carry on or superintend the business of operating the ship.[99]

In the absence of such a wider appointment, the receiver's functions will be limited to collecting the profit and disbursing ordinary running expenses pending realisation of the security.

Although it is usual to appoint a receiver in the course of foreclosure proceedings, and this will be the normal course for a mortgagee of shares or a subsequent or equitable mortgagee, nevertheless the appointment of a receiver may be employed as a remedy of itself.

A receiver will be appointed by the court at the instance of a subsequent mortgagee in an appropriate case, but subject to the right of the prior mortgagee to take possession.[100]

Where, however, a prior mortgagee has already taken possession of the mortgaged property, then a receiver will not normally be appointed at the instance of a subsequent mortgagee in the absence of gross mismanagement being established on the part of the mortgagee in possession,[101] or the prior mortgagee

---

96. (1866) L.R. 1 A. & E. 302.
97. See generally *Kerr on the Law and Practice as to Receivers* (Sweet & Maxwell, 16th ed. 1983).
98. *Re Hale, Lilley v. Foad* [1899] 2 Ch. 107 and *Gaskell v. Gosling* [1896] 1 Q.B. 669.
99. *Fairfield v. London & East Coast S.S. Co.* [1895] W.N. 64.
100. *Underhay v. Read* (1887) 20 Q.B.D. 209.
101. *Rowe v. Wood* (1822) 2 J. & W. 553.

admits to having been paid off or refuses to allow the subsequent mortgagee to pay him off.[102]

Where the court has appointed a receiver at the instance of a subsequent mortgagee and a prior mortgagee wishes to take possession, the leave of the court is customarily obtained.[103]

Foreclosure

Foreclosure is essentially the opposite of redemption. Whereas the mortgagor has the right upon payment of the mortgaged debt to redeem the property, so, too, does the mortgagee have a corresponding right upon the mortgagor's default to commence an action for foreclosure whereby the mortgagor's right of redemption is extinguished, and the mortgagee becomes absolutely entitled to the mortgaged property.

In the case of a mortgage of the whole of a ship, an action for foreclosure is rarely commenced, the more straightforward remedies of possession and sale or arrest and judicial sale being the norm. On the other hand an equitable mortgagee or a mortgagee of shares will usually be unable to realise his security effectively without resort to an action for foreclosure.

In *The "Buttermere"*[104] the registered mortgagee of 2/64th shares claimed a decree of foreclosure, or in the alternative a sale of the mortgaged shares. The mortgagor appeared in the action but made default in pleading and the court ordered that the defendant be precluded from all equity of redemption in the mortgaged shares unless he paid the amount due on the mortgage within a month.

In an action for foreclosure the court requires to have before it every person whose rights might be affected by the order sought. Thus in an action *in personam*, not only the mortgagor, but also every subsequent mortgagee and any other person interested in the equity of redemption should be named as defendants. In the case of an action *in rem*, although probably not strictly necessary, notice of the proceedings should probably be given to such persons. A second or subsequent mortgagee bringing an action for foreclosure against the mortgagor and all subsequent mortgagees, need not join or give notice to a prior mortgagee.[105]

The order initially made by the court on an application for foreclosure is an order *nisi* which directs accounts to be taken and provides for a specific period within which the mortgagor or any subsequent mortgagee may redeem the mortgaged property. Although successive periods may be granted for subsequent mortgagees to redeem, one period alone is usual.[106]

102. *Berney* v. *Sewell* (1820) J. & W. 647 and *Quarrell* v. *Beckford* (1807) 13 Ves. 377.
103. *Preston* v. *Tunbridge Wells Opera House* [1903] 2 Ch. 323.
104. 24 July 1883 (Folio 211) a case referred to in a footnote on p. 44 of the 3rd edition of Williams & Bruce's *Admiralty Practice* (1902).
105. *Richards* v. *Cooper* (1842) 5 Beav. 304.
106. *Smithett* v. *Hesketh* (1890) 44 Ch.D. 161.

If redemption does not take place within the time limited by the order *nisi,* then upon application by the mortgagee, the order will be made absolute. The effect of an order for foreclosure absolute is to divest the mortgagor and any person against whom it is made of all their estate in the mortgaged property and to transfer it to the mortgagee in whose favour the order was made.[107]

Although it is not necessary in any action for foreclosure to apply for the sale of the mortgaged property this is nevertheless frequently done, and in any event the court may at any time prior to making an order for foreclosure absolute order the property to be sold.[108]

Sale

The deed of covenants will invariably provide for the mortgagee to have a power of sale exercisable in certain circumstances. However, even in the absence of any express provision, section 35 of the 1894 Act provides that:

Every registered mortgagee shall have the power absolutely to dispose of the ship or share in respect of which he is registered, and to give effectual receipts for the purchase money; but where there are more persons than one registered as mortgagees of the same ship or share, a subsequent mortgagee shall not, except under the order of a court of competent jurisdiction, sell the ship or share, without the concurrence of every prior mortgagee.

And a similar power in respect of registered fishing vessels is granted by paragraph 5 of Schedule 3 to the 1988 Act which provides:

(1) Subject to sub-paragraph (2), every registered mortgagee shall have power, if the mortgage money or any part of it is due, to sell the vessel or share in respect of which he is registered, and to give effectual receipts for the purchase money.

(2) Where two or more mortgagees are registered in respect of the same vessel or share, a subsequent mortgagee shall not, except under the order of a court of competent jurisdiction, sell the vessel or share, without the concurrence of every prior mortgagee.

Furthermore, a mortgagee of personal chattels when in possession has an implied power of sale where the mortgagor is in default of his obligation to repay the debt secured by the mortgage or where he has acted in such a way as to imperil the security.[109]

If the mortgage does not provide for a specific date for repayment of the debt, the power of sale will nevertheless be available upon the mortgagee having given reasonable notice to the mortgagor requiring repayment and intimating to him that in default of repayment the mortgagee will sell the property.[110]

---

107. *Heath* v. *Pugh* (1881) 6 Q.B.D. 345.
108. *Union Bank of London* v. *Ingram* (1882) 20 Ch.D. 463.
109. *Wilson* v. *Tooker* (1714) 5 Bro.Parl.Cas. 193; *Lockwood* v. *Ewer* (1742) 2 Atk. 303; *Kemp* v. *Westbrook* (1749) 1 Ves.Sen. 278; *France* v. *Clark* (1883) 22 Ch.D. 830, (1884) 26 Ch.D. 257; *Re Morritt, ex. p. Official Receiver* (1886) 18 Q.B.D. 222, 223; *McHugh* v. *Union Bank of Canada* [1913] A.C. 299 and *The "Odessa"* [1916] 1 A.C. 145,159.
110. *Deverges* v. *Sandeman, Clarke & Co.* [1902] 1 Ch. 579.

Normally, the entry into possession of the mortgagee will be a prelude to his exercise of the power of sale, although he may, alternatively, have the ship arrested in a mortgage action and have the ship sold by the court.

Although the mortgagor may have been in default and the power of sale may have arisen, nevertheless if the mortgagor tenders the mortgage debt, the mortgagee has no right to proceed to sell the ship and he will be restrained by injunction.[111]

Where the mortgagee chooses to sell the ship privately, rather than through the court, he will be a constructive trustee of any surplus realised for the second or subsequent mortgagees, and ultimately for the mortgagor. See further below.[112]

He is not however a trustee of his power of sale. In *Warner* v. *Jacob*[113] Kay J. described the mortgagee's power of sale thus at page 224:

a mortgagee is strictly speaking not a trustee of the power of sale. It is a power given to him for his own benefit, to enable him the better to realise his debt. If he exercises it bona fide for that purpose, without corruption or collusion with the purchaser, the Court will not interfere even though the sale be very disadvantageous, unless indeed the price is so low as in itself to be evidence of fraud.

In *Farrar* v. *Farrars Ltd.*[114] Lindley L.J. said at page 410:

A mortgagee with a power of sale, though often called a trustee, is in a very different position from a trustee for sale. A mortgagee is under obligations to a mortgagor, but he has rights of his own which he is entitled to exercise adversely to the mortgagor. A trustee for sale has no business to place himself in such a position as to give rise to a conflict of interest and duty. But every mortgage confers upon the mortgagee the right to realise his security and to find a purchaser if he can, and if in exercise of his power he acts bona fide and takes reasonable precautions to obtain a proper price, the mortgagor has no redress, even although more might have been obtained for the property if the sale had been postponed.

In *Cuckmere Brick Co. Ltd.* v. *Mutual Finance Ltd.*,[115] Cross L.J. said at page 969:

A mortgagee exercising a power of sale is in an ambiguous position. He is not a trustee of the power for the mortgagee as it was given to him for his own benefit to enable him to obtain repayment of his loan. On the other hand he is not in the position of an absolute owner selling his own property but must undoubtedly pay some regard to the interests of the mortgagor when he comes to exercise the power.

Nevertheless, the mortgagee is under a duty to exercise his power of sale in a prudent way and he will be held liable to the mortgagor where acting imprudently he fails to realise sufficient from the sale.[116]

---

111. *McLarty* v. *Middleton* (1861) 4 L.T. 852.
112. See p. 104.
113. (1882) 20 Ch.D. 220.
114. (1888) 40 Ch.D. 395.
115. [1971] Ch. 949.
116. *The "Calm C"* [1975] 1 Lloyd's Rep. 188.

The duty of the mortgagee as regards the exercise of his power was summarised by Lord Moulton in *McHugh* v. *Union Bank of Canada*:[117]

It is well settled law that it is the duty of a mortgagee when realising the mortgaged property by sale to behave in conducting such realisation as a reasonable man would behave in the realisation of his own property, so that the mortgagor may receive credit for the fair value of the property sold.

Similarly in *Cuckmere Brick Co. Ltd.* v. *Mutual Finance Ltd.* [118] Salmon L.J. said at page 968 after considering the authorities:

I accordingly conclude both on principle and authority, that the mortgagee does owe a duty to take reasonable precautions to obtain the true market value of the mortgaged property at the date on which he decides to sell it. No doubt in deciding whether he has fallen short of that duty the facts must be looked at broadly, and he will not be adjudged to be in default unless he is plainly on the wrong side of the line.

These authorities were considered and cited with approval by the Privy Council in *Twe Kwong Lam* v. *Wong Chit Sen*.[119]

It has been held by the High Court of New Zealand that the duty of care owed by a mortgagee upon the exercise of the power of sale is owed to a guarantor as well as to the mortgagor.[120]

In exercising his power of sale the mortgagee must act *bona fide* for the purposes of realising his security and he must take reasonable precautions to secure a proper price. This duty is probably non-delegable and a mortgagee will, therefore, be liable to the mortgagor for loss caused by the negligence of his agent in carrying out his instructions to conduct a sale.[121]

Where it appears that he is not acting *bona fide* or reasonably, the mortgagor, or any other person interested in the proceeds of sale, such as a subsequent mortgagee, may be granted an injunction to restrain the mortgagee from proceeding with the sale.[122] Where the sale is tainted by fraud, provided relief is sought promptly, the court may even set aside the sale.[123]

The mortgagee may not make any charge in connection with the sale.[124] This is so even where there has been agreement between the parties for such a charge to be made. In *The "Benwell Tower"*[125] a commission of 2.5% was agreed by letter collateral to the mortgage to be payable upon the sale of the vessel by the mortgagee. Bruce J. said:

This commission ought not to be treated as part of the account current, because it only became due after the account current was closed. It is a principle well established that a mortgagee conducting a sale under his power of sale, is so far in the position of a trustee

117. [1913] A.C. 299 at p. 311.
118. *Supra.*
119. [1983] 1 W.L.R. 1349.
120. *Clark* v. *UDC Finance Ltd.* [1985] 2 N.Z.L.R. 636.
121. See *Commercial & General* v. *Nixon* (1982) C.L.R. 491 (High Court of Australia).
122. *Whitworth* v. *Rhodes* (1850) 20 L.J.Ch. 105.
123. *Haddington* v. *Hudson* [1911] A.C. 722.
124. *Matthison* v. *Clarke* (1854) 3 Drew. 3.
125. (1895) 8 Asp.M.L.C. 13.

that he can make no charge for his trouble in connection with the sale (see *Matthison* v. *Clarke*, 3 Drew. 3; *Arnold* v. *Garner*, 2 Phil. 231), and an agreement between the parties cannot, I think, render a charge of this nature valid.

He must also comply with any restrictions upon the power of sale contained in the deed of covenants. In *Broward* v. *Dumaresque*[126] the power of sale was expressed to be by "public auction" and it was held that a sale by private contract was invalid. If however the power is to sell by public auction or by private contract, there is no requirement that before selling by private contract the property should first be offered for sale by public auction.[127]

The mortgagee is not entitled in the exercise of his power of sale to sell to himself, whether alone or jointly with others, nor to any agent or trustee acting on his behalf. In *Martinson* v. *Clowes*,[128] North J. said: "It is quite clear that a mortgagee exercising his power of sale cannot purchase the property on his own account, and I think it is clear also that the solicitor or agent of such mortgagee acting for him in the matter of the sale cannot do so either."[129]

However there is nothing to prevent a subsequent mortgagee from purchasing the property even where he is in possession. If he does so he will obtain the property free from the equity of redemption in the same way as a stranger.[130]

A more difficult situation arose in *Twe Kwong Lam* v. *Wong Chit Sen*.[131] In that case the mortgagee arranged for the mortgaged property to be sold by public auction pursuant to his power of sale. Meanwhile, together with his wife, as directors of a company of which they and their children were the only shareholders, the mortgagee held a director's meeting whereat it was resolved that the wife should bid for the property on behalf of the company. At the auction there was only one bid and the property was sold to the company. It was held that there was no fixed rule which prevented a company in which the mortgagee was interested from purchasing the mortgaged property, but that there was an onus on the mortgagee to prove that he had made the sale in good faith and had taken reasonable precautions to obtain the best price reasonably attainable at the time. After considering the authorities, Lord Templeman said at page 1355:

on authority and on principle there is no hard and fast rule that a mortgagee may not sell to a company in which he is interested. The mortgagee and the company seeking to uphold the transaction must show that the sale was in good faith and that the mortgagee took reasonable precautions to obtain the best price reasonably obtainable at the time. The mortgagee is not however bound to postpone the sale in the hope of obtaining a better price or to adopt a piecemeal method of sale which could only be carried out over a substantial period or at some risk of loss . . . In the present case in which the mortgagee held a large beneficial interest in the shares of the purchasing company, was a director of the company, and was entirely responsible for financing the company, the other share-

---

126. (1841) 3 Moo.P.C. 457.

127. *Davey* v. *Durrant, Smith* v. *Durrant* (1857) 1 De G. & J. 535, 560.

128. (1882) 21 Ch.D. 857 at p. 860.

129. Similarly in *Downes* v. *Grazebrook* (1817) 3 Mer. 200; *Robertson* v. *Norris* (1857) 1 Giff. 421; *Henderson* v. *Astwood* [1894] A.C. 150 and *Hodson* v. *Deans* [1903] 2 Ch. 647.

130. *Kennedy* v. *De Trafford* [1897] A.C. 180 and *Kirkwood* v. *Thompson* (1865) 2 De G. & Sm. 613.

131. [1983] 1 W.L.R. 1349.

holders being his wife and children, the sale must be closely examined and a heavy onus lies on the mortgagee to show that in all respects he acted fairly to the borrower and used his best endeavours to obtain the best price reasonably obtainable for the mortgaged property.

Where, however, the vessel is being sold by the court[132] the mortgagee may apply to the court to be permitted to bid as a purchaser.[133]

Effect of a sale

At any time until the mortgaged property is actually sold, whether by the court or by the mortgagee, or the mortgage has been foreclosed by the court, the mortgagor, or any other person interested in the equity of redemption, may redeem the property by payment of the mortgaged debt, any interest accrued thereon, and any expenses incurred by the mortgagee in taking and remaining in possession. As has already been observed,[134] this right may be enforced through an action for redemption if the mortgagee refuses to accept tender of the full amount owing to him.

Once the sale has been completed, the mortgagor ceases to have any right to redeem, and all his rights to the mortgaged property are lost. The only right remaining in the mortgagor is to receive any balance of the proceeds of sale after deduction of the expenses of the sale, the sums due to the mortgagee and the amount of any subsequent encumbrances.

Proceeds of sale

The mortgagee on the other hand becomes a trustee of any surplus of the proceeds of sale over and above the amount required to satisfy his claim, and the surplus is bound by all the equities and other claims which bound the property itself. Thus if the mortgagee has notice of any incumbrance he is obliged to discharge it out of the surplus in his hands and then to pay over the balance thereafter remaining to the mortgagor.

In *Banner* v. *Berridge*,[135] the precise nature of the mortgagee's position of trustee of the surplus proceeds of sale was considered. In that case, the ship was sold by the first mortgagees pursuant to their statutory power of sale. An action was commenced after the expiry of the limitation period by the trustee in bankruptcy of the second mortgagees for an account of the proceeds of sale. In response to a plea by the first mortgagees that the claim was barred by the Statute of Limitations or by laches, it was argued on behalf of the second mortgagees that the first mortgagees were express trustees. The court held that on a sale by a mortgagee, there is no express trust of the proceeds of sale, but that there is a constructive trust only of the surplus and after the expiry of the limi-

---

132. For which see further below, p. 105.
133. *The "Wilsons"* (1841) 1 W.Rob. 172; *Downes* v. *Grazebrook* (1817) 3 Mer. 200.
134. See p. 133.
135. (1881) L.R. 18 Ch.D. 254.

tation period the court will not allow evidence to be gone into to show that there was a surplus for the purpose of raising such a trust. Kay J. said in the course of his judgment:

... where there is no trust expressed, either in writing or verbally, of the proceeds of the sale, no trust can possibly arise until it is shown there is a surplus. Then I am disposed to hold that there is a sufficient fiduciary relation between the mortgagor and the mortgagee to make the mortgagee constructively a trustee of the surplus. But that seems to me to be not a case of express trust at all, but of constructive trust; that is to say, a trust which only arises upon proof of the fact that there was a surplus in the hands of the mortgagee after paying himself.[136]

If the mortgagee has any doubt or difficulty in applying the surplus proceeds he should pay them into court.[137]

Court sale

As an alternative to exercising his power of sale, a mortgagee of a ship may commence an action *in rem* in the Admiralty Court and have the ship sold by the court. Generally, for commercial reasons, a mortgagee will often prefer to exercise his power of sale with a view to realising a higher sum than that likely to be achieved upon a forced sale by the court, and to avoid the additional costs and delays inherent in the system of obtaining an order for a court sale and the mechanisms of carrying it out by the Admiralty Marshal by means of prior appraisement, advertisement and sale.

However, there are certain advantages to a court sale: for example, there can be no complaint by the mortgagor against the mortgagee as to the manner in which the sale has been conducted or the price realised. A purchaser from the court is in a particularly beneficial position as he will obtain a clean title devoid of any maritime liens. In *The "Tremont"*[138] Dr Lushington stated the position as follows:

The jurisdiction of the Court in these matters, is confirmed by the municipal law of this country and by the general principles of the maritime law; and the title conferred by this Court in the exercise of this authority is a valid title against the whole world, and is recognised by the courts of this country and the courts of all other countries.

Dr Lushington's naive statement that a judicial sale by the English Admiralty Court will be recognised by the courts of all other countries is probably insupportable in the late twentieth century (even if it was true in the early nineteenth century which would appear unlikely).

As a result of this important consequence of a court sale, in *The "Acrux"*[139] where an Italian ship was sold by the Admiralty Court at the behest of Italian

---

136. Similarly in *Tanner* v. *Heard* (1857) 23 Beav. 555; *Thorne* v. *Heard & Marsh* [1895] A.C. 495 and *Thomson* v. *Bruty* (1920) 64 S.J. 375.

137. *Roberts* v. *Ball* (1855) 24 L.J.Ch. 471; *Re Walhampton Estate* (1884) 26 Ch.D. 391 and section 63 of the Trustee Act 1925.

138. (1841) 1 Wm.Rob.163.

139. [1962] 1 Lloyd's Rep. 405.

mortgagees, the court required the mortgagees to give an undertaking that they would not seek to enforce any rights outstanding after the sale against the ship in any other jurisdiction. Hewson J. said:[140]

The mortgagees, by claiming against this fund and praying the aid of this Court to recover their moneys, or such proportion of them as is possible, adopt and approbate the process of this Court in effecting the sale through its proper officer, the Marshal. The title given by such a process is a valid title and must not be disturbed by those who have knowledge or who may receive knowledge of the proceedings of this Court . . . Were such a clean title as given by this Court to be challenged or disturbed, the innocent purchaser would be gravely prejudiced. Not only that, but as a general proposition the maritime interest of the world would suffer. Were it to become established, contrary to general maritime law, that a proper sale of a ship by a competent Court did not give a clean title, those whose business it is to make advances of money in their various ways to enable ships to pursue their lawful occasions would be prejudiced in all cases where it became necessary to sell the ship under proper process of any competent Court. It would be prejudiced for this reason, that no innocent purchaser would be prepared to pay the full market price for the ship and the resultant fund, if the ship were sold, would be minimized and not represent her true value.

Mortgage of shares

Where the mortgage is of shares only and not of the whole ship, the mortgagee will be entitled, in the same circumstances as previously considered, to a proportionate share of the freight.[141]

However, a mortgagee of the shares of a part-owner is in a slightly different position from a mortgagee of the entire ship. By taking possession of the mortgaged shares and by giving notice to the managing owner, the mortgagee stands in the shoes of the mortgagor as regards dealings with the other part-owners. As to ownership, the several owners are tenants in common, although the earnings of the ship are to be dealt with according to the principles of partnership law.[142] All expenses incurred in the adventure must be deducted from the gross freight earned before any division of the earnings can take place. The mortgagee of shares in possession is only entitled to receive the net earnings after deduction of all the expenses.

In *Alexander* v. *Simms*,[143] a part-owner whose share was mortgaged agreed with a part-owner whose share was not mortgaged, to purchase guano on the joint account of the two owners and carry it to England. Upon the completion of the voyage, when the cargo was about to be discharged, the mortgagee took possession and claimed to be entitled to the freight earned on the voyage. It was held that he could at most stand in the same shoes as the mortgagor and adopt the contract so as to claim his proportionate share of the net profits. At page 65 Turner L.J. said: "What is the interest of the mortgagee? I think that by the

---

140. *Ibid.* at p. 409.
141. *Essarts* v. *Whinney* (1903) 9 Asp.M.L.C. 363.
142. *Green* v. *Briggs* (1848) 17 L.J.Ch. 323.
143. (1854) 5 De. G.M. & G. 57.

mortgage he has a lien on the share of the ship and a proportionate part of the earnings attributable to that share."[144]

In the normal course of events a mortgagee of shares will appoint a receiver to collect freight.

In *The "Faust"*,[145] the plaintiff claimed to be the equitable mortgagee of a ship and her freight. The mortgage had been given by the managing owner whom the plaintiff believed to have been the sole owner, but in fact he was only a part-owner. It was common ground that unless the advance was made to the managing owner for the necessary purposes of the ship, the mortgage could only stand as a mortgage of the managing owner's shares in the ship and freight, and not as a mortgage of the whole ship and the whole of her freight. The Court of Appeal upheld the appointment of a receiver with authority to proceed with the ship to a foreign port and there receive the whole of the ship and the whole freight, as there was a dispute as to whether the advance had been made for the necessary purposes of the ship, and, therefore, the balance of convenience lay in having a receiver to collect the whole of the freight.

In the course of giving judgment Lord Esher M.R. said:[146]

It is obvious that if it turns out that the Defendant who gave the charge was not entitled to mortgage the whole freight, he was at least entitled to mortgage his own share. In that case the Court would direct the receiver—after having paid the proper disbursements or allowed them to be paid—to keep the share of this Defendant, which would be the righteous and proper thing to do, and to pay over their respective shares to the other owners. To my mind they would not be entitled to have their shares of the profits of the voyage handed to them until the account, as between the ship's husband and the co-owners, is made out.

Although a mortgagee of shares will normally be unable to exercise his power of sale, nevertheless the court may grant a sale of the ship at the suit of a mortgagee of shares in a foreclosure action.[147]

A mortgagee of a minority of shares is entitled to his share in the distribution of the proceeds of sale.[148]

Second mortgagee

The position of a second or subsequent mortgagee was considered in *Liverpool Marine Credit* v. *Wilson*.[149] In that case, the first registered mortgagee of a ship made a further advance on the security of a mortgage comprising the ship and the freight thereof then earned or to be earned during the continuance of the security. The owner of the ship, without notice to the first mortgagee, had previously executed a second mortgage and given the second mortgagee a lien on

144. See also *Japp* v. *Campbell* (1887) 57 L.J.Q.B. 79.
145. (1887) 6 Asp.M.L.C. 126.
146. *Ibid.* at p. 128 col. 2.
147. *The "Fairlie"* (1868) 37 L.J.Adm. 66.
148. *The "Ripon City"* (*No. 2*) [1898] P. 78.
149. (1872) L.R. 7 Ch.App. 507.

the freight for a balance due to him. The second mortgagee served written notice on the charterers of his lien on the freight. The first mortgagee subsequently took possession of the ship before she reached her port of discharge. It was held that the first mortgagee was entitled to priority over the charge of the second mortgagee of the freight, not only in respect of the amount due on the first mortgage, but also in respect of the whole amount of his further advance.

The position of the second mortgagee was considered by James L.J.:[150]

What is, then, the position of a second mortgagee of a ship with respect to the freight? He has no legal right to take actual possession, and cannot therefore by his own act give himself that which is equivalent to possession. But as between himself and the mortgagor, the equitable right of the second mortgagee is the same as the legal right of the first mortgagee; just as in the case of land if the first mortgagee declines to take possession the second mortgagee may obtain a receiver and so have the possession and the benefits of a possessory right. But this is to be understood only as between the second mortgagee and the mortgagor. As regards all intervening encumbrances, interests, and titles of every kind not requiring registration, the respective positions of the first and second mortgagees are essentially different, arising from the essential difference between a legal and an equitable title. The legal owner's right is paramount to every equitable charge not affecting his own conscience; the equitable owner in the absence of special circumstances takes subject to all equities prior in date to his own estate or charge. The Courts of equity, in appointing a receiver at the instance of an equitable incumbrancer take possession in fact in behalf of all, and so as not to disturb the legal right or interfere with equitable priorities. If there be a legal mortgage of a ship, then a charge on the freight, then a second mortgage of the ship, the second mortgagee cannot by any act of his own oust the encumbrancer on the freight; and if the first mortgagee takes under these circumstances possession of the ship, his possession cannot be allowed to alter the equities of the parties. He takes both ship and freight by the same title, and there being one equitable owner of the ship, and another equitable owner of the freight, as between those equitable owners his charge must be considered as satisfied *pro rata*, just as if there was a first mortgage on Whiteacre and Blackacre belonging, subject to that mortgage, to several owners.

A second mortgagee may invoke the assistance of the court through the arrest of the ship, in which case the first mortgagee may either allow the ship to be sold and so realise his security, or he may alternatively put up bail or other security for the ship's release. If subsequently, the proceeds of sale are insufficient to satisfy the debt secured by the first mortgage, the first mortgagee will be entitled to his costs and to interest upon any sums paid into court.[151]

Costs

The successful mortgagee will be entitled to his costs in the mortgage action as of right under the provisions of R.S.C. Order 62, rule 6, unless he has acted unreasonably. Such costs will normally be taxed upon the standard basis.[152]

However, most deeds of covenants will provide expressly that the mort-

150. *Ibid.* at p. 511.
151. The "*Western Ocean*" (1870) L.R. 3 A. & E. 38.
152. The "*Kestrel*" (1866) L.R. 1 A. & E. 78.

gagee's costs are to be paid upon an indemnity basis. Such an agreement, although it will be a factor to be taken into account by the court in the exercise of its discretion, does not exclude the court's overriding discretion as to the basis of taxation upon which costs are awarded.[153]

153. *ANZ Banking Group* v. *Gibson* [1981] 2 N.Z.L.R. 513 at p. 525.

6

PRIORITIES

INTRODUCTION

Since the circumstances in which a mortgagee has to exercise his right to realise the security in order to satisfy the mortgage debt are likely to be the insolvency of the mortgagor, or his unwillingness to pay his debts, it is necessary to consider how the mortgagee's rights are affected by the conflicting claims of other creditors of the mortgagor.

In general the mortgagee will not be concerned with other judgment creditors of the mortgagor as their rights to enforce their judgments against the mortgaged property will be subject to the mortgage. This is generally the case whether or not the mortgagor is insolvent. A judgment creditor can only take in execution property belonging to the judgment debtor. Where the property against which execution is to be levied has been mortgaged, the legal ownership has been transferred to the mortgagee and the only interest left belonging to the judgment debtor is his equity of redemption. A mortgagee will be concerned with other creditors of the mortgagor where they are holding the mortgaged property under a possessory lien, such as where the ship or aircraft has been the subject of repair and the repair bill remains unsatisfied. Similarly where the ship or aircraft is the subject of some statutory detention as, for example, in respect of port or harbour charges or dues, in the case of a ship, or in respect of landing charges, in the case of an aircraft.

In the maritime context the situation is further complicated by the existence of privileged claims giving rise to rights to proceed against a ship *in rem*, which in certain cases do have priority over the rights of the mortgagee. The similar rights to proceed *in rem* against an aircraft do not generally exist in English law other than in respect of salvage of aircraft[1] or the towage or pilotage of an aircraft while waterborne.[2]

It is also necessary to consider the question of competing proprietary claims, whether of other mortgagees or other persons claiming to have ownership of the mortgaged property, or ancillary rights attaching thereto such as freight or the proceeds of insurance.

1. Section 20(2)(j) of the Supreme Court Act 1981.
2. Section 20(2)(k) and (l) of the Supreme Court Act 1981.

110

The whole question of priorities is further complicated by the fact that a ship or aircraft is by its very nature liable to travel from one jurisdiction to another. This has two main consequences. First, it may, particularly in the case of a ship, acquire various liens and claims emanating from different jurisdictions; secondly, proceedings may be brought, either in respect of the mortgage or in respect of other claims, in different jurisdictions. It is, therefore, necessary to consider the impact of private international law or conflict of laws principles on the mortgage and also on the various competing claims. This is considered in Chapter 7.

GENERAL PRINCIPLES APPLICABLE TO SHIP AND AIRCRAFT MORTGAGES

In most cases of ship and aircraft mortgages, priority will be determined by registration and as regards both ship and aircraft mortgages a registered mortgage has priority over an unregistered mortgage irrespective of notice and registered mortgages rank in order of the time of registration. This is considered further below.

Nevertheless, there may be rare cases where a mortgage is not registered and in such cases the basic scheme of priority in English law is as follows:

(i) A bona fide purchaser for value of the legal estate takes in priority over any earlier equitable incumbrance, of which he has no notice, actual or constructive.

(ii) Equitable encumbrances rank in order of creation according to the maxim "*qui prior est tempore, potior est jure*".

(iii) Priority may be lost where by reason of the conduct of the prior incumbrancer, it would be inequitable to allow him the normal priority.

It is against this background that the question of the priority of ship and aircraft mortgages will be considered in turn.

SHIP MORTGAGES

General creditors of the mortgagor

A judgment creditor has no better right in the property of the judgment debtor than the judgment debtor himself had. Accordingly, a judgment creditor obtains no priority by reason of his judgment over prior equitable interests affecting the property. This is so whether he proceeds by way of writ of *fi. fa.* or charging order.

The mortgagee of a ship or a share therein has priority over an ordinary

judgment creditor, and is not affected by the personal debts of the mortgagor.[3]
This is so even where the judgment creditor has proceeded to execution.[4]

In *Langton* v. *Horton*[5] it was held that a judgment creditor had no right to take
a ship and cargo in execution as against prior equitable mortgagees who had
given notice to the master of their assignment and had obtained possession from
him upon termination of the voyage.

In *Japp* v. *Campbell*[6] a judgment creditor obtained a garnishee order upon the
receivers of cargo in respect of freight payable by them to the owner. The court
discharged the garnishee order in favour of the mortgagee who had entered into
possession and was thus entitled to receive the freight.[7]

Insolvency of the mortgagor

Section 36 of the Merchant Shipping Act 1894 provides:

A registered mortgage of a ship or share shall not be affected by any act of bankruptcy
committed by the mortgagor after the date of the record of the mortgage, notwithstanding that the mortgagor at the commencement of his bankruptcy had the ship or share in
his possession, order, disposition, or was reputed owner thereof,[8] and the mortgagee
shall be preferred to any right, claim or interest, therein of the other creditors of the
bankrupt or any trustee or assignee on their behalf.

Thus if the mortgage is registered prior to any act of bankruptcy the mortgagee is protected. If, however, the mortgage is registered subsequent to an act
of bankruptcy on the part of the mortgagor, the mortgagee will only be protected if he has no notice of the act of bankruptcy and the registration takes
place before a receiving order is made.[9]

In *The "Thames"*[10] the owner of 42/64th shares in a ship mortgaged those
shares to the plaintiffs to secure the repayment of a debt and any subsequent
advances. The mortgage was duly registered. Prior to the date of the mortgage,
and unknown to the plaintiffs the mortgagor had committed an act of bankruptcy and a petition had been presented against him. Subsequent to the registration of the mortgage, a receiving order was made and the mortgagor
adjudicated bankrupt. On the day the receiving order was made the plaintiffs
advanced a further sum to the mortgagor pursuant to a promise so to do made
the day before. In the plaintiffs' action to establish the validity of the mortgage

3. *The "Harriet"* (1868) 18 L.T. 804 and *Dickinson* v. *Kitchen* (1858) 8 E. & B. 789 (a decision
under the corresponding section (section 70) of the Merchant Shipping Act 1854).

4. In *Dickinson* v. *Kitchen* (*ubi supra*) the mortgagee's power of sale was postponed under the mortgage to a date subsequent to the date of seizure of the ship in execution.

5. (1842) 1 Hare 549.

6. (1887) 57 L.J.Q.B. 79.

7. See also *De Wolf* v. *Pitcairn* (1869) 17 W.R. 914 and *Clydesdale Bank* v. *Walker and Bain* [1926]
S.C.72.

8. Note: The doctrine of "reputed ownership" was abolished by the Insolvency Act 1985, section
235, Schedule 10, Part III.

9. *The "Ruby" (No. 1)* (1900) 9 Asp.M.L.C. 146 and *Ponsford Baker & Co.* v. *Union Bank* [1906] 2
Ch. 444.

10. (1890) 6 Asp.M.L.C. 536.

and to recover the advances it was held that the mortgage was valid and that they were entitled to recover all the advances made thereunder including the advance made on the day the receiving order was made.

This was a decision under section 49 of the Bankruptcy Act 1883. Personal insolvency is now governed by section 342 of the Insolvency Act 1986.

According to the usual rules of priorities in insolvency, a mortgagee, as the holder of a fixed charge, will take in priority to a debenture holder who has only a floating charge. Thus in *Ward* v. *The Royal Exchange Shipping Company, ex parte Harrison*[11] an equitable mortgagee of freight took in priority to debenture holders.

After the bankruptcy or winding up of the mortgagor, the mortgagee may take proceedings for the enforcement of his security in the usual way as his action is to enforce a claim to his own property rather than that of the bankrupt or the company.[12] Where, however, some insolvency point arises the matter can and should be transferred to the Chancery Division.[13]

It should be noted however that upon the application of the liquidator or administrator the court may reopen an extortionate credit agreement with a company[14] and upon the application of a trustee in bankruptcy the court may reopen an extortionate credit agreement with a bankrupt made not more than three years before the commencement of the bankruptcy.[15]

Maritime claims against the ship

Certain maritime claims give rise to a right to proceed *in rem* against a ship and where the ship is the subject of a mortgage, a potential conflict arises with the right of the mortgagee to realise his security out of the proceeds of sale of the ship and the right of the claimants proceeding *in rem* to do likewise.

For these purposes it is necessary to distinguish three categories of maritime claims: those giving rise to a possessory lien, those giving rise to a maritime lien and those giving rise merely to a statutory right of action *in rem*.

Possessory liens

Repairer

At common law the repairer of a chattel has a possessory lien for the cost of the repairs, at least where the repairs have the effect of improving the chattel.[16] It does not matter that the repairs may not have been completed.[17] He is entitled

---

11. (1887) 6 Asp.M.L.C. 239.
12. *Re Wherly, ex p. Hirst* (1879) 11 Ch.D. 278 and *Re David Lloyd & Co., Lloyd* v. *David Lloyd & Co.* (1877) 6 Ch.D. 339.
13. See Insolvency Rules 1986, rule 7.15.
14. Insolvency Act 1986, section 244.
15. Insolvency Act 1986, section 343.
16. *Hatton* v. *Car Maintenance Co. Ltd.* [1915] 1 Ch. 621.
17. *The "Tergeste"* [1903] p. 26.

to retain possession of the ship until his charges are met.[18] Thus where a mortgagee seeks to enter into possession, he must first discharge the possessory lien.[19]

A possessory lien holder is not permitted in the exercise of his lien to sell the ship even though he may be incurring continuing expense as a result of the continued exercise of his lien.[20] Nor may the lien holder claim the costs of exercising his lien from the owner of the ship or other person who discharges the lien.[21]

The right to exercise a possessory lien may be renounced by express agreement.[22] The lien exists as long as the repairer remains in possession but it may be lost if possession is voluntarily given up.

In *The "Tergeste"*[23] Phillimore J. described the position in the following way:

It is said that they had no possessory lien, because the master and crew were on board; if that were the rule a great number of shipwright's liens would be disturbed. That man has a lien who has such control of the chattel as prevents it being taken away from his possession. He may admit other persons or workmen to access to the chattel, and other tradesmen may claim a possessory lien over the chattel or part of it, but if it cannot be got out of the dock or yard without the consent of the owner of the dock or yard, the owner of the dock will have a possessory lien . . .

In *Barr* v. *Cooper*[24] when part of the repairs to a vessel were completed, she was moved off a slip and into a dock where the repairs were completed. Whilst in the dock she was moved from time to time under the orders of the Harbour Master and it was held that the repairers had not parted with possession so as to lose their lien.[25]

Where the possessory lien holder is forced to give up his lien by judicial process such as by the arrest of the ship in an action *in rem* by another claimant, the court will nevertheless protect his rights by according him priority against all claims other than previously accrued maritime liens.[26]

In the case where it is the repairer himself who institutes the action *in rem* in which the ship is arrested the position is unclear.[27]

Where, however, the repairer does not retain possession of the ship pursuant to his lien, the position is otherwise, and the mortgagee will have priority.[28]

---

18. *The "Gustaf"* (1862) Lush. 506.
19. *Williams* v. *Allsupp* (1861) 10 C.B. (N.S.) 417; *The "Turliani"* (1875) 2 Asp.M.L.C. 603; *The "Sherbro"* (1883) 5 Asp.M.L.C. 88.
20. *Thames Ironworks* v. *Patent Derrick Co.* (1860) 29 L.J.Ch. 714.
21. *Somes* v. *British Empire Shipping Co.* (1860) 30 L.J.Q.B. 229.
22. *Raitt* v. *Mitchell* (1815) 4 Camp. 146.
23. [1903] P. 26.
24. (1875) 2 Ct. of Sess. Cas. (4th Ser.) 14.
25. *Ex p. Willoughby, re Westlake* (1881) 16 Ch.D. 604.
26. *The "Harmonie"* (1841) 1 Wm.Rob. 178; *The "Gustav"* (1862) Lush. 506 and *The "Immacolata Concezione"* (1883) 9 P.D. 37.
27. *Jacobs* v. *Latour* (1828) 5 Bing. 130; *The "Andrea Ursula"* [1971] 1 Lloyd's Rep. 145 and the Irish case *The "Acacia"* (1880) 4 Asp.M.L.C. 254.
28. See *Watkinson* v. *Bernardiston* (1762) 2 P.Wms. 367; *The "Neptune"* (1835) 3 Knapp. 94; *The "New Eagle"* (1846) 2 W.Rob. 441; *The "Scio"* (1867) L.R. 1 A. & E. 353.

Harbour authority

Most harbour authorities have a statutory right of detention and sale in respect of harbour dues outstanding on a ship which remains within their harbour. Such a right is given to them either by an express provision in their statutes or by the general incorporation in those statutes of section 44 of the Harbours, Docks and Piers Clauses Act 1847.

In addition most harbour authorities have a statutory right to recover the cost and expenses of removing a wreck within their harbour by detention and sale. Such a right is given to them either by an express provision in their statutes or by the general incorporation in those statutes of section 56 of the Harbours, Docks and Piers Clauses Act 1847.

These rights are the statutory equivalent of a possessory lien but with the addition of a power of sale and will prevail over the rights of a mortgagee to enter into possession or his priority in the proceeds of sale.

A harbour authority also has a power under section 530 of the Merchant Shipping Act 1894 to remove wrecks and to sell them in order to reimburse themselves of the cost of wreck removal. The exercise of such powers enables the authority to sell the vessel free of liens and incumbrances.[29]

Forfeiture

Under the Merchant Shipping Act 1894, a ship may be subject to forfeiture in certain circumstances. In *The "Annandale"*[30] it was held that forfeiture results immediately upon the offence being committed. Accordingly, where a ship is mortgaged subsequent to an act having been committed by the mortgagor which would render the vessel liable to be forfeit to the Crown, the ship will nevertheless be forfeit.

Maritime liens

The rule under English law is that a mortgage is postponed to all maritime liens, whether they have attached prior to the date of the mortgage or arise subsequently. The following claims are recognised in English law[31] as giving rise to a maritime lien on the ship in respect of which the claim arose:

(i) salvage[32];
(ii) damage[33];
(iii) wages[34];

29. *Manchester Ship Canal* v. *Horlock* [1914] 1 Ch. 453 (reversed on appeal on a different point: [1914] 2 Ch. 199).
30. (1877) 2 P.D. 218.
31. Also in Scots law; see *Currie* v. *McKnight* [1893] A.C. 97.
32. See *The "Veritas"* [1901] P. 304.
33. See *The "Aline"* (1839) 1 Wm.Rob. 111.
34. See *The "Feronia"* (1868) L.R. 2 A. & E. 65.

(iv) master's disbursements[35];

(v) bottomry.[36]

In addition it is provided by section 567 of the Merchant Shipping Act 1894 that a receiver of wreck has the same rights of recovery of his fees and expenses as a salvor has in respect of salvage due to him.

It is irrelevant as far as the validity or effect of maritime liens is concerned that at the time of their creation the ship was being operated by or was in the possession and under the control of charterers.[37]

This principle of priority is based upon considerations of public policy and justice. Liens arising *ex contractu* (wages and bottomry) or *quasi ex contractu* (salvage) rank in inverse order of attachment on the grounds that services which operate for the protection of prior interests should be privileged above those interests.[38] Liens arising *ex delicto* (damage) take priority over other liens and mortgages on the grounds that a person advancing money or rendering services does so voluntarily and has a choice whether or not to become a creditor of the ship, a party injured by the ship has no such choice.[39]

Maritime liens are, however, liable to be defeated by delay on the part of the lien holder in the enforcement of his claim, where the effect of such delay would render it inequitable to enforce the lien under the equitable doctrine of laches.[40]

Moreover, under section 8 of the Maritime Conventions Act 1911, a two-year time limit is generally applicable to salvage claims and to claims arising out of a collision between ships.

It should also be noted that where the holder of the maritime lien is personally liable to the mortgagee, for example, by way of guarantee, his maritime lien will be postponed to the mortgage so as to avoid circuity of action and injustice. Thus in *The "Bangor Castle"*[41] the master had personally guaranteed the mortgage and the court therefore postponed his maritime lien for wages.

Statutory rights of action in rem

No preferential status is conferred upon a claimant with a statutory right of action *in rem* unless and until a writ has been issued.[42]

---

35. See *The "Mary Ann"* (1865) L.R. 1 A. & E. 8.

36. See *The "Duke of Bedford"* (1829) 2 Hagg. 294 and *The "Staffordshire"* (1872) 2 L.R. 4 P.C. 194.

37. *The "Ticonderoga"* (1857) Swab. 215; *The "Tasmania"* (1888) 13 P.D. 110 and *Morgon* v. *Castlegate Steamship Co.* [1893] A.C. 38.

38. *The "Veritas"* [1901] P. 304. See also *The "Sydney Cove"* (1815) 2 Dods. 1; *The "Hope"* (1873) 1 Asp.M.L.C. and *The "Stream Fisher"* [1927] P. 73.

39. *The "Aline"* (1839) 1 Wm.Rob. 111; *The "Linda Flor"* (1857) Swab. 309; *The "Elino"* (1883) 8 P.D. 129 and *The "Veritas"* [1901] P. 304.

40. *The "Europa"* (1863) Br. & Lush. 89; *The "Fairport"* (1882) 8 P.D. 48; *The "Kong Magnus"* [1891] P. 223; *The "Royal Arch"* (1857) Swab. 269; *The "Rainbow"* (1885) 53 L.T. 91 and *The "Bold Buccleugh"* (1852) 7 Moo.P.C.C. 267.

41. (1876) 8 Asp.M.L.C. 156.

42. See *The "Two Ellens"* (1872) L.R. 4 P.C. 161 and *The "Monica S"* [1968] P. 741.

Accordingly, a mortgage has priority over all such claims[43] unless prior to the date of the mortgage a writ *in rem* has been issued[44] or for some other reason the mortgagee is considered to have lost his priority.[45]

Where the mortgagee is in possession of the ship it is not necessarily the case that the mortgagee will be liable for goods and materials supplied to the ship for her operation and maintenance. Such will only be the case where the agent or master ordering them is to be considered to be the agent of the mortgagee.[46]

However, the mortgagee may well lose his priority or be estopped from asserting it where with knowledge that the mortgagor was insolvent he has stood by and allowed persons to carry out repairs to the ship or to supply goods and materials which benefited his security. Although this was not established on the facts before the court, in *The "Two Ellens"* Sir Robert Phillimore at first instance[47] hinted *obiter* that this could have been the case if the facts had been established. He said:[48]

. . . the evidence before me does not sustain the position either that the mortgagee was aware that those repairs were supplied by the material men upon the credit of the ship and not upon the personal credit of the owner, or that the mortgagee stood by and looked on, giving directly, or indirectly, any sanction to the supply of these necessaries on the credit of the ship . . .

Other mortgagees

As between registered mortgages, section 33 of the Merchant Shipping Act 1894 provides:

If there are more mortgages than one registered in respect of the same ship or share, the mortgagees shall, notwithstanding any express, implied or constructive notice, be entitled in priority, one over the other, according to the date at which each mortgage is recorded in the register book, and not according to the date of each mortgage itself.

And similarly as regards registered fishing vessels. Paragraph 3 of Schedule 3 to the 1988 Act provides as follows:

Where two or more mortgages are registered in respect of the same vessel or share, the priority of the mortgagees between themselves shall (subject to paragraph 4[49]) be determined by the order in which the mortgages were registered (and not by reference to any other matter).

43. See *The "Pacific"* (1864) Br. & Lush. 243; *The "Markland"* (1871) 1 Asp.M.L.C. 44; *The "Two Ellens"* (*supra*).

44. In which case according to the rule *nemo dat quod non habet* the mortgaged property being charged with the claim, the mortgagee takes the property subject to the charge as would any other purchaser from the owner.

45. For an example of circumstances which were argued to cause the mortgagee to lose his priority, but which were not held to be established on the facts see *The "Pickaninny"* [1960] 1 Lloyd's Rep. 553.

46. See *The "Troubadour"* (1866) L.R. 1 A. & E. 302 and *Havilland v. Thompson* (1864) 3 Ct. of Sess. Cas. (3rd Ser.) 313.

47. (1871) L.R. 3 A & E. 345.

48. *Ibid.* at p. 360.

49. Which deals with notices of intending mortgages.

The effect of these sections is precisely as stated: a mortgagee obtains his priority from registration and so he will have priority over a prior unregistered equitable mortgage even though he had notice of it,[50] and over a prior equitable charge of which he has notice.[51]

In *Black* v. *Williams*[52] Vaughan Williams J. suggested that any apparent hardship was illusory and that the holders of equitable charges had only themselves to blame for not perfecting the same into a legal title and having it registered. He said:[53]

I hold therefore, that the title of the Applicants, who have got a mortgage in the statutory form which has been registered, is to be preferred to the title of the debenture holders who, having a prior equitable title, and being entitled to get that converted into a legal title in the statutory form and registered, chose not to do so. There is no hardship whatever in such a decision. The Act of Parliament was passed for the benefit of commerce, and in order that English ships might be easily dealt with by English shipowners, the Legislature has recognised that occasions arise when it is to the interest of the whole community that people should be able to raise money on ships by sale or mortgage, and in the interests of the general public it has therefore provided that registered titles in the statutory form shall have priority, thus enabling those who are disposed to purchase or lend money upon ships to do so with perfect confidence that their titles will not be overridden by priority being obtained by equitable unregistered titles which happen to be prior in point of time, and which, for reasons of their own, the owners of those equitable titles have not thought fit to convert into the legal form, or to register in the way pointed out in the statute.

In *Barclay* v. *Poole*,[54] a managing owner of a ship mortgaged his share to his bankers, who at his request did not register the mortgage. Subsequently he sold his share to other joint owners who were unaware of the mortgage and a bill of sale was duly executed and registered. It was held that the purchasers took priority to the bank under the unregistered prior mortgage.

However, although the priority of the mortgages themselves is determined by their date and time of registration, nevertheless the priority of particular advances may follow a different order.

It is a general rule of priority in respect of mortgages that a first mortgagee whose mortgage is taken to secure future advances cannot claim in priority over a second mortgagee the benefit of advances made after he had notice of the second mortgage. This was the rule laid down by the House of Lords in the case of *Hopkinson* v. *Rolt*.[55] In that case a shipbuilder granted a mortgage to the bank in order to secure monies then owing and any further advances up to a certain maximum. He subsequently granted a second mortgage over the same property to the plaintiff. Further advances were made by the bank who had notice of the plaintiff's mortgage. It was held that the bank had no priority over the plaintiff

50. *Coombes* v. *Mansfield* (1855) 24 L.J.Ch. 513.
51. *Black* v. *Williams* [1895] 1 Ch. 408.
52. *Ibid.*
53. *Ibid.* at p. 421.
54. [1907] 2 Ch. 284.
55. (1861) 9 H.L.C. 514.

in respect of the further advances made with notice of the plaintiff's mortgage. Lord Chelmsford said:[56]

As the first mortgagee is not bound to make the stipulated further advances, and with notice of a subsequent mortgage he can always protect himself by inquiries as to the state of the accounts with the second mortgagee, if he chooses to run the risk of advancing his money with the knowledge, or the means of knowledge, of his position, what reason can there be for allowing him any priority . . . But, on the other hand, if it be held that he is always to be secure of his priority, a perpetual curb is imposed on the mortgagor's right to encumber his equity of redemption.

In *West* v. *Williams*[57] it was held that the rule in *Hopkinson* v. *Rolt* applies even where a mortgagee is contractually bound to make the further advance to the mortgagor under the terms of the mortgage, provided he has notice of the subsequent mortgage.

In *The "Benwell Tower"* it was held that this rule was applicable to registered mortgages of ships, notwithstanding section 33 of the Act. Bruce J. dealt with the matter in the following way:

The case of *Hopkinson* v. *Rolt* establishes the general principle that a first mortgagee, whose mortgage is taken to cover future advances, cannot claim, in priority over a second mortgagee, the benefit of advances made after he had notice of the second mortgage. But it was contended that this principle did not apply to the registered mortgages of ships . . . But it seems to me that [section 33, MSA 1894] relates only to priorities arising from the dates of the instruments. It provides, in effect, that as regards the priorities of instruments and the rights of the parties arising therefrom, the dates of registration and not the dates of the instruments, shall be the governing dates, notwithstanding any express or implied or constructive notice of an unregistered instrument. Where priorities depend, not upon the dates of the instruments, but upon a state of facts wholly independent of the dates of the instruments, I think that the section in question does not apply.

However, where the first mortgagee does not have notice of the second mortgage at the time of the advance, he will be entitled to priority over the second mortgage in respect of the further advance.[58]

Registration only affords priority to advances made under the registered instrument. Thus in *Parr* v. *Applebee*[59] where a first registered mortgagee made further advances not under the registered mortgage, but under a separate and unregistered instrument, and another mortgagee with notice of the unregistered instrument, registered his mortgage as a second mortgage, it was held that as second registered mortgagee he had priority over the unregistered instrument held by the first registered mortgagee.

A registered mortgage or a transfer of a registered mortgage takes in priority to an unregistered mortgage, but an unregistered mortgage is good against all other persons and will be accorded the appropriate priority under the usual equitable principles. Thus as between two unregistered mortgages, the first in

56. *Ibid.* at p. 476.
57. [1899] 1 Ch. 132.
58. *Liverpool Marine Credit Co.* v. *Wilson* (1872) 7 Ch.App. 507.
59. (1855) 7 De G.M. & G. 585.

time will prevail unless there is some special reason why the first in time rule is to be displaced.

Assignees of freight

Legal assignment

In order to constitute a legal assignment of freight the formality provisions of section 136 of the Law of Property Act 1925 must be complied with, failing which the assignment will be effective only as an equitable assignment.

It is necessary to distinguish the case of a legal assignment of freight before date of the legal mortgage and an assignment of freight occurring after the mortgage.

In the latter case, where subsequent to the date of the mortgage the mortgagor in possession assigns the freight, he cannot by such assignment grant any greater right to the freight than he himself has and, accordingly, whilst the mortgagor remains in possession, the assignment is effective, but should the mortgagee enter into possession his right to receive the freight will prevail over the right of the assignee.

In *Wilson* v. *Wilson*,[60] a ship was on an outward voyage from Liverpool to Calcutta, and she was mortgaged by her owner to a bank as security for advances. The bank duly registered the mortgage. However, three days before the mortgage of the ship to the bank, the owner had mortgaged her homeward freight, and the freight of all succeeding or intermediate voyages. Upon the ship's return from Calcutta, a dispute arose between the plaintiff assignee and the defendant bank as to the freight earned. It was held that the bank was entitled to receive the freight as the registered mortgagee, having had no notice of the prior assignment. In the course of giving judgment, Malins V.-C. said:

 I do not think it material whether they took possession of the ship or not, because as owners of the ship, being mortgagees of the ship without notice, they had, in my opinion, a clear title to the plaintiff. They had a right at any time, until the money was paid which was owing by the mortgagors, to intercept it, and say that the money must be paid to them . . . it appears to me perfectly clear that the mortgage of the ship without notice of any assignment of the freight, carries with it the absolute right to receive the freight.[61]

Nevertheless, the assignee of freight does have priority over a second and subsequent mortgagee.[62]

In the case of a prior assignee of freight, the situation is different. A prior legal assignee will have priority over a subsequent legal mortgage according to the rule that as between competing legal interests the first in time prevails. But, a prior equitable assignee of freight will not prevail over a subsequent legal mort-

---

60. (1872) L.R. 14 Eq. 32.
61. See also *The "Pride of Wales"* (1867) 15 L.T. 606 and *Ward* v. *Royal Exchange Shipping Co., ex p. Harrison* (1887) 6 Asp.M.L.C. 239.
62. *Liverpool Marine Credit* v. *Wilson* (1872) 7 Ch.App. 507.

gage, provided the money is advanced under the mortgage without notice of the assignment.

The rights of a prior assignee of freight, whether legal or equitable, will prevail over all equitable mortgages.

AIRCRAFT

General creditors of the mortgagor

The same principles outlined above in relation to ship mortgages apply equally to aircraft mortgages.

Insolvency of the mortgagor

Article 15 of the Mortgaging of Aircraft Order 1972 provides:

A registered mortgage of an aircraft shall not be affected by any act of bankruptcy committed by the mortgagor after the date on which the mortgage is registered, notwithstanding that at the commencement of his bankruptcy the mortgagor had the aircraft in his possession order or disposition, or was reputed owner thereof,[63] and the mortgagee shall be preferred to any right, claim or interest therein of the other creditors of the bankrupt or any trustee or assignee on their behalf.

This provision is identical in wording to section 36 of the Merchant Shipping Act 1894 which has been considered above.[64] The cases decided under that provision in relation to ships would, therefore, apply by analogy to aircraft under this provision.

After the bankruptcy or winding up of the mortgagor, the mortgagee may take proceedings for the enforcement of his security in the usual way as his action is to enforce a claim to his own property rather than that of the bankrupt or the company.[65] Where, however, some insolvency point arises the matter can and should be transferred to the Chancery Division.[66]

It should be noted, however, that upon the application of the liquidator or administrator the court may reopen an extortionate credit agreement with a company[67] and upon the application of a trustee in bankruptcy the court may reopen an extortionate credit agreement with a bankrupt made not more than three years before the commencement of the bankruptcy.[68]

---

63. Note: the doctrine of "reputed ownership" was abolished by the Insolvency Act 1985, section 235, Schedule 10, Part III.
64. At p. 112.
65. *Re Wherly, ex p. Hirst* (1879) 11 Ch.D. 278 and *Re David Lloyd & Co., Lloyd* v. *David Lloyd & Co.* (1877) 6 Ch.D. 339.
66. See Insolvency Rules 1986, rule 7.15.
67. Insolvency Act 1986, section 244.
68. Insolvency Act 1986, section 343.

Possessory liens

The principles discussed above in relation to the ship mortgages apply, *mutatis mutandis*, to aircraft. The priority of the possessory lien of a repairer and of one exercising a power of statutory detention is in fact given express statutory force by Article 14(5) of the Mortgaging of Aircraft Order 1972 which provides:

Nothing in this Article[69] shall be construed as giving a registered mortgage any priority over any possessory lien in respect of work done on the aircraft (whether before or after the creation or the registration of the mortgage) on the express or implied authority of any persons lawfully entitled to possession of the aircraft or over any right to detain the aircraft under any Act of Parliament.

In the United Kingdom there is power under section 88 of the Civil Aviation Act 1982 to detain an aircraft in respect of airport charges. Section 88 provides as follows:

88.—(1) Where default is made in the payment of airport charges incurred in respect of any aircraft at an aerodrome to which this section applies, the aerodrome authority may, subject to the provisions of this section—
(a) detain, pending payment, either—
  (i) the aircraft in respect of which the charges were incurred (whether or not they were incurred by the person who is the operator of the aircraft at the time when the detention begins); or
  (ii) any other aircraft of which the person in default is the operator at the time when the detention begins; and
(b) if the charges are not paid within 56 days of the date when the detention begins, sell the aircraft in order to satisfy the charges.
(2) An aerodrome authority shall not detain or continue to detain an aircraft under this section by reason of any alleged default in the payment of airport charges if the operator of the aircraft or any other person claiming an interest therein—
(a) disputes that the charges, or any of them, are due or, if the aircraft is detained under subsection (1)(a)(i) above, that the charges in question were incurred in respect of that aircraft; and
(b) gives to the authority, pending the determination of the dispute, sufficient security for the payment of the charges which are alleged to be due.
(3) An aerodrome authority shall not sell an aircraft under this section without the leave of the court; and the court shall not give leave except on proof—
(a) that a sum is due to the authority for airport charges;
(b) that default has been made in the payment thereof; and
(c) that the aircraft which the authority seek leave to sell is liable to sale under this section by reason of the default.
(4) An aerodrome authority proposing to apply for leave to sell an aircraft under this section shall take such steps as may be prescribed—
(a) for bringing the proposed application to the notice of persons whose interests may be affected by the determination of the court thereon; and
(b) for affording to any such person an opportunity of becoming a party to the proceedings on the application;
and, if leave is given, the aerodrome authority shall secure that the aircraft is sold for the best price that can reasonably be obtained.

---

69. Which deals with the priority of registered mortgages of aircraft. See further, p. 125.

(5) Failure to comply with any requirement of subsection (4) above in respect of any sale, while actionable as against the aerodrome authority concerned at the suit of any person suffering loss in consequence thereof, shall not, after the sale has taken place, be a ground for impugning its validity.

(6) The proceeds of any sale under this section shall be applied as follows, and in the following order, that is to say—

(a) in payment of any duty (whether of customs or excise) chargeable on imported goods or value added tax which is due in consequence of the aircraft's having been brought into the United Kingdom;

(b) in payment of the expenses incurred by the aerodrome authority in detaining, keeping and selling the aircraft, including their expenses in connection with the application to the court;

(c) in payment of the airport charges which the court has found to be due;

(d) in payment of any charge in respect of the aircraft which is due by virtue of regulations under section 73 above;

and the surplus, if any, shall be paid to or among the person or persons whose interests in the aircraft have been divested by reason of the sale.

(7) The power of detention and sale conferred by this section in respect of an aircraft extends to the equipment of the aircraft and any stores for use in connection with its operation (being equipment and stores carried in the aircraft) whether or not the property of the person who is its operator, and references to the aircraft in subsections (2) to (6) above include, except where the context otherwise requires, references to any such equipment and stores.

(8) The power of detention conferred by this section in respect of an aircraft extends to any aircraft documents carried in it, and any such documents may, if the aircraft is sold under this section, be transferred by the aerodrome authority to the purchaser.

(9) The power conferred by this section to detain an aircraft in respect of which charges have been incurred may be exercised on the occasion on which the charges have been incurred or on any subsequent occasion when the aircraft is on the aerodrome on which those charges were incurred or on any other aerodrome owned or managed by the aerodrome authority concerned.

(10) This section applies to any aerodrome owned or managed by any government department, the BAA or a local authority, other than a district council in Scotland, and to any other aerodrome designated for the purposes of this section by an order made by the Secretary of State; and in this section—

"aerodrome authority" in relation to any aerodrome, means the person owning or managing it;

"airport charges" means charges payable to an aerodrome authority for use of, or for services provided at, an aerodrome but does not include charges payable by virtue of regulations under section 73 above;

"aircraft documents", in relation to any aircraft, means any certificate of registration, maintenance or airworthiness of that aircraft, any log book relating to the use of that aircraft or its equipment and any similar document;

"the court" means—

(a) as respects England and Wales, the High Court; and

(b) as respects Scotland, the Court of Session.

(11) The Secretary of State may, after consultation with any local authority which appears to him to be concerned, by order repeal any enactment in a local Act which appears to the Secretary of State to be unnecessary having regard to the provisions of this section or to be inconsistent therewith.

(12) Nothing in this section shall prejudice any right of an aerodrome authority to recover any charges, or any part thereof, by action.

There is also a power of detention and sale in respect of navigation services under Articles 10 to 18 of the Civil Aviation (Navigation Services Charges) Regulations 1986 which provide as follows:

10. Where default is made in the payment of charges incurred in respect of any aircraft under these Regulations, the Authority or an authorised person may, subject to the provisions of this and the following regulations, take such steps as are necessary to detain, pending payment, either—

(a) the aircraft in respect of which the charges were incurred (whether or not they were incurred by the person who is the operator of the aircraft at the time when the detention begins); or

(b) any other aircraft of which the person in default is the operator at the time when the detention begins;

and if the charges are not paid within 56 days of the date when the detention begins, the Authority may sell the aircraft in order to satisfy the charges.

11. The Authority or authorised person concerned shall not detain, or continue to detain, an aircraft under these Regulations by reason of any alleged default in the payment of charges payable under these Regulations if the operator of the aircraft or any other person claiming an interest therein—

(a) disputes that the charges, or any of them, are due or, if the aircraft is detained under regulation 10(a) of these Regulations, that the charges in question were incurred in respect of that aircraft; and

(b) gives to the Authority, pending the determination of the dispute, sufficient security for the payment of the charges which are alleged to be due.

12. The Authority shall not sell an aircraft under these Regulations without the leave of the court; and the court shall not give leave except on proof that a sum is due to the Authority for charges under these Regulations, that default has been made in the payment thereof and that the aircraft which the Authority seeks leave to sell is liable to sale under these Regulations by reason of the default.

13. The Authority shall, before applying to the court for leave to sell an aircraft under these Regulations, take such steps for bringing the proposed application to the notice of interested persons and for affording them an opportunity of becoming a party to the proceedings as are set forth in Schedule 2 of these Regulations. If such leave is given, the Authority shall secure that the aircraft is sold for the best price that can be reasonably obtained; but failure to comply with any requirement of this regulation or of the said Schedule in respect of any sale, while actionable as against the Authority at the suit of any person suffering loss in consequence thereof, shall not, after the sale has taken place, be a ground for impugning its validity.

14. The proceeds of any sale under these Regulations shall be applied as follows, and in the following order, that is to say—

(a) in payment of any customs duty which is due in consequence of the aircraft having been brought into the United Kingdom;

(b) in payment of the expenses incurred by the Authority in detaining, keeping and selling the aircraft, including its expenses in connection with the application to the court;

(c) in payment of the charges in respect of any aircraft which the court has found to be due from the operator by virtue of these or any other Regulations under section 73 of the Civil Aviation Act 1982;

(d) in payment of any airport charges incurred in respect of the aircraft which are due from the operator of the aircraft to the person owning or managing the aerodrome at which the aircraft was detained under these Regulations;

and the surplus, if any, shall be paid to or among the person or persons whose interests in the aircraft have been divested by reason of the sale.

15. The power of detention and sale conferred by these Regulations in respect of an aircraft extends to the equipment of the aircraft and any stores for use in connection with its operation (being equipment and stores carried in the aircraft) whether or not the property of the person who is its operator, and references to the aircraft in regulations 11 to 14 of these Regulations include, except where the context otherwise requires, references to any such equipment and stores.

16. The power of detention conferred by these Regulations in respect of an aircraft extends to any aircraft documents carried in it, and any such documents may, if the aircraft is sold under these Regulations, be transferred by the Authority to the purchaser.

17. The power conferred by these Regulations to detain an aircraft may be exercised on any occasion when the aircraft is on any aerodrome referred to in the Table in regulation 2(1) of these Regulations or to which section 88 of the Civil Aviation Act 1982 for the time being applies.

18. Nothing in these Regulations shall prejudice any right of the Authority to recover any charges, or any part thereof, by action.

Other mortgagees

Article 14 of the Mortgaging of Aircraft Order 1972 provides:

(1) Subject to the following provisions of this article, a mortgage of an aircraft entered in the Register shall have priority over any other mortgage of or charge on that aircraft, other than another mortgage entered in the Register . . . [transitional provisions no longer relevant].

(2) Subject to the following provisions of this article, where two or more mortgages of an aircraft are entered in the Register, those mortgages shall as between themselves have priority according to the times at which they were respectively entered in the Register.

Provided that:

(i) [transitional provisions no longer relevant];

(ii) without prejudice to proviso (i), where a priority notice has been entered in the Register and the contemplated mortgage referred to therein is made and entered in the Register within 14 days thereafter that mortgage shall be deemed to have priority from the time when the priority notice was registered.

(3) In reckoning the period of 14 days under the preceding paragraph of this article, there shall be excluded any day which the Authority has by notice in its Official Record specified as a day on which its office is not open for the registration of mortgages.

(4) The priorities provided for by the preceding provisions of this article shall have effect notwithstanding any express, implied or constructive notice affecting the mortgagee.

7

CONFLICT OF LAWS

INTRODUCTION

It is in the very nature of ships and aircraft that they may travel from one jurisdiction to another and at common law a mortgagee has no right to restrain a
ship from going on a foreign voyage merely because this will take the ship out of
the jurisdiction and render enforcement of the security more difficult.[1] The
same principle would appear to be equally applicable to mortgages of aircraft.

This international aspect to mortgages of ships and aircraft has two main
features. First, the mortgagee may need to enforce his mortgage in a foreign
court. This raises the problem of jurisdiction in relation to the court in which
the mortgagee is seeking enforcement, and also the problem of recognition of
foreign judgments should it ever become necessary to rely in the courts of one
jurisdiction upon a judgment obtained in the courts of another jurisdiction.
Secondly, in the course of its voyages, a ship, and to a lesser extent, an aircraft,
may attract claims against it of various descriptions. Claims of a particular description may be granted a different priority in one jurisdiction to another, and
the courts of different jurisdictions may apply different conflict of laws rules in
order to determine the appropriate priority which the particular claim attracts:
the priority granted by the law of the claim or that granted by the law of the
forum.[2]

Unfortunately, there is at present no uniform and international approach to
either of these problems and none appears likely in the foreseeable future.
Although two international Conventions have resulted from conferences convened to consider these problems, they have not gained widespread acceptance.
The International Convention for the Unification of Certain Rules of Law relating to Maritime Liens and Mortgages, signed at Brussels, 10 April 1926[3] and
the International Convention for the Unification of Certain Rules of Law relat-

---

1. *The "Innisfallen"* (1886) L.R. 1 A. & E. 72.
2. Compare the differing decisions (on facts which were to all intents and purposes identical) by
the Supreme Court of Canada in *The "Ioannis Daskalelis"* [1974] S.C.R. 1248 and the Privy Council
in *The "Halcyon Isle"* [1980] 2 Lloyd's Rep. 325 (on appeal from Singapore Court of Appeal).
3. See Appendix 6.

ing to Maritime Liens and Mortgages, done at Brussels on 27 May 1967[4] have not been ratified by the major maritime nations of the world and in particular they have not been ratified by the U.S.A., Canada, or the United Kingdom.

It is, therefore, not possible to advise any mortgagee with certainty generally as to his position, as it is likely to depend upon the jurisdiction in which the ship or aircraft happens to be at any given moment of time. A mortgagee is best advised to seek local advice appropriate to the jurisdiction concerned before taking any particular course of action.

JURISDICTION

In personam

The mortgagee may of course sue the mortgagor for the debt secured by the mortgage upon his personal covenant and jurisdiction may in such case be established in the English High Court if the mortgagor is to be found within the jurisdiction, or subject to the provisions of the Civil Jurisdiction and Judgments Act 1982, if the provisions of R.S.C., Order 11, rule 1(1)(a) or (d) or (m), are satisfied, and in the exercise of its discretion the court grants leave to serve the writ out of the jurisdiction.

In rem

Usually, however, a mortgagee will wish to enforce his rights *in rem* against the ship or aircraft so as to realise his security. In this context the treatment of ships and aircraft is not the same, and they will therefore be considered in turn.

SHIPS

In the case of a ship, the Admiralty Court is given jurisdiction by section 20 of the Supreme Court Act 1981 which provides:

(1) The Admiralty jurisdiction of the High Court shall be as follows, that is to say—
   (a) jurisdiction to hear and determine any of the questions and claims mentioned in subsection (2);
. . .
(2) The questions and claims referred to in subsection (1)(a) are—
   (c) any claim in respect of a mortgage of or charge on a ship or any share therein;
. . .
(7) The preceding provisions of this section apply—
   (a) in relation to all ships and aircraft,[5] whether British or not and whether registered or not and wherever the residence or domicile of their owners may be;
   (b) in relation to all claims, wherever arising, . . .

4. See Appendix 7.
5. This applies only to claims for salvage, towage and pilotage of aircraft and does not extend to claims in respect of mortgages of aircraft. See *The Glider Standard Austria SH* [1965] P. 463.

(c) so far as they relate to mortgages and charges, to all mortgages or charges, whether registered or not and whether legal or equitable, including mortgages and charges created under foreign law;

Section 21 of the Act provides:

(1) Subject to section 22,[6] an action in personam may be brought in the High Court in all cases within the Admiralty Jurisdiction of that Court.

(2) In the case of any claim as is mentioned in section 20(2) . . . (c) . . . an action in rem may be brought in the High Court against the ship or property in connection with which the claim arises.

Co-extensive with the right to proceed *in rem*, the ship may be arrested by the Admiralty Marshal pursuant to R.S.C., Order 75, rule 5, and if necessary appraised and sold by him.[7]

Accordingly, if the mortgaged ship is within the jurisdiction, the mortgagee may found jurisdiction against it by an Admiralty action *in rem* whether or not the mortgagor is or is not domiciled within the jurisdiction, whether or not the ship is a British ship, and whether or not the mortgage is governed by English law.

For example, in a Canadian case, *Orient Leasing Co. Ltd.* v. *The ship "Kosei Maru"*[7a] the Federal Court held that it had jurisdiction under the Canadian equivalents of sections 20(2)(c), 20(7)(c) and 21(2) of the Supreme Court Act[8] to hear and determine foreclosure proceedings brought by Japanese mortgages against a Japanese ship arrested in Canada.

The Admiralty Court regularly gives judgments against foreign ships in favour of foreign mortgagees and in respect of foreign mortgages and orders such ships to be appraised and sold.

AIRCRAFT

There is no equivalent right of action *in rem* against an aircraft in respect of mortgage[9] and the mortgagee of an aircraft must therefore commence an ordinary mortgage action under R.S.C., Order 88. This will usually be done by originating summons in the Chancery Division. If the mortgagor is within the jurisdiction the originating summons may be served on him in the usual way. If he is not within the jurisdiction, the High Court will have jurisdiction, and leave to serve the originating summons out of the jurisdiction may be sought under

6. Restrictions on actions *in personam* in collision actions etc.
7. See generally Meeson, *The Practice and Procedure of the Admiralty Court* (Lloyd's of London Press, 1986).
7a. (1979) 94 D.L.R. (3d) 658.
8. Namely, sections 22(2)(c), 22(3)(d) and 43(2) of the Federal Court Act.
9. See *The Glider Standard Austria SH* [1965] P. 463.

R.S.C., Order 11 if the mortgagor is domiciled in England[11] or if there is an express jurisdiction agreement or if the aircraft is within the jurisdiction.[12]

If necessary, an *ex parte* injunction may be obtained to prevent the aircraft from leaving the jurisdiction, pending the hearing of the originating summons.

FOREIGN JUDGMENTS

A mortgagee, having his debt secured on the ship or aircraft the subject of the mortgage, is not generally concerned with *in personam* foreign judgments affecting the mortgagor. He will however be concerned with any judgment purporting to be *in rem* and binding upon the whole world which affects his security.

This distinction was described by Lord Blackburn in *Castrique* v. *Imrie*[13] where he said:

When a tribunal, no matter whether in England or a foreign country, has to determine between two parties and between them only, the decision of that tribunal, though in general binding between the parties and privies, does not affect the rights of third parties, and if in execution of the judgment of such a tribunal process issues against the property of one of the litigants, and some particular thing is sold as being his property, there is nothing to prevent any third person setting up his claim to that thing, for the tribunal neither had jurisdiction to determine nor did determine more than that the litigant's property should be sold, and did not do more than sell the litigant's interest, if any, in the thing . . . But when the tribunal has jurisdiction to determine not merely the rights of the parties, but also on the disposition of the thing, and does in the exercise of that jurisdiction direct that the thing, and not merely the interest of any particular party in it, be sold or transferred, the case is very different.

The English courts will recognise a foreign judgment operating *in rem* against the mortgaged property if at the time of the foreign proceedings the mortgaged property was situate in the foreign country.[14]

Thus in *Castrique* v. *Imrie*[15] a British ship which was mortgaged to an English mortgagee was sold by a French court to another British subject in an action brought by a ship repairer. The House of Lords held that the judgment of the French court *in rem* was binding upon the mortgagee.

In *Simpson* v. *Fogo*[16] a mortgaged British ship was attached by creditors in New Orleans. The law of New Orleans did not recognise a mortgage of chattels and the court, therefore, disregarded the claim of the English mortgagees intervening in the proceedings and duly sold the ship to another British subject. In the mortgagees' action in England to enforce their mortgage, the court held that the judgment of the New Orleans court was *in personam* and accordingly not

11. Ord. 11(1)(a).
12. Ord. 11(1)(i).
13. (1869) L.R. 4 H.L. 414.
14. See Dicey & Morris, *The Conflict of Laws*, Rule 182.
15. (1869) L.R. 4 H.L. 414.
16. (1860) 29 L.J.Ch. 657.

binding upon persons not parties to the action. It was further held that the mortgagees had not become parties to the action by their intervention.

THE MORTGAGE

It is necessary in this context to distinguish two separate questions. First, the question what is the applicable law governing the formal validity of the mortgage? Secondly, the question what is the applicable law governing the respective rights and obligations of the parties under the mortgage?

According to general principles, the answer to the first of these questions is the *lex situs* and the answer to the second is the proper law of the contract.

In the context of the mortgages of ships and aircraft, the registration provisions as regards the ownership and mortgaging of ships and aircraft which have been enacted in most jurisdictions mean that ships and aircraft have a permanent nationality independent of their geographical location. Accordingly their *situs* for these purposes is fixed, and questions regarding formal validity will be governed by the law of the state of registration, often referred to as "the law of the flag". This will also, *prima facie*, be the proper law of the mortgage, unless there is an express choice of law clause in the mortgage deed[17] or other indications suggesting some other law.

Thus in *The "Angel Bell"*[18] Donaldson J. had to consider whether the proper law of a mortgage was English or Panamanian. He said:[19]

A ship is, in effect, a floating piece of the nation whose flag it wears and there is, therefore, an analogy between foreign land and foreign ships.

I accept that it is possible to have an English contract for the mortgage of foreign land which will result in the mortgage being governed inter partes by English law, while being perfected according to foreign law: *British South African Co. Ltd.* v. *De Beers Consolidated Mines Ltd* [1910] 2 Ch. 502. But prima facie mortgages of either foreign land or ships will be governed by the law of their situs or flag.

In *The "Arosa Kulm"*[20] Hewson J. had to consider the validity of mortgage bearer bonds under Panamanian law where the original mortgagees were in fact the owners of the mortgaged property. He held that such a mortgage was valid under Panamanian law and referred to the English case of *Black* v. *Williams*[21] where by a trust deed a shipowner undertook to execute a legal mortgage of his ships to trustees to secure the interests of debenture holders.

In *The "Pacific Challenger"*[22] a question arose as to the validity of a Liberian mortgage which the court decided upon affidavit evidence of Liberian law.

---

17. This may not be possible in some jurisdictions which require mortgages of their ships to be governed by their law.
18. [1979] 2 Lloyd's Rep. 491.
19. At page 495, col. 2.
20. [1959] 1 Lloyd's Rep. 212.
21. [1895] 1 Ch. 408.
22. [1960] 1 Lloyd's Rep. 99.

It is important however to distinguish questions of formal validity, which in general will be relevant only as regards effectiveness of the mortgage as against third parties, and questions arising under the mortgage between the mortgagor and the mortgagee.

As between the mortgagor and the mortgagee, their respective rights and obligations will depend upon the proper law of the mortgage which may well be different from the law of the flag.

Many mortgages will have an express choice of law clause, often providing for English law to be the proper law of the mortgage. Without intending to be unduly chauvinistic, it is a fact that at least as regards ship mortgages, England has a long and unrivalled history and experience of dealing with such matters. In the U.S.A. for example, ship mortgages were not given legal recognition until 1920.

COMPETING CLAIMS

This is the most difficult area in which to determine the appropriate law to be applied. Lord Diplock summarised the problem in *The "Halcyon Isle"*[23] at page 230B to D:

In the case of a ship . . . the classification of claims against her former owners for the purposes of determining priorities to participate in the proceeds of her sale may raise a further problem of conflict of laws, since claims may have arisen as a result of events that occurred not only on the high seas but also within the territorial jurisdictions of a number of different foreign states. So the lex causae of one claim may differ from the lex causae of another, even though the events which gave rise to the claim in each of those foreign states are similar in all respects except their geographical location; the leges causarum of various claims, of which under English conflict rules the "proper law" is that of different states may assign different legal consequences to different events.

The two basic principles to be applied in the resolution of this problem are clear:

(i) The actual validity of a particular claim and the substantive rights of a claimant will be governed by the *proper law* (in the case of a contractual claim) or the *lex loci delicti commissii*[24] (in the case of a tort claim).

(ii) The determination of the priority of one particular claim against another is governed by the *lex fori*.[25]

However, in the case of a maritime lien a difficulty arises as to whether it is to be classified as part of the substantive claim in the same way that the security interest created by a mortgage is so treated, or whether it is looked upon simply as a procedural device.

There is at present an unfortunate divergence of judicial opinion in common

23. [1981] A.C. 221 (P.C.).
24. Subject to certain qualifications. See further Dicey & Morris, *Conflict of Laws*, Chapter 35.
25. "Whatever related to the remedy to be enforced, must be determined by the *lex fori*", *per* Lord Brougham in *Don* v. *Lippmann* (1837) 5 Cl. & Fin. 1 at p. 13.

law jurisdictions as to the correct approach to adopt. In England the majority decision of the Privy Council in *The "Halcyon Isle"*[26] decided that a maritime lien was procedural only.

The facts in *The "Halcyon Isle"*[27] may be stated simply: the *"Halcyon Isle"* was arrested in Singapore in an action brought by her mortgagees and she was sold by the court. The proceeds of sale were insufficient to satisfy all the creditors. American ship repairers applied to the court for a declaration that they had a maritime lien, and the mortgagees applied for determination of priorities. Under United States law a ship repairer has a maritime lien in respect of a claim for repairs, but under Singapore (and English) law he does not. On appeal to the Privy Council, the majority comprising Lords Diplock, Elwyn Jones and Lane held that the ship repairer had no maritime lien and therefore the mortgagee had priority. Lords Salmon and Scarman dissented.

The fundamental policy problem which faced their lordships was summarised by Lord Salmon at page 244D to G:

> Whether it be put in terms of the law of the sea or the rules of private international law, the question has to be asked and answered in this appeal: does English and Singapore law recognise a foreign maritime lien, where none would exist, had the claim arisen in England or Singapore? Whatever the answer the result is unsatisfactory. If in the affirmative, maritime states may be tempted to pass "chauvinistic" laws conferring liens on a plurality of claims so that the claimants may obtain abroad a preference denied to domestic claimants; if in the negative, claimants who have given the ship credit in reliance upon their lien may find themselves sorely deceived. If the law of the sea were a truly universal code, those dangers would disappear. Unfortunately the maritime nations, though they have tried, have failed to secure uniformity in their rules regarding maritime liens.

The policy distinction between the minority and the majority decision lies in the basic question whether, in the absence of any international Convention or consensus as to what claims give rise to maritime liens, the court should adopt a broad international approach based upon comity or whether it should adopt a narrow view based upon purely domestic policy considerations. It was the difference in attitude to this policy question that really determined whether a maritime lien was seen as procedural or substantive, even though much mention is made in both the majority and minority judgments of "principle" and "authority".

There are two main practical arguments in favour of the majority decision. It provides for simplicity of application and certainty for litigants in the English Admiralty Court. In addition, there is a basic policy argument in its favour in that it prevents foreign claimants being afforded greater priority than their English counterparts.

Simplicity was a matter considered by Lord Diplock at the beginning of his judgment.

26. [1981] A.C. 221.
27. *Ibid.*

The choice would appear to lie between (1) on the one hand classifying by reference to the events on which each claim was founded and giving to it the priority to which it would be entitled under the lex fori if those events had occurred within the territorial jurisdiction of the distributing Court; or (2) on the other hand applying a complicated partial renvoi by (i) first ascertaining in respect of each foreign claim the legal consequences other than those relating to priorities in the distribution of a limited fund, that would be attributed under its own lex causae to the events on which the claim is founded; and (ii) then giving to the foreign claim the priority accorded under the lex fori to claims arising from events, however dissimilar, which would have given rise to the same or analogous legal consequences if they had occurred within the territorial jurisdiction of the distributing Court.

Certainty arises because in English law the classes of claim which give rise to a maritime lien are limited and strictly defined.

The arguments in favour of the minority view are based on history and principle. As Lords Salmon and Scarman concluded:

A maritime lien is a right of property given by way of security for a maritime claim . . . A maritime lien validly conferred by the lex loci is as much a part of the claim as is a mortgage similarly valid by the lex loci. Each is a limited right of property securing the claim. The lien travels with the claim, as does the mortgage: and the claim travels with the ship. It would be a denial of history and principle, in the present chaos of the law of the sea governing the recognition and priority of maritime liens and mortgages, to refuse the aid of private international law.

This view also has academic support.[28]

As far as authority is concerned, there is no clear guidance to be obtained and both the majority and the minority views considered their position to be supported by authority.

The majority view finds support in earlier decisions in Bermuda[29] and the East African Court of Appeal.[30]

In South Africa, the position is that after a vigorous defence of the minority view by Munnick J.P., sitting in the Cape Provincial Division, in *The "Khalij Sky"*,[31] the majority view has now been supported, first by Marais J., also sitting in the Cape Provincial Division, in *The "Andrico Unity"*[32] and subsequently by Leon J., sitting in the Durban and Coast Local Division, in *The "Kalantiao"*.[33] It is, however, important to note the proper jurisdictional context of these cases. The question to be decided in *The "Khalij Sky"*[34] was what the position in English admiralty law was as of July 1891, although it has to be said that the judgment contains a full debate as to the relative merits of the majority and minority views. In the other two cases, the question was what the position in English

---

28. See Jackson, *Enforcement of Maritime Claims* (Lloyd's of London Press, 1985), pp. 221–223; Thomas, *Maritime Liens*, paragraphs 578–579; Beazley (1978) *Malaya Law Review* 111; Owen [1985] L.M.C.L.Q. 424; Stanilands [1986] S.A.L.J. 542.
29. See *The "Christine Isle"* [1974] A.M.C. 331 (Bermuda Supreme Court) (pre *"Halcyon Isle"*).
30. *Coal Export v. Notias* [1962] E.A. 220.
31. [1986] 1 S.A.L.R. 485.
32. [1987] 3 S.A.L.R. 794.
33. [1987] 4 S.A.L.R. 250.
34. [1986] 1 S.A.L.R. 485.

admiralty law was as of 1 November 1983. In *The "Kalantiao"*[35] it was expressly stated that the case was decided on the narrow question of what would an English court have held in 1983. Nevertheless, the judgment in *The "Andrico Unity"*[36] is a reasoned defence of the majority concluding that it was: "not in conflict with prior English authorities and rests upon readily understandable considerations of policy".[37]

Other common law jurisdictions, notably Canada and the United States, subscribe to the minority view.[38]

35. [1987] 4 S.A.L.R. 250.
36. [1987] 3 S.A.L.R. 794.
37. Ibid. p. 821I.
38. In the United States see *The "Leah"* [1984] A.M.C. 2089 (4th Circuit Court of Appeals) and *The "Seisho Maru"*, 744 F. 2d 461 (5th Circuit Court of Appeals). In Canada see *The "Har Rai"* [1984] A.M.C. 1649 (C.A.) affirmed by the Supreme Court without opinion [1987] 1 S.C.R. 57.

MERCHANT SHIPPING ACT 1894,[1] PART I

AS AMENDED BY THE
MERCHANT SHIPPING ACT 1988

PART I. REGISTRY

Qualification for owning British Ships

Qualification for owning British Ship

1. [Repealed.][2]

Obligation to register British Ships

Obligation to register British Ships

2. [Repealed.][3]

Exemptions from registry

3. [Repealed.][3]

Procedure for registration

Registrars of British Ships

4.—(1) The following persons shall be registrars of British ships:—
   (a) At any port in the United Kingdom, . . . , approved by the [Commissioners of Customs and Excise] for the registry of ships, *the chief officer of customs* [any officer (whether at that port or elsewhere) appointed for the purpose by the Commisioners]:
  (aa) At any port in the Isle of Man approved by the Governor in Council for the registry of ships, such officer of the Isle of Man Harbour Board as may be appointed for the purpose by the Governor in Council:]
   (b) In Guernsey and Jersey, the chief officers of customs together with the governor:
   (c) In Malta and Gibraltar, the governor:
   (d) At Calcutta, Madras, and Bombay, the port officer:
   (e) At any other port in any British possession approved by the governor of the

---

1. Chapter 60.
2. Replaced by sections 2 and 3 of the Merchant Shipping Act 1988.
3. Replaced by sections 4–8 of the Merchant Shipping Act 1988.

possession for the registry of ships, the chief officer of customs, or, if there is no such officer there resident, the governor of the possession in which the port is situate, or any officer appointed for the purpose by the governor:

(f) At a port of registry established by Order in Council under this Act, persons of the description in that behalf declared by the Order.

(2) [Repealed.]

(3) A registrar shall not be liable to damages or otherwise for any loss accruing to any person by reason of any act done or default made by him in his character of registrar, unless the same has happened through his neglect or wilful act.

Register book

5. Every registrar of British ships shall keep a book to be called the register book, and entries in that book shall be made in accordance with the following provisions:—

(i) The property in a ship shall be divided into sixty-four shares:

(ii) Subject to the provisions of this Act with respect to joint owners by transmission, not more than sixty-four individuals shall be entitled to be registered at the same time as owners of any one ship; but this rule shall not affect the beneficial title of any number of persons or any company represented by or claiming under or through any registered owner or joint owner:

(iii) A person shall not be entitled to be registered as owner of a fractional part of a share in a ship; but any number of persons not exceeding five may be registered as joint owners of a ship or of any share or shares therein:

(iv) Joint owners shall be considered as constituting one person only as regards the persons entitled to be registered, and shall not be entitled to dispose in severalty of any interest in a ship, or in any share therein in respect of which they are registered:

(v) A corporation may be registered as owner by its corporate name.

Survey and measurement of ship

6. Every ship shall before registry be surveyed by a surveyor of ships and her tonnage ascertained in accordance with the tonnage regulations of this Act, and the surveyor shall grant his certificate specifying the ship's tonnage and build, and such other particulars descriptive of the identity of the ship as may for the time being be required by the Board of Trade, and such certificate shall be delivered to the registrar before registry.

Marking of ship

7.—(1) Every ship shall before registry be marked permanently and conspicuously to the satisfaction of the Board of Trade as follows:—

(a) Her name shall be marked on each of her bows, and her name and the name of her port of registry must be marked on her stern, on a dark ground in white or yellow letters, or on a light ground in black letters, such letters to be of a length not less than [one decimetre], and of proportionate breadth:

(b) Her official number and the number denoting her registered tonnage shall be cut in on her main beam:

(c) [In the case of every such ship registered before the 1st day of January 1974] A scale of feet denoting her draught of water shall be marked on each side of her stem and of her stern post in Roman capital letters or in figures, not less than six inches in length, the lower line of such letters or figures to coincide with the draught line denoted thereby, and those letters or figures must be marked by being cut in and painted white or yellow on a dark ground, or in such other way as the Board of Trade approve.

[(d) In the case of every such ship registered on or after that date, a scale of decimetres, or of metres and decimetres, denoting a draught of water shall be marked on each side of her stem and of her stern post—

    (i) in figures at two-decimetre intervals, if the scale is in decimetres; and

    (ii) in figures at each metre interval and at intervening two-decimetre intervals, if the scale is in metres and decimetres;

the capital letter "M" being placed after each metre figure; the top figure of the scale showing both the metre and (except where it marks a full metre interval) the decimetre figure; the lower line of the figures, or figures and letters (as the case may be), coinciding with the draft line denoted thereby; the figures and letters being not less than one decimetre in length and being marked by being cut in and painted white or yellow on a dark ground, or in such other way as the Secretary of State approves.

(e) In the case of every such ship registered after that date but before the 31st day of December 1974 a scale shall be marked either in accordance with paragraph (c) of this sub-section, or in accordance with paragraph (d) of this sub-section.]

(2) [Repealed.]

(3) If the scale . . . showing the ship's draught of water is in any respect inaccurate, so as to be likely to mislead, the owner of the ship shall be liable to a fine not exceeding [level 3 on the standard scale].

(4) The marks required by this section shall be permanently continued, and no alteration shall be made therein, except in the event of any of the particulars thereby denoted being altered in the manner provided by this Act.

(5) If an owner or master of a British ship neglects to cause his ship to be marked as required by this section, or to keep her so marked, or if any person conceals, removes, alters, defaces, or obliterates, or suffers any person under his control to conceal, remove, alter, deface, or obliterate any of the said marks, except in the event aforesaid, or except for the purpose of escaping capture by an enemy, that owner, master, or person shall for each offence be liable to a fine not exceeding [level 3 on the standard scale], and on a certificate from a surveyor of ships, or Board of Trade inspector under this Act, that a ship is insufficiently or inaccurately marked the ship may be detained until the insufficiency or inaccuracy has been remedied.

Application for registry

8. An application for registry of a ship shall be made in the case of individuals by the person requiring to be registered as owner, or by some one or more of the persons so requiring if more than one, or by his or their agent, and in the case of corporations by their agent, and the authority of the agent shall be testified by writing, if appointed by individuals, under the hands of the appointers, and, if appointed by a corporation, under the common seal of that corporation.

Declaration of ownership on registry

9. A person shall not be entitled to be registered as owner of a ship or of a share therein until he, or in the case of a corporation the person authorised by this Act to make declarations on behalf of the corporation, has made and signed a declaration of ownership, referring to the ship as described in the certificate of the surveyor, and containing the following particulars:—

    (i) A statement of his qualification to own a British ship, or in the case of a corporation, of such circumstances of the constitution and business thereof as prove it to be qualified to own a British ship:

(ii) A statement of the time when and the place where the ship was built, or, if the ship is foreign built, and the time and place of building unknown, a statement that she is foreign built, and that the declarant does not know the time or place of her building; and, in addition thereto, in the case of a foreign ship, a statement of her foreign name, or, in the case of a ship condemned, a statement of the time, place, and court at and by which she was condemned:

(iii) [Repealed.]

(iv) A statement of the number of shares in the ship of which he or the corporation, as the case may be, is entitled to be registered as owner:

(v) A declaration that, to the best of his knowledge and belief, no unqualified person or body of persons is entitled as owner to any legal or beneficial interest in the ship or any share therein.

Evidence on first registry

10.—(1) On the first registry of a ship the following evidence shall be produced in addition to the declaration of ownership:—

(a) In the case of a British-built ship, a builder's certificate, that is to say, a certificate signed by the builder of a ship, and containing a true account of the proper denomination and of the tonnage of the ship, as estimated by him, and of the time when and the place where she was built, and of the name of the person (if any) on whose account the ship was built, and if there has been any sale, the bill of sale under which the ship, or a share therein, has become vested in the applicant for registry:

(b) In the case of a foreign-built ship, the same evidence as in the case of a British-built ship, unless the declarant who makes the declaration of ownership declares that the time and place of her building are unknown to him, or that the builder's certificate cannot be procured, in which case there shall be required only the bill of sale under which the ship, or a share therein, became vested in the applicant for registry:

(c) In the case of a ship condemned by any competent court, an official copy of the condemnation.

(2) The builder shall grant the certificate required by this section, and such person as the [Commissioners of Customs and Excise] recognise as carrying on the business of the builder of a ship, shall be included, for the purposes of this section, in the expression "builder of the ship".

(3) If the person granting a builder's certificate under this section wilfully makes a false statement in that certificate he shall for each offence be liable to a fine not exceeding [level 4 on the standard scale].

Entry of particulars in register

11. As soon as the requirements of this Act preliminary to registry have been complied with the registrar shall enter in the register the following particulars respecting the ship:—

(a) The name of the ship and the name of the port to which she belongs:

(b) The details comprised in the surveyor's certificate:

(c) The particulars respecting her origin stated in the declaration of ownership: and

(d) The name and description of her registered owner or owners, and if there are more owners than one, the proportions in which they are interested in her.

Documents to be retained by registrar

12. On the registry of a ship the registrar shall retain in his possession the following documents: namely, the surveyor's certificate, the builder's certificate, any bill of sale of the ship previously made, the copy of the condemnation (if any), and all declarations of ownership.

Port of registry

13. The port at which a ship is registered for the time being shall be deemed her port of registry and the port to which she belongs.

Certificate of Registry

Certificate of registry

14. On completion of the registry of a ship, the registrar shall grant a certificate of registry comprising the particulars respecting her entered in the register book, with the name of her master.

Custody of certificate

15.—(1) The certificate of registry shall be used only for the lawful navigation of the ship, and shall not be subject to detention by reason of any title, lien, charge, or interest whatever had or claimed by any owner, mortgagee, or other person to, on, or in the ship.

(2) If any person, whether interested in the ship or not, refuses on request to deliver up the certificate of registry when in his possession or under his control to the person entitled to the custody thereof for the purposes of the lawful navigation of the ship, or to any registrar, [officer of customs and excise], or other person entitled by law to require such delivery, any justice by warrant under his hand and seal, or any court capable of taking cognizance of the matter, may summon the person so refusing to appear before such justice or court, and to be examined touching such refusal, and unless it is proved to the satisfaction of such justice or court that there was reasonable cause for such refusal, the offender shall be liable to a fine not exceeding [level 3 on the standard scale], but if it is shown to such justice or court that the certificate is lost, the person summoned shall be discharged, and the justice or court shall certify that the certificate of registry is lost.

(3) If the person so refusing is proved to have absconded so that the warrant of a justice or process of a court cannot be served on him, or if he persists in not delivering up the certificate, the justice or court shall certify the fact, and the same proceedings may then be taken as in the case of a certificate mislaid, lost, or destroyed, or as near thereto as circumstances permit.

Penalty for use of improper certificate

16. If the master or owner of a ship uses or attempts to use for her navigation a certificate of registry not legally granted in respect of the ship, he shall, in respect of each offence, be guilty of a misdemeanour, and the ship shall be subject to forfeiture under this Act.

Power to grant new certificate

17. The registrar of the port of registry of a ship may, with the approval of the [Commissioners of Customs and Excise], and on the delivery up to him of the certificate of registry of a ship, grant a new certificate in lieu thereof.

Provision for loss of certificate

18.—(1) In the event of the certificate of registry of a ship being mislaid, lost, or destroyed, the registrar of her port of registry shall grant a new certificate of registry in lieu of her original certificate.

(2) If the port (having a British registrar or consular officer) at which the ship is at the time of the event, or first arrives after the event—

    (a) is not in the United Kingdom, where the ship is registered in the United Kingdom; or,

    (b) is not in the British possession in which the ship is registered; or,

    (c) where the ship is registered at a port of registry established by Order in Council under this Act, is not that port;

then the master of the ship, or some other person having knowledge of the facts of the case, shall make a declaration stating the facts of the case, and the names and descriptions of the registered owners of such ship to the best of the declarant's knowledge and belief, and the registrar or consular officer, as the case may be, shall thereupon grant a provisional certificate, containing a statement of the circumstances under which it is granted.

(3) The provisional certificate shall within ten days after the first subsequent arrival of the ship at her port of discharge in the United Kingdom, where she is registered in the United Kingdom, or in the British possession in which she is registered, or where she is registered at a port of registry established by Order in Council under this Act at that port, be delivered up to the registrar of her port of registry, and the registrar shall thereupon grant the new certificate of registry; and if the master without reasonable cause fails to deliver up the provisional certificate within the ten days aforesaid, he shall be liable to a fine not exceeding [level 3 on the standard scale].

Endorsement of change of master on certificate

19. [Repealed.]

Endorsement of change of ownership on certificate

20.—(1) Whenever a change occurs in the registered ownership of a ship, the change of ownership shall be endorsed on her certificate of registry either by the registrar of the ship's port of registry or by the registrar of any port at which the ship arrives who has been advised of the change by the registrar of the ship's port of registry.

(2) The master shall, for the purpose of such endorsement by the registrar of the ship's port of registry, deliver the certificate of registry to the registrar, forthwith after the change if the change occurs when the ship is at her port of registry, and if it occurs during her absence from that port and the endorsement under this section is not made before her return then upon her first return to that port.

(3) The registrar of any port, not being the ship's port of registry, who is required to make an endorsement under this section may for that purpose require the master of the ship to deliver to him the ship's certificate of registry, so that the ship be not thereby detained, and the master shall deliver the same accordingly.

(4) If the master fails to deliver to the registrar the certificate of registry as required by this section he shall, for each offence, be liable to a fine not exceeding [level 3 on the standard scale].

Delivery up of certificate of ship lost or ceasing to be British owned

21.—(1) In the event of a registered ship being either actually or constructively lost, taken by the enemy, burnt, or broken up, or ceasing by reason of a transfer to persons not qualified to be owners of British ships, or otherwise, to be a British ship, every owner of the ship or any share in the ship shall, immediately on obtaining knowledge of the event, if no notice thereof has already been given to the registrar, give notice thereof to the registrar at her port of registry, and that registrar shall make an entry thereof in the register book [and the registry of the ship in that book shall be considered as closed except so far as relates to any unsatisfied mortgages or existing certificates of mortgages entered therein].

(2) In any such case, except where the ship's certificate of registry is lost or destroyed, the master of the ship shall, if the event occurs in port immediately, but if it occurs elsewhere then within ten days after his arrival in port, deliver the certificate to the registrar, or, if there is none, to the British consular officer there, and the registrar, if he is not himself the registrar of her port of registry, or the British consular officer, shall forthwith forward the certificate delivered to him to the registrar of her port of registry.

(3) If any such owner or master fails, without reasonable cause, to comply with this section, he shall for each offence be liable to a fine not exceeding [level 3 on the standard scale].

Provisional certificate for ships becoming British owned abroad

22.—(1) If at a port not within Her Majesty's dominions and not being a port of registry established by Order in Council under this Act, a ship becomes the property of persons qualified to own a British ship, the British consular officer there may grant to her master, on his application a provisional certificate, stating—

    (a) the name of the ship;

    (b) the time and place of her purchase, and the names of her purchasers;

    (c) the name of her master; and

    (d) the best particulars respecting her tonnage, build, and description which he is able to obtain;

and shall forward a copy of the certificate at the first convenient opportunity to the Registrar-General of Shipping and Seamen.

(2) Such a provisional certificate shall have the effect of a certificate of registry until the expiration of six months from its date, or until the ship's arrival at a port where there is a registrar (whichever first happens), and on either of those events happening shall cease to have effect.

Temporary passes in lieu of certificates of registry

23. Where it appears to the [Commissioners of Customs and Excise] that by reason of special circumstances it would be desirable that permission should be granted to any British ship to pass, without being previously registered, from any port in Her Majesty's dominions to any other port within Her Majesty's dominions, the Commissioners may grant a pass accordingly, and that pass shall, for the time and within the limits therein mentioned, have the same effect as a certificate of registry.

Transfers and transmissions

Transfer of ships or shares

24.—(1) A registered ship or share therein (when disposed of to a person qualified to own a British ship) shall be transferred by a bill of sale.

(2) The bill of sale shall contain such description of the ship as is contained in the surveyor's certificate, or some other description sufficient to identify the ship to the satisfaction of the registrar, . . . and shall be executed by the transferor in the presence of, and be attested by, a witness or witnesses.

Declaration of transfer

25. Where a registered ship or a share therein is transferred, the transferee shall not be entitled to be registered as owner thereof until he, or, in the case of a corporation, the person authorised by this Act to make declarations on behalf of the corporation, has made and signed a declaration (in this Act called a declaration of transfer) referring to the ship, and containing—
  (a) a statement of the qualification of the transferee to own a British ship, or if the transferee is a corporation, of such circumstances of the constitution and business thereof as prove it to be qualified to own a British ship; and
  (b) a declaration that, to the best of his knowledge and belief, no unqualified person or body of persons is entitled as owner to any legal or beneficial interest in the ship or any share therein.

Registry of transfer

26.—(1) Every bill of sale for the transfer of a registered ship or of a share therein, when duly executed, shall be produced to the registrar of her port of registry, with the declaration of transfer, and the registrar shall thereupon enter in the register the name of the transferee as owner of the ship or share, and shall endorse on the bill of sale the fact of that entry having been made, with the day and hour thereof.

(2) Bills of sale of a ship or of a share therein shall be entered in the register in the order of their production to the registrar.

Transmission of property in ship on death, bankruptcy, marriage, etc.

27.—(1) Where the property in a registered ship or share therein is transmitted to a person qualified to own a British ship on the marriage, death, or bankruptcy of any registered owner, or by any lawful means other than by a transfer under this Act—
  (a) That person shall authenticate the transmission by making and signing a declaration (in this Act called a declaration of transmission) identifying the ship and containing the several statements hereinbefore required to be contained in a declaration of transfer, or as near thereto as circumstances admit, and also a statement of the manner in which and the person to whom the property has been transmitted.
  (b) [Repealed.]
  (c) If the transmission is consequent on bankruptcy, the declaration of transmission shall be accompanied by such evidence as is for the time being receivable in courts of justice as proof of the title of persons claiming under a bankruptcy.
  (d) If the transmission is consequent on death, the declaration of the transmission shall be accompanied by the instrument of representation, or an official extract therefrom.

(2) The registrar, on receipt of the declaration of transmission so accompanied, shall enter in the register the name of the person entitled under the transmission as owner of the ship or share the property in which has been transmitted, and, where there is more than one such person, shall enter the names of all such persons, but those persons, how-

ever numerous, shall, for the purpose of the provision of this Act with respect to the number of persons entitled to be registered as owners, be considered as one person.

Order for sale on transmission to unqualified person

28.—(1) Where the property in a registered ship or share therein is transmitted on marriage, death, bankruptcy, or otherwise to a person not qualified to own a British ship, then—

if the ship is registered in England or Ireland, the High Court; or

if the ship is registered in Scotland, the Court of Session; or

if the ship is registered in any British possession, the court having the principal civil jurisdiction in that possession;

if the ship is registered in a port of registry established by Order in Council under this Act, the British court having the principal civil jurisdiction there;

may on application by or on behalf of the unqualified person, order a sale of the property so transmitted, and direct that the proceeds of the sale, after deducting the expenses thereof, be paid to the person entitled under such transmission or otherwise as the court direct.

(2) The court may require any evidence in support of the application they think requisite and may make the order on any terms and conditions they think just, or may refuse to make the order, and generally may act in the case as the justice of the case requires.

(3) Every such application for sale must be made within four weeks after the occurrence of the event on which the transmission has taken place, or within such further time (not exceeding in the whole one year from the date of the occurrence) as the court allow.

(4) If such an application is not made within the time aforesaid, or if the court refuse an order for sale, the ship or share transmitted shall thereupon be subject to forfeiture under this Act.

Transfer of ship or sale by order of court

29. Where any court, whether under the preceding sections of this Act or otherwise, order the sale of any ship or share therein, the order of the court shall contain a declaration vesting in some person named by the court the right to transfer that ship or share, and that person shall thereupon be entitled to transfer the ship or share in the manner and to the same extent as if he were the registered owner thereof; and every registrar shall obey the requisition of the person so named in respect of any such transfer to the same extent as if such person were the registered owner.

Power of court to prohibit transfer

30. Each of the following courts; namely, —
- (a) In England or Ireland the High Court,
- (b) In Scotland the Court of Session,
- (c) In any British possession the court having the principal civil jurisdiction in that possession; and
- (d) In the case of a port of registry established by Order in Council under this Act, the British court having the principal civil jurisdiction there,

may, if the court think fit (without prejudice to the exercise of any other power of the court), on the application of any interested person make an order prohibiting for a time specified any dealing with a ship or any share therein, and the court may make the order on any terms or conditions they think just, or may refuse to make the order, or may discharge the order when made, with or without costs, and generally may act in the case as the justice of the case requires; and every registrar, without being made a party to the proceeding, shall on being served with the order or an official copy thereof obey the same.

Mortgages

Mortgage of ship or share

31.—(1) A registered ship or a share therein may be made a security for a loan or other valuable consideration, and the instrument creating the security (in this Act called a mortgage) shall be in the form marked B in the first part of the First Schedule to this Act, or as near thereto as circumstances permit, and on the production of such instrument the registrar of the ship's port of registry shall record it in the register book.

(2) Mortgages shall be recorded by the registrar in the order in time in which they are produced to him for that purpose, and the registrar shall by memorandum under his hand notify on each mortgage that it has been recorded by him, stating the day and hour of that record.

Entry of discharge of mortgage

32. Where a registered mortgage is discharged, the registrar shall, on the production of the mortgage deed, with a receipt for the mortgage money endorsed thereon, duly signed and attested, make an entry in the register to the effect that the mortgage has been discharged, and on that entry being made the estate (if any) which passed to the mortgagee shall vest in the person in whom (having regard to intervening acts and circumstances, if any), it would have vested if the mortgage had not been made.

Priority of mortgages

33. If there are more mortgages than one registered in respect of the same ship or share, the mortgagees shall, notwithstanding any express, implied, or constructive notice, be entitled in priority, one over the other, according to the date at which each mortgage is recorded in the register and not according to the date of each mortgage itself.

Mortgagee not treated as owner

34. Except as far as may be necessary for making a mortgaged ship or share available as a security for the mortgage debt, the mortgagee shall not by reason of the mortgage be deemed the owner of the ship or share, nor shall the mortgagor be deemed to have ceased to be owner thereof.

Mortgagee to have power of sale

35. Every registered mortgagee shall have power absolutely to dispose of the ship or share in respect of which he is registered, and to give effectual receipts for the purchase money; but where there are more persons than one registered as mortgagees of the same ship or share, a subsequent mortgagee shall not, except under the order of a court of competent jurisdiction, sell the ship or share, without the concurrence of every prior mortgagee.

Mortgage not affected by bankruptcy

36. A registered mortgage of a ship or share shall not be affected by any act of bankruptcy committed by the mortgagor after the date of the record of the mortgage, notwithstanding that the mortgagor at the commencement of his bankruptcy had the ship or share in his possession, order or disposition, or was reputed owner thereof, and the mortgage shall be preferred to any right, claim, or interest therein of the other creditors of the bankrupt or any trustee or assignee on their behalf.

Transfer of mortgages

37. A registered mortgage of a ship or share may be transferred to any person, and the instrument affecting the transfer shall be in the form marked C in the first part of the First Schedule to this Act, or as near thereto as circumstances permit, and on the production of such instrument the registrar shall record it by entering in the register book the name of the transferee as mortgagee of the ship or share, and shall by memorandum under his hand notify on the instrument of transfer that it has been recorded by him, stating the day and hour of the record.

Transmission of interest in mortgage by death, bankruptcy, marriage, etc.

38.—(1) Where the interest of a mortgagee in a ship or share is transmitted on death, or bankruptcy, or by any lawful means, other than by a transfer under this Act, the transmission shall be authenticated by a declaration of the person to whom the interest is transmitted, containing a statement of the manner in which and the person to whom the property has been transmitted, and shall be accompanied by the like evidence as is by this Act required in case of a corresponding transmission of the ownership of a ship or share.

(2) The registrar on the receipt of the declaration, and the production of the evidence aforesaid, shall enter the name of the person entitled under the transmission in the register as mortgagee of a ship or share.

Certificates of Mortgage and Sale

Powers of mortgage and sale may be conferred by certificate

39. [Repealed.]

Requisites for certificates of mortgage and sale

40. [Repealed.]

Restrictions on certificates of mortgage and sale

41. [Repealed.]

Contents of certificates of mortgage and sale

42. [Repealed.]

Rules as to certificates of mortgage

43. [Repealed.]

Rules as to certificates of sale

44. [Repealed.]

Powers of Commissioners of Customs in case of loss of certificate of mortgage or sale

45. [Repealed.]

Revocation of certificates of mortgage and sale

46. [Repealed.]

Name of Ship

Rules as to name of ship

47.—(1) A ship shall not be described by any name other than that by which she is for the time being registered.

(2) A change shall not be made in the name of a ship without the previous written permission of the Board of Trade.

(3) Application for that permission shall be in writing, and if the Board are of opinion that the application is reasonable they may entertain it, and thereupon require notice thereof to be published in such form and manner as they think fit.

(4) On permisssion being granted to change the name, the ship's name shall forthwith be altered in the register, in the ship's certificate of registry, and on her bows and stern.

(5) If it is shown to the satisfaction of the Board of Trade that the name of any ship has been changed without their permission they shall direct that her name be altered into that which she bore before the change, and the name shall be altered in the register, in the ship's certificate of registry, and on her bows and stern accordingly.

(6) Where a ship having once been registered has ceased to be so registered no person unless ignorant of the previous registry (proof whereof shall lie on him) shall apply to register, and no registrar shall knowingly register, the ship, except by the name by which she was previously registered, unless with the previous written permission of the Board of Trade.

(7) Where a foreign ship, not having at any previous time been registered as a British ship, becomes a British ship, no person shall apply to register, and no registrar shall knowingly register, the ship, except by the name which she bore as a foreign ship immediately before becoming a British ship, unless with the previous written permission of the Board of Trade.

(8) If any person acts, or suffers any person under his control to act, in contravention of this section, or omits to do, or suffers any person under his control to omit to do, anything required by this section, he shall for each offence be liable to a fine not exceeding [level 3 on the standard scale], and (except in the case of an application being made under the section with respect to a foreign ship which not having at any previous time been registered as a British ship has become a British ship) the ship may be detained until this section is complied with.

Registry of Alterations, Registry anew, and Transfer of Registry

Registry of alterations

48.—(1) When a registered ship is so altered as not to correspond with the particulars relating to her tonnage or description contained in the register, then, if the alteration is made at any port having a registrar, that registrar, or, if it is made elsewhere, the registrar of the first port having a registrar at which the ship arrives after the alteration, shall, on application being made to him, and on receipt of a certificate from the proper surveyor stating the particulars of the alteration, either cause the alteration to be registered, or direct that the ship be registered anew.

[(2) If default is made in registering anew a ship, or in registering an alteration of a ship so altered as aforesaid, the owner of the ship shall be liable on summary conviction to a fine not exceeding [level 3 on the standard scale], and, in addition, to a fine not exceeding [twenty pounds] for every day during which the offence continues after conviction.]

Regulations for registry of alteration

49.—(1) For the purpose of the registry of an alteration in a ship, the ship's certificate of registry shall be produced to the registrar, and the registrar shall, in his discretion, either retain the certificate of registry and grant a new certificate of registry containing a description of the ship as altered, or endorse and sign on the existing certificate a memorandum of the alteration.

(2) The particulars of the alteration so made, and the fact of the new certificate having been granted, or endorsement having been made, shall be entered by the registrar of the ship's port of registry in his register book; and for that purpose the registrar to whom the application for the registry of the alteration has been made (if he is not the registrar of the ship's port of registry), shall forthwith report to the last-mentioned registrar the particulars and facts as aforesaid, accompanied, where a new certificate of registry has been granted, by the old certificate of registry.

Provisional certificate and endorsement where ship is to be registered anew

50.—(1) Where any registrar, not being the registrar of the ship's port of registry, on an application as to an alteration in a ship directs the ship to be registered anew, he shall either grant a provisional certificate, describing the ship as altered, or provisionally endorse the particulars of the alteration on the existing certificate.

(2) Every such provisional certificate, or certificate provisionally endorsed, shall, within ten days after the first subsequent arrival of the ship at her port of discharge in the United Kingdom, if she is registered in the United Kingdom, or, if she is registered in a British possession, at her port of discharge in that British possession, or, if she is registered at a port of registry established by Order in Council under this Act, at that port, be delivered up to the registrar thereof, and that registrar shall cause the ship to be registered anew.

(3) The registrar granting a provisional certificate under this section, or provisionally endorsing a certificate, shall add to the certificate or endorsement a statement that the same is made provisionally, and shall send a report of the particulars of the case to the registrar of the ship's port of registry, containing a similar statement as the certificate or endorsement.

Registry anew on change of ownership

51. Where the ownership of any ship is changed, the registrar of the port at which the ship is registered may, on the application of the owners of the ship, register the ship anew, although registration anew is not required under this Act.

Procedure for registry anew

52.—(1) Where a ship is to be registered anew, the registrar shall proceed as in the case of first registry, and on the delivery up to him of the existing certificate of registry, and on the other requisites to registry, or in the case of a change of ownership such of them as he thinks material, being duly complied with, shall make such registry anew, and grant a certificate thereof.

(2) When a ship is registered anew, her former register shall be considered as closed, except so far as relates to any unsatisfied mortgage or existing certificates of sale or mortgage entered thereon, but the names of all persons appearing on the former register to be interested in the ship as owners or mortgagees shall be entered on the new register, and the registry anew shall not in any way affect the rights of any of those persons.

Transfer of registry

53.—(1) The registry of any ship may be transferred from one port to another on the application to the registrar of the existing port of registry of the ship made by declaration in writing of all persons appearing on the register to be interested therein as owners or mortgagees, but that transfer shall not in any way affect the rights of those persons or any of them, and those rights shall in all respects continue in the same manner as if no such transfer had been effected.

(2) On any such application the registrar shall transmit notice thereof to the registrar of the intended port of registry with a copy of all particulars relating to the ship, and the names of all persons appearing on the register to be interested therein as owners or mortgagees.

(3) The ship's certificate of registry shall be delivered up to the registrar either of the existing or intended port of registry, and, if delivered up to the former, shall be transmitted to the registrar of the intended port of registry.

(4) On the receipt of the above documents the registrar of the intended port of registry shall enter in his register book all the particulars and names so transmitted as aforesaid, and grant a fresh certificate of registry, and thenceforth such ship shall be considered as registered at the new port of registry, and the name of the ship's new port of registry shall be substituted for the name of her former port of registry on the ship's stern.

Restrictions on re-registration of abandoned ships

54. [Repealed.]

Incapacitated Persons

Provision for cases of infancy or other incapacity

55. [Repealed.]

(1) Where by reason of infancy, lunacy, or any other cause any person interested in any ship, or any share therein, is incapable of making any declaration or doing anything required or permitted by this Act to be made or done in connexion with the registry of the ship or share, the guardian or committee, if any, of that person, or, if there is none, any person appointed on application made on behalf of the incapable person, or of any other person interested, by any court or judge having jurisdiction in respect of the property of incapable persons, may make such declaration, or a declaration as nearly corresponding thereto as circumstances permit, and do such act or thing in the name and on behalf of the incapable person; and all acts done by the substitute shall be as effectual as if done by the person for whom he is substituted.

(2) The Trustee Act 1850, and the Acts amending the same, shall, so far as regards the court exercising jurisdiction in lunacy in Ireland, apply to shares in ships registered under this Act as if they were stock as defined by that Act.

Trusts and Equitable Rights

Notices of trusts not received

56. No notice of any trust, express, implied, or constructive, shall be entered in the register or be receivable by the registrar, and, subject to any rights and powers appearing by the register book to be vested in any other person, the registered owner of a ship or of a share therein shall have powers absolutely to dispose in manner in this Act provided of the ship or share, and to give effectual receipts for any money paid or advanced by way of consideration.

Equities not excluded by Act

57. The expression "beneficial interest," where used in this Part of this Act, includes interests arising under contract and other equitable interests; and the intention of this Act is, that without prejudice to the provisions of this Act for preventing notice of trusts from being entered in the register or received by the registrar, and without prejudice to the powers of disposition and of giving receipts conferred by this Act on registered owners and mortgagees, and without prejudice to the provisions of this Act relating to the exclusion of unqualified persons from the ownership of British ships, interests arising under contract or other equitable interests may be enforced by or against owners and mortgagees of ships in respect of their interest therein in the same manner as in respect of any other personal property.

Liability of Beneficial Owner

Liability of owners

58. Where any person is beneficially interested, otherwise than by way of mortgage, in any ship or share in a ship registered in the name of some other person as owner, the person so interested shall, as well as the registered owner, be subject to all pecuniary penalties imposed by this or any other Act on the owners of ships or shares therein, so nevertheless that proceedings may be taken for the enforcement of any such penalties against both or either of the aforesaid parties, with or without joining the other of them.

Managing Owner

Ship's managing owner or manager to be registered

59.—(1) The name and address of the managing owner for the time being of every ship registered at a port in the United Kingdom shall be registered at the custom house of that port.

(2) Where there is not a managing owner there shall be so registered the name of the ship's husband or other person to whom the management of the ship is entrusted by or on behalf of the owner; and any person whose name is so registered shall, for the purposes of this Act, be under the same obligations, and subject to the same liabilities, as if he were the managing owner.

(3) If default is made in complying with this section the owner shall be liable, or if there are more owners than one each owner shall be liable in proportion to his interest in the ship, to a fine not exceeding in the whole [level 3 on the standard scale] each time the ship leaves any port in the United Kingdom.

Appendix 1

Declarations, Inspection of Register, and Fees

Power of registrar to dispense with declarations and other evidence

60. When, under this Part of the Act, any person is required to make a declaration on behalf of himself or of any corporation, or any evidence is required to be produced to the registrar, and it is shown to the satisfaction of the registrar that from any reasonable cause that person is unable to make the declaration, or that the evidence cannot be produced, the registrar may, with the approval of the [Commissioners of Customs and Excise], and on the production of such evidence, and subject to such terms as they may think fit, dispense with the declaration or evidence.

Mode of making declarations

61.—(1) [Repealed.]

(2) Declarations required by this Part of this Act may be made on behalf of a corporation by the secretary or any other officer of the corporation authorised by them for the purpose.

Application of fees

62. All fees authorised to be taken under this Part of this Act, shall, except where otherwise in this Act provided, be applied in payment of the general expenses of carrying into effect this Part of this Act, or otherwise as the Treasury may direct.

Returns, Evidence, and Forms

Returns to be made by registrars

63.—(1) Every registrar shall at the expiration of every month transmit to him a full return, in such form as the said Registrar-General may direct, of all registries, transfers, transmissions, mortgages, and other dealings with ships which have been registered by or communicated to him in his character of registrar, and of the names of the persons concerned in the same, and of such other particulars as may be directed by the said Registrar-General.

(2) Every registrar shall on or before the first day of February and the first day of August in every year transmit to the Registrar-General of Shipping and Seamen a list of all ships registered at that port, and also of all ships whose registers have been transferred or cancelled at that port since the last preceding return.

Evidence of register books, certificate of registry, and other documents

64.—(1) A person, on payment of a fee . . . to be fixed by the [Commissioners of Customs and Excise], may, on application to the registrar at a reasonable time during the hours of his official attendance, inspect any register book.

(2) The following documents shall be admissible in evidence in manner provided by this Act; namely,—

(a) [Repealed.]
(b) A certificate of registry under this Act purporting to be signed by the registrar or other proper officer;

(c) An endorsement on a certificate of registry purporting to be signed by the registrar or other proper officer;

(d) Every declaration made in pursuance of this Part of this Act.

(3) A copy or transcript of the register of British ships kept by the Registrar-General of Shipping and Seamen under the direction of the Board of Trade shall be admissible in evidence in manner provided by this Act, and have the same effect to all intents as the original register of which it is a copy or transcript.

Forms of documents, and instructions as to registry

65.—(1) The several instruments and documents specified in the second part of the First Schedule to this Act shall be in the form prescribed by the [Commissioners of Customs and Excise], with the consent of the Board of Trade, or as near thereto as circumstances permit; and the [Commissioners of Customs and Excise] may, with the consent of the Board of Trade, make such alterations in the forms so prescribed as they may deem requisite.

(2) A registrar shall not be required without the special direction of the [Commissioners of Customs and Excise] to receive and enter in the register any bill of sale, mortgage or other instrument for the disposal or transfer of any ship or share, or any interest therein, which is made in any form other than that for the time being required under this Part of this Act, or which contains any particulars other than those contained in such form; but the said Commissioners shall, before altering the forms, give such public notice thereof as may be necessary in order to prevent inconvenience.

(3) [Repealed.]

(4) The [Commissioners of Customs and Excise], with the consent of the Board of Trade, may also, for carrying into effect this Part of this Act, give such instructions to their officers as to the manner of making entries in the register, as to the execution and attestation of powers of attorney, as to any evidence required for identifying any person, as to the referring to themselves of any question involving doubt or difficulty, and generally as to any act or thing to be done in pursuance of this Part of this Act, as they think fit.

Forgery and false Declarations

False declarations

67.—(1) If any person in the case of any declaration made in the presence of or produced to a registrar under this Part of this Act, or in any document or other evidence produced to such registrar—

(i) wilfully makes, or assists in making, or procures to be made any false statement concerning the title to or ownership of, or the interest existing in any ship, or any share in a ship; or

(ii) utters, produces, or makes use of any declaration, or document containing any such false statement knowing the same to be false,

he shall in respect of each offence be guilty of a misdemeanour.

(2) If any person wilfully makes a false declaration touching the qualification of himself or of any other person or of any corporation to own a British ship or any share therein, he shall for each offence be guilty of a misdemeanour, and that ship or share shall be subject to forfeiture under this Act, to the extent of the interest therein of the declarant, and also, unless it is proved that the declaration was made without authority, of any person or corporation on behalf of whom the declaration is made.

National Character and Flag

National character of ship to be declared before clearance

68.—(1) An [officer of customs and excise] shall not grant a clearance or transire for any ship until the master of such ship has declared to that officer the name of the nation to which he claims that she belongs, and that officer shall thereupon inscribe that name on the clearance or transire.

(2) If a ship attempts to proceed to sea without such clearance or transire, she may be detained until the declaration is made.

Penalty for unduly assuming British character

69.—(1) If a person uses the British flag and assumes the British national character on board a ship owned in whole or in part by any persons not qualified to own a British ship, for the purpose of making the ship appear to be a British ship, the ship shall be subject to forfeiture under this Act, unless the assumption has been made for the purpose of escaping capture by an enemy or by a foreign ship of war in the exercise of some belligerent right.

(2) In any proceeding for enforcing any such forfeiture the burden of proving a title to use the British flag and assume the British national character shall lie upon the person using and assuming the same.

Penalty for concealment of British or assumption of foreign character

70. If the master or owner of a British ship does anything or permits anything to be done, or carries or permits to be carried any papers or documents, with intent to conceal the British character of the ship from any person entitled by British law to inquire into the same, or with intent to assume a foreign character, or with intent to deceive any person so entitled as aforesaid, the ship shall be subject to forfeiture under this Act; and the master, if he commits or is privy to the commission of the offence, shall in respect of each offence be guilty of a misdemeanour.

Penalty for acquiring ownership if unqualified

71. [Repealed.]

Liabilities of ships not recognised as British

72. Where it is declared by this Act that a British ship shall not be recognised as a British ship, that ship shall not be entitled to any benefits, privileges, advantages, or protection usually enjoyed by British ships nor to use the British flag or assume the British national character, but so far as regards the payment of dues, the liability to fines and forefeiture, and the punishment of offences committed on board such ship, or by any persons belonging to her, such ship shall be dealt with in the same manner in all respects as if she were a recognised British ship.

National colours for ships, and penalty on carrying improper colours

73.—(1) The red ensign usually worn by merchant ships, without any defacement or modification whatsoever, is hereby declared to be the proper national colours for all ships and boats belonging to any British subject, except in the case of Her Majesty's ships or in the case of any other ship for the time being allowed to wear any other national colours in pursuance of a warrant from Her Majesty or from the Admiralty.

(2) If any distinctive national colours, except such red ensign or except the Union Jack with a white border, or if any colours usually worn by Her Majesty's ships or resembling those of Her Majesty, or if the pendant usually carried by Her Majesty's ships or any pendant resembling that pendant, are or is hoisted on board any ship or boat belonging to any British subject without warrant from Her Majesty or from the Admiralty, the master of the ship, or the owner thereof, if on board the same, and every other person hoisting the colours or pendant, shall for each offence [be liable on conviction on indictment to a fine or on summary conviction to a fine not exceeding the statutory maximum].

(3) Any commissioned officer on full pay in the military or naval service of Her Majesty, or any officer of customs in Her Majesty's dominions, or any British consular officer, may board any ship on which any colours or pendant are hoisted contrary to this Act, and seize and take away the colours or pendant, and the colours or pendant shall be forfeited to Her Majesty.

(4), (5) . . .

Penalty on ship not showing colours

74.—(1) A ship belonging to a British subject shall hoist the proper national colours—

(a) on a signal being made to her by one of Her Majesty's ships (including any vessel under the command of an officer of Her Majesty's navy on full pay), and

(b) on entering or leaving any foreign port, and

(c) if of fifty tons gross tonnage or upwards, on entering or leaving any British port.

(2) If default is made on board any such ship in complying with this section, the master of the ship shall for each offence be liable to a fine not exceeding [level 3 on the standard scale].

(3) This section shall not apply to a fishing boat duly entered in the fishing boat register and lettered and numbered as required by the Fourth Part of this Act.

Saving for Admiralty

75. The provisions of this Act with respect to colours worn by merchant ships shall not affect any other power of the Admiralty in relation thereto.

Forfeiture of Ship

Proceedings on forfeiture of ship

76.—(1) Where any ship has either wholly or as to any share therein become subject to forfeiture under this Part of this Act,

(a) any commissioned officer on full pay in the military or naval service of Her Majesty;

(b) any officer of customs in Her Majesty's dominions; or

(c) any British consular officer,

may seize and detain the ship, and bring her for adjudication before the High Court in England or Ireland, or before the Court of Session in Scotland, and the court may thereupon adjudge the ship with her tackle, apparel, and furniture to be forfeited to Her Majesty, and make such order in the case as to the court seems just, and may award to the officer bringing in the ship for adjudication such portion of the proceeds of the sale of the ship, or any share therein, as the court think fit.

(2) Any such officer as in this section mentioned shall not be responsible either civilly or criminally to any person whomsoever in respect of any such seizure or detention as

aforesaid notwithstanding that the ship has not been brought in for adjudication, or if so brought in is declared not liable to forfeiture, if it is shown to the satisfaction of the court before whom any trial relating to such ship or such seizure or detention is held that there were reasonable grounds for such seizure or detention; but if no such grounds are shown the court may award costs and damages to any party aggrieved, and make such other order in the premises as the court thinks just.

Measurement of Ship and Tonnage

Tonnage once ascertained to be the tonnage of ship

82. Whenever the tonnage of any ship has been ascertained and registered in accordance with the tonnage regulations of this Act, the same shall thenceforth be deemed to be the tonnage of the ship, and shall be repeated in every subsequent registry thereof, unless any alteration is made in the form or capacity of the ship, or unless it is discovered that the tonnage of the ship has been erroneously computed; and in either of those cases the ship shall be remeasured, and her tonnage determined and registered according to the tonnage regulations of this Act.

Fees for measurement

83. Such fees as the Board of Trade determine shall be paid in respect of the measurement of a ship's tonnage . . . , and those fees shall be paid into the Mercantile Marine Fund.

Tonnage of ships of foreign countries adopting tonnage regulations

84.—(1) Whenever it appears to Her Majesty the Queen in Council that the tonnage regulations of this Act have been adopted by any foreign country, and are in force there, Her Majesty in Council may order that the ships of that country shall, without being remeasured in Her Majesty's dominions, be deemed to be of the tonnage denoted in their certificates of registry or other national papers, in the same manner, to the same extent, and for the same purposes as the tonnage denoted in the certificate of registry of a British ship is deemed to be the tonnage of that ship, . . . [and any space shown by the certificate of registry or other national papers of any such ship as deducted from the tonnage shall, where a similar deduction in the case of a British ship depends on compliance with any conditions or on the compliance being evidenced in any manner, be deemed to comply with those conditions and be so evidenced, unless a surveyor of ships certifies to the Board of Trade that the construction and the equipment of the ship as respects that space do not come up to the standards which would be required if the ship were a British ship registered in the United Kingdom].

(2) Her Majesty in Council may limit the time during which the Order is to remain in operation, and make the Order subject to such conditions and qualifications (if any) as Her Majesty may deem expedient, and the operation of the Order shall be limited and modified accordingly.

(3) If it is made to appear to Her Majesty that the tonnage of any foreign ship, as measured by the rules of the country to which she belongs, materially differs from that which would be her tonnage if measured under this Act, Her Majesty in Council may order that, notwithstanding any Order in Council for the time being in force under this section, any of the ships of that country may, for all or any of the purposes of this Act, be re-measured in accordance with this Act.

Space occupied by deck cargo to be liable to dues

85. [Repealed.]

Levy of tonnage rates under local Acts on the registered tonnage

87. Any persons having power to levy tonnage rates on ships may, if they think fit, with the consent of the Board of Trade, levy those tonnage rates upon the registered tonnage of the ships as determined by the tonnage regulations of this Act, notwithstanding that any local Act under which those rates are levied provides for levying the same upon some different system of tonnage measurement.

Ports of Registry in Place under Foreign Jurisdiction Act

Foreign ports of registry

88. [Repealed.]

Registry in Colonies

Powers of governors in colonies

89. [Repealed.]

Terminable certificates of registry for small ships in colonies

90. [Repealed.]

Application of Part I

Application of Part I

91. [Repealed.]

MERCHANT SHIPPING ACT 1988[1]
PARTS I AND II, SCHEDULES 2 AND 3

PART I. REGISTRATION OF BRITISH SHIPS

Preliminary

Effect of Part I and interpretation

1.—(1) In this Part—
(a) sections 2 and 3 have effect in place of section 1 of the Merchant Shipping Act 1894 (qualification for owning British ship); and
(b) sections 4 to 8 have effect in place of sections 2 and 3 of that Act (obligation to register British ships and exemptions from registry) and for otherwise regulating the registration of ships under Part I of that Act in the United Kingdom.

(2) In this Part, unless the context otherwise requires—
"length", in relation to a ship, has the same meaning as in the tonnage regulations of the 1894 Act;
"owner", in relation to a registered ship, means registered owner;
"registered" and "registration" mean respectively registered and registration under Part I of the 1894 Act in the United Kingdom;
"representative person" means a person appointed (or treated as appointed) as such under section 5.

(3) References in this Part to a ship being entitled to be registered shall be construed in accordance with section 4.

British ships

2.—(1) A ship shall be a British ship for the purposes of the Merchant Shipping Acts if—
(a) the ship is registered in the United Kingdom under any of the following enactments, namely—
(i) Part I of the 1894 Act or section 5 of the Merchant Shipping Act 1983 (registration of small ships), or
(ii) Part II of this Act (registration of British fishing vessels); or
(b) the ship is registered in the United Kingdom in pursuance of an Order in Council under section 80 of the Merchant Shipping Act 1906 (Government ships); or
(c) the ship is a fishing vessel within the meaning of Part II of this Act which is eligible to be registered under that Part of this Act by virtue of section 14 below, but—
(i) is excluded from registration under that Part of this Act by regulations made under section 13 below, and

1. Chapter 12.

(ii) is not registered under the law of any country outside the United Kingdom; or

(d) the ship is registered under the law of a relevant overseas territory; or

(e) the ship is less than 24 metres in length and—

(i) is not a fishing vessel within the meaning of Part II of this Act, and

(ii) is not registered in the United Kingdom under an enactment falling within paragraph (a)(i) above or under the law of any country outside the United Kingdom, but

(iii) is wholly owned by one or more persons qualified to be owners of British ships by virtue of section 3(1) below.

(2) This section shall have effect in relation to any time before the end of the period referred to in section 13(3)(b) below as if the enactments falling within subsection (1)(a)(i) included Part IV of the 1894 Act (registration of British fishing boats).

Persons qualified to be owners of British ships

3.—(1) For the purposes of Part I of the 1894 Act the following persons are persons qualified to be owners of British ships, namely—

(a) British citizens;

(b) British Dependent Territories citizens;

(c) British Overseas citizens;

(d) persons who under the British Nationality Act 1981 are British subjects;

(e) persons who under the Hong Kong (British Nationality) Order 1986 are British Nationals (Overseas);

(f) bodies corporate incorporated in the United Kingdom or in any relevant overseas territory and having their principal place of business in the United Kingdom or in any such territory; and

(g) citizens of the Republic of Ireland.

(2) Subject to subsection (3) below, references (however phrased) in any statutory provision to persons who are, for the purposes of Part I of the 1894 Act, qualified to be owners of British ships shall be construed in accordance with subsection (1) above.

(3) For the purposes of section 5 of the Merchant Shipping Act 1983 the following persons are persons qualified to be owners of British ships, namely—

(a) persons falling within paragraphs (a) to (e) and (g) of subsection (1) above; and

(b) Commonwealth citizens not falling within those paragraphs.

(4) It is hereby declared that a person who is not qualified under subsection (1) above to be an owner of a British ship may nevertheless be one of the owners of such a ship if—

(a) a majority interest in the ship (within the meaning of section 4 below) is owned by persons who are qualified to be owners of British ships; and

(b) the ship is registered, in accordance with the provisions of that section, under Part I of the 1894 Act.

Registration under Part I of 1894 Act

Entitlement to registration under Part I of 1894 Act

4.—(1) Subject to sections 6 and 7 below, this section has effect for the purpose of determining whether a ship is entitled to be registered under Part I of the 1894 Act in the United Kingdom.

(2) Subject to subsection (3), a ship shall be entitled to be registered if a majority interest in the ship is owned by one or more persons qualified to be owners of British ships by virtue of section 3(1)(a),(b),(e) or (f) above.

(3) Where—

(a) a ship falling within subsection (2) is 24 metres or more in length, and

(b) the person, or (as the case may be) each of the persons, by whom the majority interest in the ship is owned is not resident in the United Kingdom,

the ship shall only be entitled to be registered if a representative person is appointed in relation to the ship.

(4) Where a majority interest in a ship is owned by one or more persons qualified to be owners of British ships by virtue of section 3(1)(c), (d) or (g) above, the ship shall be entitled to be registered—

(a) if that person, or (as the case may be) any of those persons, is resident in the United Kingdom, or

(b) (where that condition is not satisfied) if the Secretary of State furnishes him or them with a declaration that he consents to the ship being registered, and, in addition, a representative person is appointed in relation to the ship.

(5) Where a majority interest in a ship is owned by the following persons, namely—

(a) one or more persons qualified to be owners of British ships by virtue of section 3(1)(a), (b), (e) or (f), and

(b) one or more persons so qualified by virtue of section 3(1)(c), (d) or (g),

the ship shall be entitled to be registered—

(i) if any of those persons is resident in the United Kingdom, or

(ii) (where that condition is not satisfied) if a representative person is appointed in relation to the ship.

(6) A ship shall, in accordance with section 13(2)(a) below, not be entitled to be registered if it is a fishing vessel within the meaning of Part II.

(7) For the purposes of this section—

(a) one or more persons shall be treated as owning a majority interest in a ship if there is vested in that person or in those persons, taken together, the legal title to 33 or more of the 64 shares into which the property in the ship is divided, for the purposes of registration, in accordance with section 5 of the 1894 Act (there being left out of account for this purpose any share in which any beneficial interest is owned by a person who is not qualified to be an owner of a British ship); and

(b) a body corporate shall be treated as resident in the United Kingdom if it is incorporated in the United Kingdom and has its principal place of business there.

(8) Nothing in this section applies to a ship to which section 80 of the Merchant Shipping Act 1906 applies (Government ships).

Representative persons

5.—(1) Where the entitlement of any ship to be registered is, by virtue of any provision of section 4, conditional on the appointment of a representative person in relation to the ship, the owner of the ship shall—

(a) before applying for the ship to be registered, appoint an individual or body corporate satisfying the prescribed requirements to be the representative person in relation to the ship, and

(b) secure that, so long as the ship remains registered, an individual or body corporate satisfying those requirements is so appointed.

(2) For the purposes of subsection (1) the prescribed requirements are—

(a) that the representative person is either—

(i) an individual resident in the United Kingdom, or

(ii) a body corporate incorporated in the United Kingdom and having its principal place of business there; and

(b) such other requirements as the Secretary of State may by regulations prescribe.

(3) Where subsection (1) applies to a ship, any person who is registered under section 59(2) of the 1894 Act (registration of ship's manager) in relation to the ship shall, if that person is such an individual or body corporate as is mentioned in subsection (2)(a)(i) or (ii) above, be treated for the purposes of this Part of this Act as the representative person for the time being appointed in relation to the ship.

(4) The owner of any ship in relation to which any representative person is for the time being appointed shall—

    (a) on applying for the ship to be registered, notify the registrar to whom the application is made of the name and address of the representative person; and

    (b) in the event of any change in the identity, or in the address, of the representative person so appointed, notify the registrar of the ship's port of registry of the name and address of the new representative person, or (as the case may be) of the new address, as soon as practicable after the change occurs;

and the registrar in question shall record any particulars notified to him in pursuance of this section in the register kept by him under Part I of the 1894 Act.

(5) Any document required or authorised, by virtue of any statutory provision, to be served for the purpose of the institution of, or otherwise in connection with, proceedings for an offence under the Merchant Shipping Acts, or under any instrument in force under those Acts, shall, where the person to be served is the owner of a registered ship, be treated as duly served on him if—

    (a) delivered to any representative person for the time being appointed in relation to the ship, or

    (b) sent to any such person by post at the address notified (or, as the case may be, last notified) to the registrar under subsection (4) in relation to that person, or

    (c) left for any such person at that address.

(6) Any person who contravenes subsection (1)(b) or (4)(b) above shall be guilty of an offence and liable on summary conviction to a fine not exceeding the third level on the standard scale.

Refusal of registration

6.—(1) If for any reason it appears to the Secretary of State that a ship in respect of which an application for registration has been made may not be entitled to be registered, he may by notice served on—

    (a) the applicant, or

    (b) any representative person for the time being appointed in relation to the ship,

require that person to furnish him with such information as he thinks necessary for the purpose of determining whether the ship is entitled to be registered.

(2) Where the Secretary of State has served a notice under subsection (1) with respect to any ship, then, unless he has become satisfied that the ship is entitled to be registered, he shall, as soon as practicable after the end of the period of 30 days beginning with the date of service of that notice, give to registrars of British ships generally a direction requiring them not to register the ship.

(3) Notwithstanding that any ship in respect of which an application for registration has been made is entitled to be registered, the Secretary of State may give to registrars of British ships generally a direction requiring them not to register the ship if he is satisfied that, having regard—

    (a) to the condition of the ship so far as relevant to its safety or to any risk of pollution, or

    (b) to the safety, health and welfare of persons employed or engaged in any capacity on board the ship,

it would be inappropriate for the ship to be registered.

Power of Secretary of State to direct removal from the register

7.—(1) If for any reason it appears to the Secretary of State that a registered ship may no longer be entitled to be registered, he may by notice served on—

(a) the owner of the ship, or

(b) any representative person for the time being appointed in relation to the ship,

require that person to furnish him with such information as he thinks necessary for the purpose of determining whether the ship is entitled to be registered.

(2) Where the Secretary of State has served a notice under subsection (1) with respect to any ship, then, unless he has become satisfied that the ship is entitled to be registered, he shall, as soon as practicable after the end of the period of 30 days beginning with the date of service of that notice, serve a notice under subsection (4) on the owner or on any representative person for the time being appointed in relation to the ship.

(3) Where the Secretary of State is satisfied—

(a) that, having regard to the matters mentioned in paragraph (a) or (b) of section 6(3), it would be inappropriate for a registered ship to continue to be registered, or

(b) that any penalty imposed on the owner of a registered ship in respect of a contravention of the Merchant Shipping Acts, or of any instrument in force under those Acts, has remained unpaid for a period of more than three months (and no appeal against the penalty is pending), or

(c) that any summons for any such contravention has been duly served on the owner of a registered ship but the owner failed to appear at the time and place appointed for the trial of the information or complaint in question and a period of not less than three months has elapsed since that time,

the Secretary of State shall serve a notice under subsection (4) either on the owner or on any representative person for the time being appointed in relation to the ship.

(4) A notice under this subsection is a notice stating—

(a) that the Secretary of State is not satisfied that the ship in question is entitled to be registered or (as the case may be) that he is satisfied as mentioned in paragraph (a), (b) or (c) of subsection (3); and

(b) that he intends, after the end of the period of 30 days beginning with the date of service of the notice, to direct that the ship in question should cease to be registered unless he is satisfied that it would be inappropriate to do so by any representations made to him by or on behalf of the owner within that period.

(5) As soon as practicable after the end of that period the Secretary of State shall accordingly direct the registrar of the ship's port of registry to terminate the ship's registration unless he is satisfied that it would be inappropriate to do so by any such representations.

(6) Where the registration of any ship has terminated by virtue of this section, the Secretary of State may subsequently, if he is satisfied that it would be appropriate to do so, direct the registrar of the ship's former port of registry to restore the ship's registration.

**Offences relating to furnishing of information, and
duty to comply with directions**

8.—(1) Any person who—

(a) in purported compliance with the requirements of a notice under section 6(1) or 7(1), or

(b) in connection with the making of any representations in pursuance of section 7(4)(b),

knowingly or recklessly furnishes information which is false in a material particular shall be guilty of an offence and liable—

  (i) on summary conviction, to a fine not exceeding the statutory maximum;
  (ii) on conviction on indictment, to a fine.
(2) It shall be the duty of any person to whom the Secretary of State gives a direction under this Part to give effect to that direction.

Duty of owner of registered ship to secure termination of any overseas registration

9.—(1) Where a ship becomes registered at a time when it is already registered under the law of any country outside the United Kingdom, the owner of the ship shall take all reasonable steps to secure the termination of the ship's registration under the law of that country.

(2) Any person who contravenes subsection (1) shall be guilty of an offence and liable on summary conviction to a fine not exceeding the third level on the standard scale.

(3) Subsection (1) does not apply to a ship which becomes registered in pursuance of section 53B of the 1894 Act (transfer of registration under that Act from overseas territory).

Amendments of Part I of 1894 Act

10.—(1) Part I of the 1894 Act shall have effect subject to the amendments specified in Schedule 1 to this Act, which include amendments—
  (a) restricting the scope of operation of that Part of that Act to registration in the United Kingdom;
  (b) restricting the grant of provisional certificates of registration under section 22 of that Act (ships becoming British-owned abroad); and
  (c) enabling ships to be registered otherwise than in register books;
as well as amendments consequential on the preceding provisions of this Part of this Act.
(2) In Part I of the 1894 Act—
  (a) references to registration or to registered ships or registered owners shall accordingly (unless the context otherwise requires) be construed as references to registration, or to ships or owners registered, under that Part of that Act in the United Kingdom;
  (b) references to registrars of British ships shall accordingly be construed as references to registrars of British ships in the United Kingdom;
  (c) references to a ship being entitled to be registered shall be construed in accordance with section 4 of this Act; and
  (d) references to the ownership of a majority interest in a ship shall be construed in accordance with subsection (7)(a) of that section.

Registration in overseas territories

Regulation of registration in overseas territories by reference to categories of registries

11.—(1) Her Majesty may by Order in Council make provision for regulating the registration of ships under Part I of the 1894 Act in relevant overseas territories by reference to categories of registries established by the Order.
(2) Any such Order may—
  (a) establish different categories of registries to which different restrictions on the registration of ships under Part I of the 1894 Act apply, being restrictions framed by reference to—
    (i) ships' tonnages, or

(ii) types of ships, or

(iii) any other specified matter, or

(iv) any combination of matters falling within one or more of the preceding sub-paragraphs,

as well as a category of registries to which no such restriction applies;

(b) assign any relevant overseas territory to such one of the categories so established as appears to Her Majesty to be appropriate;

(c) provide that, where a relevant overseas territory has been assigned to a category to which any such restriction on registration as is mentioned in paragraph (a) applies, no ship covered by that restriction shall be registered under Part I of the 1894 Act in that territory;

(d) specify circumstances in which ships may be exempted from any provision made by virtue of paragraph (c).

(3) Any provision made by virtue of subsection (2)(c) shall be expressed to be without prejudice to the operation of any provision for the time being in force under the law of any such territory as is mentioned in subsection (2)(c) by virtue of which the registration of ships under Part I of the 1894 Act in that territory is, or may be, further restricted.

(4) An Order in Council under this section—

(a) may make such transitional, incidental or supplementary provision as appears to Her Majesty to be necessary or expedient; and

(b) shall be subject to annulment in pursuance of a resolution of either House of Parliament.

PART II. REGISTRATION OF BRITISH FISHING VESSELS

Preliminary

Interpretation of Part II, etc.

12.—(1) In this Part (unless the context otherwise requires)—

"fishing vessel" means a vessel for the time being used (or, in the context of an application for registration, intended to be used) for or in connection with fishing for sea fish, other than a vessel used (or intended to be used) for fishing otherwise than for profit;

"fishing vessel survey rules" has the meaning given by section 2 of the Fishing Vessels (Safety Provisions) Act 1970, and any reference to a survey under the fishing vessel survey rules is a reference to such a survey carried out in the United Kingdom;

"owner", in relation to a registered fishing vessel, means registered owner;

"prescribed" means prescribed by regulations under section 13;

"the register" means the register of British fishing vessels referred to in section 13(1)(a);

"the register" and "registration" mean respectively registered and registration in the register;

"sea fish" includes shellfish, salmon and migratory trout (as defined by section 44 of the Fisheries Act 1981);

"share", in relation to a fishing vessel, means one of the shares into which the property in the vessel is divided, for the purposes of registration, in accordance with section 18.

(2) It is hereby declared that a vessel for the time being used (or intended to be used) wholly for the purpose of conveying persons wishing to fish for pleasure is not a fishing vessel for the purposes of this Part.

(3) References in this Part to a fishing vessel being eligible to be registered as a British fishing vessel shall be construed in accordance with section 14.

(4) For the purposes of this Part the beneficial ownership of a fishing vessel shall be determined by reference to every beneficial interest in that vessel, however arising (whether held by a trustee or nominee or arising under a contract or otherwise), other than an interest held by any person as mortgagee.

New system of registration for fishing vessels

Separate registration of fishing vessels

13.—(1) The Secretary of State shall by regulations make provision—
  (a) for the establishment and maintenance of a register of British fishing vessels; and
  (b) for the registration in that register of fishing vessels which are, by virtue of section 14, eligible to be registered as British fishing vessels.

(2) Subject to subsection (3), a fishing vessel shall no longer be capable of being registered under any of the following enactments, namely—
  (a) Part I of the 1894 Act;
  (b) section 373 of that Act (registry of British fishing boats); or
  (c) the Sea Fishing Boats (Scotland) Act 1886.

(3) Where any fishing vessel is registered under any of those enactments immediately before the commencement of this Part, the registration of the vessel under that enactment shall (notwithstanding any repeals made by this Act) continue in force until—
  (a) the vessel (being eligible to be registered as a British fishing vessel) is registered under this Part in accordance with regulations under this section, or
  (b) the end of such period beginning with the commencement of this Part as may be prescribed,
whichever first occurs.

(4) Any fishing vessel whose registration under any of those enactments continues in force by virtue of subsection (3) shall be deemed to be a vessel registered under this Part for the purposes of sections 19, 20 and 22 below.

(5) Where a fishing vessel becomes registered under this Part at a time when it is already registered under the law of any country outside the United Kingdom, the owner of the vessel shall take all reasonable steps to secure the termination of the vessel's registration under the law of that country.

(6) Any person who contravenes subsection (5) shall be guilty of an offence and liable on summary conviction to a fine not exceeding the third level on the standard scale.

(7) Schedule 2 shall have effect for the purpose of supplementing this section.

Eligibility for registration as British fishing vessel

14.—(1) Subject to subsections (3) and (4), a fishing vessel shall only be eligible to be registered as a British fishing vessel if—
  (a) the vessel is British-owned;
  (b) the vessel is managed, and its operations are directed and controlled, from within the United Kingdom; and
  (c) any charterer, manager or operator of the vessel is a qualified person or company.

(2) For the purposes of subsection (1)(a) a fishing vessel is British-owned if—
  (a) the legal title to the vessel is vested wholly in one or more qualified persons or companies; and

    (b) the vessel is beneficially owned—
        (i) as to not less than the relevant percentage of the property in the vessel, by one or more qualified persons, or
        (ii) wholly by a qualified company or companies, or
        (iii) by one or more qualified companies and, as to not less than the relevant percentage of the remainder of the property in the vessel, by one or more qualified persons.

(3) The Secretary of State may by regulations specify further requirements which must be satisfied in order for a fishing vessel to be eligible to be registered as a British fishing vessel, being requirements imposed—

    (a) in connection with the implementation of any of the requirements specified in subsection (1)(a) to (c), or
    (b) in addition to the requirements so specified,

and appearing to the Secretary of State to be appropriate for securing that such a vessel has a genuine and substantial connection with the United Kingdom.

(4) Where, in the case of any fishing vessel, the Secretary of State is satisfied that—

    (a) the vessel would be eligible to be registered as a British fishing vessel but for the fact that any particular individual, or (as the case may be) each of a number of particular individuals, is not a British citizen (and is accordingly not a qualified person), and
    (b) it would be appropriate to dispense with the requirement of British citizenship in the case of that individual or those individuals, in view of the length of time he has or they have resided in the United Kingdom and been involved in the fishing industry of the United Kingdom,

the Secretary of State may determine that that requirement should be so dispensed with; and, if he does so, the vessel shall, so long as paragraph (a) above applies to it and such determination remains in force, be treated for the purposes of this Part as eligible to be registered as a British fishing vessel.

(5) Where any share in a vessel is beneficially owned jointly by persons not all of whom are qualified persons or companies, then, for the purposes of this section, the whole of that share shall be treated as beneficially owned by persons who are not qualified persons or companies.

(6) For the purpose of determining whether a fishing vessel is eligible to be registered as a British fishing vessel, the Secretary of State may, if he thinks fit, appoint a person—

    (a) to investigate the eligibility of the vessel to be so registered, and
    (b) to make a report of his conclusions to the Secretary of State;

and any person so appointed shall, for the purpose of conducting the investigation, have the powers conferred on an inspector by the provisions of section 27 of the Merchant Shipping Act 1979 (other than paragraphs (d) to (h) of subsection (1) of that section).

(7) In this section—

    "qualified company" means a company which satisfies the following conditions, namely—

        (a) it is incorporated in the United Kingdom and has its principal place of business there;
        (b) at least the relevant percentage of its shares (taken as a whole), and of each class of its shares, is legally and beneficially owned by one or more qualified persons or companies; and
        (c) at least the relevant percentage of its directors are qualified persons;

    "qualified person" means—

        (a) a person who is a British citizen resident and domiciled in the United Kingdom, or
        (b) a local authority in the United Kingdom; and

"the relevant percentage" means 75 per cent. or such greater percentage (which may be 100 per cent.) as may for the time being be prescribed.

Grant or refusal of applications for registration of fishing vessels

15.—(1) If, on an application for the registration of a fishing vessel made in accordance with regulations under section 13, the Secretary of State is satisfied—

    (a) that the vessel is eligible to be registered as a British fishing vessel, and

    (b) that any relevant requirements of any such regulations have been complied with in relation to the vessel,

he shall (subject to subsection (2)) cause the vessel to be registered as a British fishing vessel.

(2) Notwithstanding that the Secretary of State is so satisfied, he may refuse any such application if he is satisfied that there is not in force in respect of the vessel any certificate required to be so in force by virtue of section 4 of the Fishing Vessels (Safety Provisions) Act 1970 (prohibition on going to sea without appropriate certificates).

(3) If, on any such application, the Secretary of State is not satisfied as mentioned in subsection (1), he shall refuse the application.

Termination of registration where vessel is not eligible for registration or is not certificated

16.—(1) If for any reason it appears to the Secretary of State that a registered vessel may no longer be eligible to be registered as a British fishing vessel, he may by notice served on—

    (a) the owner of the vessel, or

    (b) any charterer, manager or operator of the vessel,

require that person, at such time or times as may be specified in the notice—

    (i) to produce to the Secretary of State such documents or descriptions of documents specified in the notice, and

    (ii) to furnish to him, in such form as may be specified in the notice such accounts, estimates, returns or other information (of whatever nature) specified in the notice,

as the Secretary of State thinks necessary for the purpose of determining whether the vessel is eligible to be so registered.

(2) In a case where the owner of a registered vessel is a company, subsection (1) shall apply to any person holding any shares in the company as it applies to the company.

(3) Where the Secretary of State has served a notice under subsection (1) with respect to any vessel, then, unless he has become satisfied that the vessel is eligible to be registered as a British fishing vessel—

    (a) he shall, as soon as practicable after the end of the period of 30 days beginning with the date of service of that notice, serve a notice under subsection (6) on the owner of the vessel, and

    (b) the vessel's registration shall terminate by virtue of this subsection at the relevant time.

(4) Where it appears to the Secretary of State that there is not in force in respect of any registered vessel any such certificate as is mentioned in section 15(2), he may by notice served on the owner of the vessel require the vessel to be presented for a survey under the fishing vessel survey rules within the period of 30 days beginning with the date of service of the notice.

(5) If the vessel is not presented for such a survey within that period—

    (a) the Secretary of State shall serve a notice under subsection (6) on the owner of the vessel, and

    (b) the vessel's registration shall terminate by virtue of this subsection at the relevant time.

(6) A notice under this subsection is a notice stating—

    (a) that the Secretary of State is not satisfied that the vessel in question is eligible to be registered as a British fishing vessel, or

    (b) that the vessel has not been presented for a survey as required by a notice under subsection (4),

as the case may be, and that the vessel's registration will accordingly terminate at the relevant time by virtue of subsection (3) or (5).

(7) In this section "the relevant time", in relation to a notice under subsection (6), means the end of the period of 14 days beginning with the date of service of that notice.

Consequences of termination of registration by virtue of s. 16

17.—(1) Where the registration of any vessel has terminated by virtue of section 16(3) or (5), then, without prejudice to the operation of any other provision of this Part of this Act or of regulations under section 13, the vessel shall not again be registered as a British fishing vessel unless—

    (a) the Secretary of State is satisfied that the earlier failure of the vessel to be eligible to be so registered or (as the case may be) to be presented for a survey was due to inadvertence, and (in the latter case) that the vessel has since been presented for a survey, or

    (b) the Secretary of State consents to the vessel being so registered, or

    (c) in the case of a vessel whose registration terminated by virtue of section 16(3), the Secretary of State is satisfied that the vessel has been disposed of by its former registered owner by means of a transaction at arm's length and that no person who for the time being is a relevant owner of the vessel was a relevant owner of it at the time when its registration terminated.

(2) In subsection (1)(a) "survey" means a survey under the fishing vessel survey rules.

(3) For the purposes of subsection (1)(c) a person is a relevant owner of a vessel at any time if at that time—

    (a) the legal title to the vessel or any share in it is vested in that person, or

    (b) the vessel or any share in it is beneficially owned by that person, or

    (c) any shares in a company falling within paragraph (a) or (b) above are legally or beneficially owned by that person,

whether vested in, or (as the case may be) owned by, that person alone or together with any other person or persons.

Registration of property in fishing vessels

18.—(1) For the purposes of the registration of a fishing vessel—

    (a) the property in the vessel shall be divided into 64 shares;

    (b) except as provided by paragraph (c), the number of persons registered as owners of the vessel shall not at any time exceed 64;

    (c) any number of persons not exceeding five may be registered as joint owners of the vessel or of any share in the vessel (but for the purposes of paragraph (b) the registered joint owners of any such share shall be treated as constituting one person);

    (d) a registered joint owner of the vessel or of any share in the vessel shall not be entitled to dispose of his interest in the vessel or share separately from the interest or interests in it of the other joint owner or joint owners; and

(e) a person shall not be entitled to be registered as the owner of a fractional part of a share in the vessel.

(2) Subsection (1)(b) and (c) do not prejudice any beneficial interest of any person represented by or claiming under or through a registered owner (including a registered joint owner).

Transfers etc. of registered vessels

Transfer of vessel or share by bill of sale

19.—(1) Any transfer of—

(a) a registered vessel (not being a vessel registered in pursuance of paragraph 2(c) of Schedule 2), or

(b) a share in any such vessel,

shall be effected by a bill of sale satisfying the requirements specified in subsection (2), unless the transfer will result in the vessel ceasing to be British-owned for the purposes of section 14(1)(a).

(2) Those requirements are that the bill of sale—

(a) is in such form as may be prescribed or approved by the Secretary of State; and

(b) contains a description of the vessel sufficient to identify the vessel to the satisfaction of the Secretary of State.

(3) Where any such vessel or share has been transferred in accordance with subsection (1), the transferee shall not be registered as owner of the vessel or share unless—

(a) he has made an application for the purpose in accordance with regulations under section 13 and has produced to the Secretary of State the bill of sale by which the vessel or share has been so transferred, and

(b) the Secretary of State is satisfied as mentioned in section 15(1);

and section 15(2) and (3) shall apply in relation to an application under this subsection as they apply in relation to an application for the registration of a fishing vessel.

(4) If an application under subsection (3) is granted by the Secretary of State, the Secretary of State shall—

(a) register the bill of sale referred to in paragraph (a) of that subsection by causing the applicant's name to be entered in the register as owner of the vessel or share in question, and

(b) endorse on the bill of sale the fact that that entry has been made, together with the date and time when it was made.

(5) Bills of sale shall be registered under subsection (4) in the order in which they are produced to the Secretary of State for the purposes of registration.

(6) If on an application under subsection (3) the Secretary of State is not satisfied that the vessel with respect to which the application is made is eligible to be registered as a British fishing vessel—

(a) the Secretary of State shall serve a notice under subsection (7) on the owner of the vessel; and

(b) the vessel's registration shall terminate by virtue of this subsection at the end of the period of 14 days beginning with the date of service of that notice.

(7) A notice under this subsection is a notice stating—

(a) that the Secretary of State is not satisfied that the vessel in question is eligible to be registered as a British fishing vessel; and

(b) that the vessel's registration will accordingly terminate by virtue of subsection (6) at the end of the period referred to in that subsection.

Transmission of property in vessel or share other than under s. 19

20.—(1) Where a registered vessel, or a share in a registered vessel, is transmitted to any person by any lawful means other than by a transfer under section 19, that person shall not be registered as owner of the vessel or share unless—
  (a) he has made an application for the purpose in accordance with regulations under section 13 and has produced to the Secretary of State such evidence of the transmission as may be prescribed; and
  (b) the Secretary of State is satisfied as mentioned in section 15(1);
and section 15(2) and (3) shall apply in relation to an application under this subsection as they apply in relation to an application for the registration of a fishing vessel.

(2) If an application under subsection (1) is granted by the Secretary of State, he shall cause the applicant's name to be entered in the register as owner of the vessel or share.

(3) The preceding provisions of this section shall apply in relation to the transmission of the interest of a joint owner in a registered vessel or in a share in any such vessel as they apply in relation to the transmission of any such vessel or share, except that anything required to be done by virtue of subsection (1)(a) shall be done by both or all of the joint owners of the vessel or share.

(4) If on an application under subsection (1) the Secretary of State is not satisfied that the vessel with respect to which the application is made is eligible to be registered as a British fishing vessel—
  (a) the Secretary of State shall serve a notice under subsection (5) on the owner of the vessel; and
  (b) the vessel's registration shall terminate by virtue of this subsection at the end of the period of 14 days beginning with the date of service of that notice.

(5) A notice under this subsection is a notice stating—
  (a) that the Secretary of State is not satisfied that the vessel in question is eligible to be registered as a British fishing vessel; and
  (b) that the vessel's registration will accordingly terminate by virtue of subsection (4) at the end of the period referred to in that subsection.

Mortgages of registered vessels

Mortgages of registered vessels

21.—(1) Schedule 3 to this Act (which makes provision with respect to the registration of mortgages) shall have effect.

(2) Where the registration of any fishing vessel terminates by virtue of any provision of this Act, the termination of that registration shall not affect any entry made in the register under Schedule 3 so far as relating to any undischarged registered mortgage of that vessel or of any share in it.

(3) In subsection (2) "registered mortgage" has the same meaning as in Schedule 3.

Unregistered fishing vessels

Offences relating to, and liabilities of, unregistered fishing vessels

22.—(1) If any fishing vessel to which this subsection applies fishes for profit—
  (a) the skipper, the owner and any charterer of the vessel shall each be guilty of an offence; and
  (b) the vessel shall be liable to forfeiture.

(2) Subsection (1) applies to any fishing vessel which is either—
  (a) eligible to be registered under this Part, or

(b) wholly owned by one or more persons qualified to be owners of British ships for the purposes of Part I of the 1894 Act,

but is neither registered under this Part nor excluded from registration by regulations under section 13 nor registered under the law of any country outside the United Kingdom.

(3) Subsection (1) also applies to any fishing vessel which (notwithstanding that it is not entitled to be so registered) is for the time being registered in the United Kingdom under Part I of the 1894 Act or section 5 of the Merchant Shipping Act 1983 (registration of small ships).

(4) Subject to subsection (8), if any prescribed marks are displayed on a fishing vessel which is not a registered vessel, the skipper, the owner and any charterer of the vessel shall each be guilty of an offence.

(5) If the skipper or owner of a fishing vessel which is not a registered vessel does anything, or permits anything to be done, for the purpose of causing the vessel to appear to be a registered vessel, then (subject to subsection (8))—

(a) the skipper, the owner and any charterer of the vessel shall each be guilty of an offence; and

(b) the vessel shall be liable to forfeiture.

(6) Where a fishing vessel is not a British ship and is not registered under the law of any country outside the United Kingdom, but—

(a) it is eligible to be registered under this Part, or

(b) it is wholly owned by one or more such persons as are mentioned in subsection (2)(b), or

(c) (subject to subsection (8)) any prescribed marks are displayed on it,

then (notwithstanding that the vessel is not entitled to any benefits, privileges, advantages or protection usually enjoyed by a British ship) the vessel shall, for the purposes mentioned in subsection (7), be dealt with in the same manner in all respects as if the vessel were a British ship.

(7) Those purposes are—

(a) the payment of dues, fees or other charges;

(b) liablility to fines and forfeiture; and

(c) the punishment of offences committed on board the vessel, or by any persons belonging to it.

(8) Where the registration of any vessel has terminated by virtue of any provision of this Part, any prescribed marks displayed on the vessel within the period of 14 days beginning with the date of termination of that registration shall be disregarded for the purposes of subsections (4) to (6).

(9) Subsections (1), (4) and (5)(a) apply to offences falling within those provisions wherever committed.

(10) Section 76 of the 1894 Act (proceedings on forfeiture of ship) shall apply to any vessel liable to forfeiture under this section as it applies to any such ship as is mentioned in subsection (1) of that section.

Supplemental

Notification of changes in ownership etc., and offences relating to furnishing of information.

23.—(1) If at any time there occurs, in relation to a registered vessel—

(a) any change affecting the eligibility of the vessel to be registered as a British fishing vessel, or

(b) any change (not falling within paragraph (a)) in the percentage of the property

in the vessel which is beneficially owned by persons who are qualified persons or companies within the meaning of section 14,
the owner of the vessel shall, as soon as practicable after the change occurs, notify the Secretary of State in writing of that change.

(2) Any person who contravenes subsection (1) shall be guilty of an offence.

(3) Any person who—

(a) in connection with the registration of any vessel or the making of any other entry in the register in pursuance of this Part, or

(b) in purported compliance with the requirements of any notice under section 16(1),

knowingly or recklessly furnishes information which is false in a material particular shall be guilty of an offence.

(4) Any person who intentionally alters, suppresses, conceals or destroys a document which he has been required to produce by a notice under section 16(1) shall be guilty of an offence.

Penalties for offences under s. 22 or 23 and other provisions relating to such offences

24.—(1) Any person guilty of an offence under section 22 or 23 shall be liable—

(a) on summary conviction, to a fine not exceeding £50,000;

(b) on conviction on indictment, to imprisonment for a term not exceeding two years or a fine, or both.

(2) Proceedings for an offence under section 22 or 23 shall not be instituted—

(a) in England and Wales, except by or with the consent of the Attorney General, the Secretary of State or the Minister; or

(b) in Northern Ireland, except by or with the consent of the Attorney General for Northern Ireland, the Secretary of State or the Minister.

(3) Proceedings for an offence under section 22 may be taken, and the offence may for all incidental purposes be treated as having been committed, in any place in the United Kingdom.

(4) In this section "the Minister"—

(a) in relation to England and Wales, means the Minister of Agriculture, Fisheries and Food; and

(b) in relation to Northern Ireland, means the Secretary of State concerned with sea fishing in Northern Ireland.

Application of other enactments, etc.

25.—(1) Any reference (however phrased) in any statutory provision not contained in this Act to the registration of a fishing vessel under any of the enactments specified in section 13(2) shall, so far as the context permits, be construed as, or as including, a reference to the registration of a fishing vessel under this Part; and connected phrases shall be construed accordingly.

(2) The following provisions of the 1894 Act, namely—

(a) section 69 (penalty for unduly assuming British character), and

(b) section 71 (penalty for acquiring ownership if unqualified),

shall not apply to a registered vessel; and section 72 of that Act (liabilities of unregistered ships) shall not apply to a fishing vessel (whether registered or not).

(3) Sections 8 and 9 of the Sea Fisheries Act 1968 (general powers of British sea-fishery officers and powers of sea-fishery officers to enforce conventions) shall apply in relation to—

(a) this Part of this Act, and

(b) any regulations made under it,

as they apply in relation to any order mentioned in section 8 of that Act and in relation to any convention mentioned in section 9 of that Act respectively; and sections 10 to 12 and 14 of that Act (offences and supplemental provisions as to legal proceedings) shall apply accordingly.

(4) A document purporting to be a copy of any information contained in an entry in the register and to be certified as a true copy by an authorised officer of the Secretary of State shall be evidence (and, in Scotland, sufficient evidence) of the matters stated in the document.

SCHEDULE 2. REGISTRATION OF FISHING VESSELS: SUPPLEMENTARY PROVISIONS (SECTION 13)

Interpretation

1. In this Schedule—
    "declaration of British character" means a declaration, in such form as may be prescribed, relating to the eligibility of a fishing vessel to be registered as a British fishing vessel;
    "regulations" means regulations made under section 13;
    "relevant statutory provision" means any provision of this Part or of regulations;
    "specified" means specified in regulations.

Regulations: general provisions

2. Regulations may make provision—
    (a) for the persons by whom and the manner in which applications in connection with registration are to be made (including provision limiting the persons who may apply for registration, whether by reference to residence or place of business or otherwise);
    (b) for the information and evidence to be provided in connection with such applications and for such supplementary information or evidence as may be required by any authority specified in the regulations for the purpose to be so provided, and for the production, in connection with such applications, of declarations of British character;
    (c) for the registration of vessels as vessels to which the provisions of this Part relating to transfers by bill of sale and the registration of mortgages do not apply;
    (d) for the issue of certificates of registration (including temporary certificates), their production and surrender;
    (e) for the marking of registered vessels;
    (f) for the period for which the registration of a vessel is to remain effective without renewal;
    (g) for matters arising out of the expiration or termination of registration (including the removal of marks and the cancellation of certificates);
    (h) for declarations of British character to be produced to the Secretary of State, as respects registered vessels, at specified intervals or at the request of the Secretary of State;
    (i) for the payment of fees determined with the approval of the Treasury;
    (j) excluding from registration, or from any provision of the regulations, any specified class or description of vessel;
    (k) for the manner in which notices or other documents required or authorised to

be given or served by virtue of any relevant statutory provision are to be given or served;
   (l) for prescribing anything which is authorised to be prescribed under this Part;
   (m) for any of the provisions of Part I of the 1894 Act to have effect in relation to the registration of fishing vessels subject to such modifications (if any) as may be specified;
   (n) for any other matters relating to the establishment and maintenance of the register (including its inspection).

Provisional registration

3. Regulations may make provision—
   (a) for fishing vessels acquired outside the United Kingdom which are eligible to be registered as British fishing vessels to be provisionally registered as such pending their registration in the register;
   (b) for any such provisional registration to terminate in specified circumstances (including failure to comply with requirements imposed by or under the regulations).

Transfers of registration

4.—(1) Regulations may make provision with respect to the transfer to the register of—
   (a) fishing vessels to which section 13(3) applies where those vessels are eligible to be registered as British fishing vessels, and
   (b) undischarged mortgages affecting those vessels,
and with respect to matters consequential on the termination of the registration of fishing vessels under any of the enactments specified in section 13(2) (including vessels which are not transferred to the register).
   (2) Any such regulations may make provision—
   (a) for any of the matters specified in sub-paragraphs (a), (b) and (i) of paragraph 2;
   (b) for applications under sections 19(3) and 20(1) to be treated, in cases where those provisions apply by virtue of section 13(4), as applications for registration of the vessels in question;
   (c) for the issue of certificates of registration under this Part (including temporary certificates) and for the surrender of certificates of registration issued under any of the enactments specified in section 13(2);
   (d) for preserving the effect of entries in any register kept under either of the enactments specified in section 13(2)(a) and (c) so far as those entries relate to undischarged mortgages affecting vessels which are not transferred to the register kept under this Part.
   (3) Nothing in this paragraph prejudices the generality of paragraph 2.

Offences

5.—(1) Regulations may provide for the creation of offences and their punishment on summary conviction in any of the following cases—
   (a) where a person with intent to deceive, uses, or lends to or allows to be used by another, a certificate of registration, whether in force or not;

(b) where a person required by regulations to ensure that any requirement of the regulations as to the marking of a fishing vessel is satisfied fails to ensure that that requirement is satisfied;

(c) where a person required by regulations to surrender a certificate of registration fails without reasonable excuse to surrender the certificate.

(2) Any such regulations shall—

(a) in the case of an offence created by virtue of sub-paragraph (1)(a), provide for the offence to be punishable with a fine not exceeding the fifth level on the standard scale; and

(b) in the case of an offence created by virtue of sub-paragraph (1)(b) or (c), provide for it to be punishable with a fine not exceeding the third level on the standard scale.

(3) Regulations providing for the creation of an offence by virtue of sub-paragraph (1)(b) shall provide that it shall be a defence for a person charged with the offence to prove that he took all reasonable precautions and exercised all due diligence to avoid the commission of the offence.

Operation of regulations in territorial waters

6. Regulations may provide for any of their provisions to extend to the territorial sea of the United Kingdom.

Discharge of functions by persons appointed by Secretary of State

7.—(1) The Secretary of State may appoint persons to discharge such functions in connection with—

(a) applications for registration, or

(b) the issue, production or surrender of certificates of registration,

as he may specify; and regulations may provide for references to the Secretary of State in any relevant statutory provision to be read as, or as including, references to any person so appointed.

(2) Sub-paragraph (1) does not authorise the appointment of any person to determine applications for registration.

Construction of references in other enactments to fishing vessels excluded from registration

8. References in any statutory provision (apart from section 2(1)(c)) to fishing vessels excluded from registration by regulations under section 13 shall be construed as references to fishing vessels which, being eligible to be registered under this Part by virtue of section 14, are excluded from registration by such regulations (and are not registered under the law of any country outside the United Kingdom).

SCHEDULE 3. MORTGAGES OF REGISTERED FISHING VESSELS (SECTION 21)

Interpretation

1. In this Schedule—

"mortgage" shall be construed in accordance with paragraph 2(2) below;

"registered mortgage" means a mortgage registered in pursuance of paragraph 2(3) below; and

"registered vessel" means a vessel registered otherwise than in pursuance of paragraph 2(c) of Schedule 2.

Mortgages of registered vessels

2.—(1) Any registered vessel or share in a registered vessel may be made a security for the repayment of a loan or the discharge of any other obligation.

(2) The instrument creating any such security (referred to in this Schedule as a mortgage) shall be in such form as is prescribed or approved by the Secretary of State.

(3) Where a mortgage executed in accordance with sub-paragraph (2) is produced to the Secretary of State, he shall—

(a) register the mortgage by causing it to be recorded in the register, and

(b) endorse on it the fact that it has been recorded, together with the date and time when it was recorded.

(4) Mortgages shall be registered under sub-paragraph (3) in the order in which they are produced to the Secretary of State for the purposes of registration.

Priority of registered mortgages

3. Where two or more mortgages are registered in respect of the same vessel or share, the priority of the mortgagees between themselves shall (subject to paragraph 4) be determined by the order in which the mortgages were registered (and not by reference to any other matter).

Notices by intending mortgagees

4.—(1) Where any person who is an intending mortgagee under a proposed mortgage of—

(a) a registered vessel, or

(b) a share in a registered vessel,

notifies the Secretary of State in writing of the interest which it is intended that he should have under the proposed mortgage, the Secretary of State shall cause that interest to be recorded in the register.

(2) Where any person who is an intending mortgagee under a proposed mortgage of—

(a) a fishing vessel which is not for the time being a registered vessel, or

(b) a share in any such vessel,

notifies the Secretary of State in writing of the interest which it is intended that he should have under the proposed mortgage and furnishes him with such particulars of that vessel as may be prescribed, the Secretary of State—

(i) shall cause that interest to be recorded in the register, and

(ii) if the vessel is subsequently registered (otherwise than in pursuance of paragraph 2(c) of Schedule 2), shall cause the vessel to be registered subject to that interest or, if the mortgage has by then been executed in accordance with paragraph 2(2) and produced to the Secretary of State, subject to that mortgage.

(3) In a case where—

(a) paragraph 3 operates to determine the priority between two or more mortgagees, and

(b) any of those mortgagees gave a notification under sub-paragraph (1) or (2) above with respect to his mortgage, paragraph 3 shall have effect in relation to that mortgage as if it had been registered at the time when the relevant entry was made in the register under sub-paragraph (1) or (2) above.

(4) Any notification given by a person under sub-paragraph (1) or (2) (and anything done as a result of it) shall cease to have effect—

(a) if the notification is withdrawn, or

(b) at the end of the period of 30 days beginning with the date of the notification, unless the notification is renewed in accordance with sub-paragraph (5).

(5) The person by whom any such notification is given may renew or further renew the notification, on each occasion for a period of 30 days, by notice in writing given to the Secretary of State—

(a) before the end of the period mentioned in sub-paragraph (4)(b), or

(b) before the end of the current period of renewal,

as the case may be.

(6) Any notification or notice purporting to be given under this paragraph (and anything done as a result of it) shall not have any effect if the Secretary of State determines that it was not validly given.

Registered mortgagee's power of sale

5.—(1) Subject to sub-paragraph (2), every registered mortgagee shall have power, if the mortgage money or any part of it is due, to sell the vessel or share in respect of which he is registered, and to give effectual receipts for the purchase money.

(2) Where two or more mortgagees are registered in respect of the same vessel or share, a subsequent mortgagee shall not, except under an order of a court of competent jurisdiction, sell the vessel or share without the concurrence of every prior mortgagee.

Transfer of registered mortgage

6.—(1) A registered mortgage may be transferred by an instrument made in such form as is prescribed or approved by the Secretary of State.

(2) Where any such instrument is produced to the Secretary of State, he shall—

(a) cause the name of the transferee to be entered in the register as mortgagee of the vessel or share in question, and

(b) endorse on the instrument the fact that that entry has been made, together with the date and time when it was made.

Transmission of registered mortgage by operation of law

7. Where the interest of a mortgagee in a registered mortgage is transmitted to any person by any lawful means other than by a transfer under paragraph 6, the Secretary of State shall, on production of such evidence of the transmission as may be prescribed, cause the name of that person to be entered in the register as mortgagee of the vessel or share in question.

Discharge of registered mortgage

8. Where a registered mortgage has been discharged, the Secretary of State shall, on production of the mortgage deed with such evidence of the discharge of the mortgage as

is prescribed, cause an entry to be made in the register to the effect that the mortgage has been discharged.

Transfer of mortgages from one system of registration to another

9.—(1) Regulations may provide—
    (a) for the transfer to the register of undischarged mortgages that have been registered under Part I of the 1894 Act and affect ships registered under that Part of that Act which become registered vessels otherwise than in pursuance of paragraph 4 of Schedule 2 to this Act; and
    (b) for any provisions of this Part to have effect in relation to any such mortgages, or in relation to any mortgages transferred in pursuance of paragraph 4 of that Schedule, subject to such modifications as may be specified in the regulations.
(2) Regulations may also provide—
    (a) for the transfer to registers kept under Part I of the 1894 Act of undischarged registered mortgages affecting registered vessels which become ships registered under that Part of that Act; and
    (b) for any provisions of that Part of that Act to have effect in relation to any such mortgages subject to such modifications as may be specified in the regulations.
(3) Without prejudice to the generality of sub-paragraphs (1) and (2)—
    (a) regulations made by virtue of sub-paragraph (1) may make provision, in connection with the transfer of mortgages in pursuance of that sub-paragraph, for the transmission of information relating to such mortgages which is recorded in registers kept under Part I of the 1894 Act, and for the recording of such information in the register kept under this Part; and
    (b) regulations made by virtue of sub-paragraph (2) may make corresponding provision, in connection with the transfer of mortgages in pursuance of that sub-paragraph, for the transmission and recording of information relating to such mortgages which is recorded in the register kept under this Part.
(4) In this paragraph "regulations" means regulations made under section 13.

APPENDIX 3

CIVIL AVIATION ACT 1982[1]
ss. 60 AND 86–91

PART III. REGULATION OF CIVIL AVIATION

General

Power to give effect to Chicago Convention and to regulate air navigation, etc.

60.—(1) Subject to section 11(7) above, Her Majesty may by Order in Council under this section (in this Act referred to as "an Air Navigation Order") make such provision as is authorised by subsections (2) and (3) below or otherwise by this Act or any other enactment.

(2) An Air Navigation Order may contain such provision as appears to Her Majesty in Council to be requisite or expedient—

    (a) for carrying out the Chicago Convention, any Annex thereto relating to international standards and recommended practices (being an Annex adopted in accordance with the Convention) and any amendment of the Convention or any such Annex made in accordance with the Convention; or

    (b) generally for regulating air navigation.

(3) Without prejudice to the generality of subsection (2) above or to any other provision of this Act, an Air Navigation Order may contain provision—

    (a) as to the registration of aircraft in the United Kingdom;

    (b) for prohibiting aircraft from flying unless certificates of airworthiness issued or validated under the Order are in force with respect to them and except upon compliance with such conditions as to maintenance or repair as may be specified in the Order;

    (c) for the licensing, inspection and regulation of aerodromes, for access to aerodromes and places where aircraft have landed, for access to aircraft factories for the purpose of inspecting work therein carried on in relation to aircraft or parts thereof and for prohibiting or regulating the use of unlicensed aerodromes;

    (d) for prohibiting persons from engaging in, or being employed in or (except in the maintenance at unlicensed aerodromes of aircraft not used for or in connection with commercial, industrial or other gainful purposes) in connection with air navigation in such capacities as may be specified in the Order except in accordance with provisions in that behalf contained in the Order, and for the licensing of those employed at aerodromes licensed under the Order in the inspection or supervision of aircraft;

    (e) as to the conditions under which, and in particular the aerodromes to or from which, aircraft entering or leaving the United Kingdom may fly, and as to the

1. Chapter 16.

177

conditions under which aircraft may fly from one part of the United Kingdom to another;

(f) as to the conditions under which passengers and goods may be carried by air and under which aircraft may be used for other commercial, industrial or gainful purposes, and for prohibiting the carriage by air of goods of such classes as may be specified in the Order;

(g) for minimizing or preventing interference with the use or effectiveness of apparatus used in connection with air navigation, and for prohibiting or regulating the use of such apparatus as aforesaid and the display of signs and lights liable to endanger aircraft;

(h) generally for securing the safety, efficiency and regularity of air navigation and the safety of aircraft and of persons and property carried therein, for preventing aircraft endangering other persons and property and, in particular, for the detention of aircraft for any of the purposes specified in this paragraph;

(i) for requiring persons engaged in, or employed in or in connection with, air navigation to supply meteorological information for the purposes of air navigation;

(j) for regulating the making of signals and other communications by or to aircraft and persons carried therein;

(k) for regulating the use of the civil air ensign and any other ensign established by Her Majesty in Council for purposes connected with air navigation;

(l) for prohibiting aircraft from flying over such areas in the United Kingdom as may be specified in the Order;

(m) for applying, adapting or modifying the enactments for the time being in force relating to customs or excise in relation to aerodromes and to aircraft and to persons and property carried therein and for preventing smuggling by air, and for permitting in connection with air navigation, subject to such conditions as appear to Her Majesty in Council to be requisite or expedient for the protection of the revenue, the importation of goods into the United Kingdom without payment of duty;

(n) as to the manner and conditions of the issue, validation, renewal, extension or variation of any certificate, licence or other document required by the Order (including the examinations and tests to be undergone), and as to the form, custody, production, cancellation, suspension, endorsement and surrender of any such document;

(o) for regulating the charges that may be made for the use of, and for services provided at, an aerodrome licensed under the Order or so much of any aerodrome (whether or not so licensed) as consists of buildings or other works maintained by a local authority by virtue of section 30 above at an aerodrome which is not an aerodrome maintained by that authority;

(p) for specifying, subject to the consent of the Treasury the fees to be paid in respect of the issue, validation, renewal, extension or variation of any certificate, licence or other document or the undergoing of any examination or test required by the Order and in respect of any other matters in respect of which it appears to Her Majesty in Council to be expedient for the purpose of the Order to charge fees;

(q) for exempting from the provisions of the Order or any of them any aircraft or persons or classes of aircraft or persons;

(r) for prohibiting aircraft from taking off or landing in the United Kingdom unless there are in force in respect of those aircraft such certificates of compliance with standards as to noise as may be specified in the Order and except upon compliance with the conditions of those certificates; and

(s) for regulating or prohibiting the flight of aircraft over the United Kingdom at speeds in excess of Flight Mach 1.

(4) An Air Navigation Order may make different provision with respect to different classes of aircraft, aerodromes, persons or property and with respect to different circumstances and with respect to different parts of the United Kingdom but shall, so far as practicable, be so framed as not to discriminate in like circumstances between aircraft registered in the United Kingdom operated on charter terms by one air transport undertaking and such aircraft so operated by another such undertaking.

(5) The powers conferred by the preceding provisions of this section may be exercised so as to provide for the licensing of any aerodrome in Northern Ireland notwithstanding that the aerodrome is owned or managed by a Northern Ireland department and so as to impose duties on any such department as licensee of any such aerodrome, including duties as to the charges which may be made for the use of, or for services provided at, any such aerodrome.

(6) In this section a reference to goods shall include a reference to mails or animals.

Rights etc. in relation to aircraft

Power to provide for the mortgaging of aircraft

86.—(1) Her Majesty may by Order in Council make provision for the mortgaging of an aircraft registered in the United Kingdom or capable of being so registered.

(2) Without prejudice to the generality of the powers conferred by subsection (1) above, an Order in Council under this section may, in particular—

(a) include provisions which correspond (subject to such modifications as appear to Her Majesty in Council to be necessary or expedient) to any of the provisions of the Merchant Shipping Act 1894 relating to the mortgaging of ships;

(b) make provision as respects the rights and liabilities of mortgagors and mortgagees of such aircraft as are mentioned in subsection (1) above, and as respects the priority inter se of such rights and the relationship of such rights to other rights in or over such aircraft, including possessory liens for work done to such aircraft and rights under section 88 below or under regulations made by virtue of section 74(4) above;

(c) make provision as respects the operation, in relation to such aircraft as aforesaid, of any of the enactments in force in any part of the United Kingdom relating to bills of sale or the registration of charges on the property or undertaking of companies;

(d) provide for the rights of mortgagees of such aircraft to be exercisable, in such circumstances as may be specified in the Order, in relation to payments for the use of the aircraft;

(e) confer on courts in the United Kingdom powers in respect of any register maintained in pursuance of the Order and in respect of transactions affecting aircraft registered therein;

(f) make provision for enabling the mortgage of an aircraft to extend to any store of spare parts for that aircraft and for applying, for that purpose, to any such spare parts provisions such as are mentioned in the preceding paragraphs of this subsection;

(g) make provision specifying, subject to the consent of the Treasury, the fees to be paid in respect of the making or deletion of entries in any such register as aforesaid and in respect of any other matters in respect of which it appears to Her Majesty in Council to be expedient for the purposes of the Order to charge fees;

(h) provide for the imposition of penalties in respect of the making of false statements in connection with matters dealt with in the Order and in respect of the forgery of documents relating to such matters.

Application of law of wreck and salvage to aircraft

87.—(1) Any services rendered in assisting, or in saving life from, or in saving the cargo or apparel of, an aircraft in, on or over the sea of any tidal water, or on or over the shores of the sea or any tidal water, shall be deemed to be salvage services in all cases in which they would have been salvage services if they had been rendered in relation to a vessel.

(2) Where salvage services are rendered by an aircraft to any property or person, the owner of the aircraft shall be entitled to the same reward for those services as he would have been entitled to if the aircraft had been a vessel.

(3) Subsections (1) and (2) above shall have effect notwithstanding that the aircraft concerned is a foreign aircraft and notwithstanding that the services in question are rendered elsewhere than within the limits of the territorial waters adjacent to any part of Her Majesty's dominions.

(4) Her Majesty may by Order in Council direct that any provisions of any Act for the time being in force which relate to wreck, to salvage of life or property or to the duty of rendering assistance to vessels in distress shall, with such modifications, if any, as may be specified in the Order apply in relation to aircraft as those provisions apply in relation to vessels.

(5) For the purposes of this section—

   (a) any provisions of an Act which relate to vessels laid by or neglected as unfit for sea service shall be deemed to be provisions relating to wreck; and

   (b) "Act" shall include any local or special Act and any provisions of the Harbours, Docks and Piers Clauses Act 1847, as incorporated with any local or special Act, whenever passed.

Detention and sale of aircraft for unpaid airport charges

88.—(1) Where default is made in the payment of airport charges incurred in respect of any aircraft at an aerodrome to which this section applies, the aerodrome authority may, subject to the provisions of this section—

   (a) detain, pending payment, either—

      (i) the aircraft in respect of which the charges were incurred (whether or not they were incurred by the person who is the operator of the aircraft at the time when the detention begins); or

      (ii) any other aircraft of which the person in default is the operator at the time when the detention begins; and

   (b) if the charges are not paid within 56 days of the date when the detention begins, sell the aircraft in order to satisfy the charges.

(2) An aerodrome authority shall not detain or continue to detain an aircraft under this section by reason of any alleged default in the payment of airport charges if the operator of the aircraft or any person claiming an interest therein—

   (a) disputes that the charges, or any of them, are due or, if the aircraft is detained under subsection (1)(a)(i) above, that the charges in question were incurred in respect of that aircraft; and

   (b) gives to the authority, pending the determination of the dispute, sufficient security for the payment of the charges which are alleged to be due.

(3) An aerodrome authority shall not sell an aircraft under this section without the leave of the court; and the court shall not give leave except on proof—

   (a) that a sum is due to the authority for airport charges;

   (b) that default has been made in the payment thereof; and

   (c) that the aircraft which the authority seek leave to sell is liable to sale under this section by reason of the default.

(4) An aerodrome proposing to apply for leave to sell an aircraft under this section shall take such steps as may be described—
  (a) for bringing the proposed application to the notice of persons whose interests may be affected by the determination of the court thereon; and
  (b) for affording to any such person an opportunity of becoming a party to the proceedings on the application;
and, if leave is given, the aerodrome authority shall secure that the aircraft is sold for the best price that can reasonably be obtained.

(5) Failure to comply with any requirement of subsection (4) above in respect of any sale, while actionable as against the aerodrome authority concerned at the suit of any person suffering loss in consequence thereof, shall not, after the sale has taken place, be a ground for impugning its validity.

(6) The proceeds of any sale under this section shall be applied as follows, and in the following order, that is to say—
  (a) in payment of any duty (whether of customs or excise) chargeable on imported goods or value added tax which is due in consequence of the aircraft's having been brought into the United Kingdom;
  (b) in payment of the expenses incurred by the aerodrome authority in detaining, keeping and selling the aircraft, including their expenses in connection with the application to the court;
  (c) in payment of the airport charges which the court has found to be due;
  (d) in payment of any charge in respect of the aircraft which is due by virtue of regulations under section 73 above;
and the surplus, if any, shall be paid to or among the person or persons whose interests in the aircraft have been divested by reason of the sale.

(7) The power of detention and sale conferred by this section in respect of an aircraft extends to the equipment of the aircraft and any stores for use in connection with its operation (being equipment and stores carried in the aircraft) whether or not the property of the person who is its operator, and references to the aircraft in subsections (2) to (6) above include, except where the context otherwise requires, references to any such equipment and stores.

(8) The power of detention conferred by this section in respect of an aircraft extends to any aircraft documents carried in it, and any such documents may, if the aircraft is sold under this section, be transferred by the aerodrome authority to the purchaser.

(9) The power conferred by this section to detain an aircraft in respect of which charges have been incurred may be exercised on the occasion on which the charges have been incurred or on any subsequent occasion when the aircraft is on the aerodrome on which those charges were incurred or on any other aerodrome owned or managed by the aerodrome authority concerned.

(10) This section applies to any aerodrome owned or managed by any government department, the BAA or a local authority, other than a district council in Scotland, and to any other aerodrome designated for the purposes of this section by an order made by the Secretary of State; and in this section—
  "aerodrome authority" in relation to any aerodrome, means the person owning or managing it;
  "airport charges" means charges payable to an aerodrome authority for the use of, or for services provided at, an aerodrome but does not include charges payable by virtue of regulations under section 73 above;
  "aircraft documents", in relation to any aircraft, means any certificate of registration, maintenance or airworthiness of that aircraft, any log book relating to the use of that aircraft or its equipment and any similar document;
  "the court" means—

    (a) as respects England and Wales, the High Court; and

    (b) as respects Scotland, the Court of Session.

(11) The Secretary of State may, after consultation with any local authority which appears to him to be concerned, by order repeal any enactment in a local Act which appears to the Secretary of State to be unnecessary having regard to the provisions of this section or to be inconsistent therewith.

(12) Nothing in this section shall prejudice any right of an aerodrome authority to recover any charges, or any part thereof, by action.

Exemption of aircraft and parts thereof from seizure on patent claims

89.—(1) Any lawful entry into the United Kingdom or any lawful transit across the United Kingdom, with or without landings, of an aircraft to which this section applies shall not entail any seizure or detention of the aircraft or any proceedings being brought against the owner or operator thereof or any other interference therewith by or on behalf of any person in the United Kingdom, on the ground that the construction, mechanism, parts, accessories or operation of the aircraft is or are an infringement of any patent, design or model.

(2) Subject to subsection (3) below, the importation into, and storage in, the United Kingdom of spare parts and spare equipment for an aircraft to which this section applies and the use and installation thereof in the repair of such an aircraft shall not entail any seizure or detention of the aircraft or of the spare parts or spare equipment or any proceedings being brought against the owner or operator of the aircraft or the owner of the spare parts or spare equipment or any other interference with the aircraft by or on behalf of any person in the United Kingdom on the ground that the spare parts or spare equipment or their installation are or is an infringement of any patent, design or model.

(3) Subsection (2) above shall not apply in relation to any spare parts or spare equipment which are sold or distributed in the United Kingdom or are exported from the United Kingdom for sale or distribution.

(4) This section applies—

    (a) to an aircraft other than an aircraft used in military, customs or police services, registered in any country or territory in the case of which there is for the time being in force a declaration made by Her Majesty by Order in Council with a view to the fulfilment of the provisions of the Chicago Convention to which this section relates, that the benefits of those provisions apply to that country or territory; and

    (b) to such other aircraft as Her Majesty may by Order in Council specify.

(5) Schedule 12 to this Act shall have effect with respect to detention on patent claims in respect of foreign aircraft other than aircraft to which this section applies.

Power to give effect to Convention on rights in aircraft

90.—(1) Her Majesty may by Order in Council[2] make such provision as appears to Her Majesty in Council to be necessary or expedient for giving effect to the Convention on the International Recognition of Rights in Aircraft which was signed at Geneva on behalf of the United Kingdom on 19th June 1948.

(2) Without prejudice to the generality of the powers conferred by subsection (1) above, an Order in Council under this section may, in particular, make provision—

    (a) for the recognition in the United Kingdom of rights of the kind specified in the Convention in or over aircraft registered in other states party to the Convention, being rights registered or recorded in those states in accordance with the Conven-

2. The power has not been exercised.

tion and recognised as valid by the law of the state party to the Convention in which the aircraft in question was registered when the rights were constituted;

(b) for subordinating to any such rights as aforesaid, to such extent as may be required under the Convention, any other rights in or over such aircraft as aforesaid, including possessory liens for work done to such aircraft and rights under section 88 above or under regulations made by virtue of section 74(4) above;

(c) as respects the operation, in relation to such aircraft as aforesaid, of any of the enactments in force in any part of the United Kingdom relating to bills of sale or the registration of charges on the property or undertaking of companies;

(d) for prohibiting the sale in execution of any such aircraft as aforesaid without an order of a court, and otherwise for safeguarding in the case of such a sale any such rights as are mentioned in paragraph (a) above;

(e) for the recognition in the United Kingdom, in priority to other rights in or over any such aircraft as aforesaid or any aircraft registered in the United Kingdom or a relevant overseas territory, of any charge consequent on salvage or similar operations in respect of the aircraft, being a charge arising in accordance with the law of any other state party to the Convention in which those operations terminated;

(f) for the application, in accordance with the Convention, of provisions corresponding to those made by virtue of paragraphs (a) to (d) above to cases where a right such as is mentioned in the said paragraph (a) (being a right created as security for the payment of indebtedness) extends to any store of spare parts for the aircraft in question.

Jurisdiction, etc.

Jurisdiction in civil matters

91. Her Majesty may by Order in Council[3] make provision as to the courts in which proceedings may be taken for enforcing any claim in respect of aircraft, and in particular may provide—

(a) for conferring jurisdiction in any such proceedings on any court exercising Admiralty jurisdiction; and

(b) for applying to such proceedings any rules of practice or procedure applicable to proceedings in Admiralty.

---

3. The power has not been exercised.

AIR NAVIGATION ORDER 1985[1]
PART I (ARTICLES 3–5), SCHEDULE 1

PART I. REGISTRATION AND MARKING OF AIRCRAFT

Aircraft to be registered

3.—(1) An aircraft shall not fly in or over the United Kingdom unless it is registered in:

(a) some part of the Commonwealth; or

(b) a Contracting State; or

(c) some other country in relation to which there is in force an agreement between Her Majesty's Government in the United Kingdom and the Government of that country which makes provision for the flight over the United Kingdom of aircraft registered in that country:

Provided that:

(i) a glider may fly unregistered, and shall be deemed to be registered in the United Kingdom for the purposes of articles 13, 14, 19 and 32 of this Order, on any flight which—

(a) begins and ends in the United Kingdom without passing over any country, and

(b) is not for the purpose of public transport or aerial work;

(ii) any aircraft may fly unregistered on any flight which:

(a) begins and ends in the United Kingdom without passing over any other country, and

(b) is in accordance with the "B Conditions" set forth in Schedule 2 to this Order;

(iii) this paragraph shall not apply to any kite or captive balloon.

(2) If an aircraft flies over the United Kingdom in contravention of paragraph (1) of this article in such manner or circumstances that if the aircraft had been registered in the United Kingdom an offence against this Order or any regulations made thereunder would have been committed, the like offence shall be deemed to have been committed in respect of that aircraft.

Registration of aircraft in the United Kingdom

4.—(1) The Authority shall be the authority for the registration of aircraft in the United Kingdom and shall keep the register on its premises and may record therein the

---

1. S.I. 1985 1643.

particulars specified in paragraph (7) of this article in a legible or non legible form so long as the recording is capable of being reproduced in a legible form.

(2) Subject to the provisions of this article, an aircraft shall not be registered or continue to be registered in the United Kingdom if it appears to the Authority that:

(a) the aircraft is registered outside the United Kingdom and that such registration does not cease by operation of law upon the aircraft being registered in the United Kingdom; or

(b) an unqualified person holds any legal or beneficial interest by way of ownership in the aircraft or any share therein; or

(c) the aircraft could more suitably be registered in some other part of the Commonwealth; or

(d) it would be inexpedient in the public interest for the aircraft to be or to continue to be registered in the United Kingdom.

(3) The following persons and no others shall be qualified to hold a legal or beneficial interest by way of ownership in an aircraft registered in the United Kingdom or a share therein—

(a) the Crown in right of Her Majesty's Government in the United Kingdom;

(b) Commonwealth citizens;

(c) citizens of the Republic of Ireland;

(d) British protected persons;

(e) bodies incorporated in some part of the Commonwealth and having their principal place of business in any part of the Commonwealth;

(f) firms carrying on business in Scotland.

In this sub-paragraph "firm" has the same meaning as in the Partnership Act 1890.

(4) If an unqualified person residing or having a place of business in the United Kingdom holds a legal or beneficial interest by way of ownership in an aircraft, or a share therein, the Authority, upon being satisfied that the aircraft may otherwise be properly so registered, may register the aircraft in the United Kingdom. The person aforesaid shall not cause or permit the aircraft, while it is registered in pursuance of this paragraph, to be used for the purpose of public transport or aerial work.

(5) If the aircraft is chartered by demise to a person qualified as aforesaid the Authority may, whether or not an unqualified person is entitled as owner to a legal or beneficial interest therein, register the aircraft in the United Kingdom in the name of the charterer upon being satisfied that the aircraft may otherwise be properly so registered, and subject to the provisions of this article the aircraft may remain so registered during the continuation of the charter.

(6) Application for the registration of an aircraft in the United Kingdom shall be made in writing to the Authority, and shall include or be accompanied by such particulars and evidence relating to the aircraft and the ownership and chartering thereof as it may require to enable it to determine whether the aircraft may properly be registered in the United Kingdom and to issue the certificate referred to in paragraph (8) of this Article. In particular, the application shall include the proper description of the aircraft according to column 4 of the "General Classification of Aircraft" set forth in Part A of Schedule 1 to this Order.

(7) Upon receiving an application for the registration of an aircraft in the United Kingdom and being satisfied that the aircraft may properly be so registered, the Authority shall register the aircraft, wherever it may be, and shall include in the register the following particulars:

(a) the number of the certificate;

(b) the nationality mark of the aircraft, and the registration mark assigned to it by the Authority;

(c) the name of the constructor of the aircraft and its designation;

   (d) the serial number of the aircraft;

   (e) (i) the name and address of every person who is entitled as owner to a legal interest in the aircraft or a share therein, or, in the case of an aircraft which is the subject of a charter by demise, the name and address of the charterer by demise; and

         (ii) in the case of an aircraft registered in pursuance of paragraph (4) or (5) of this article, an indication that it is so registered.

(8) The Authority shall furnish to the person in whose name the aircraft is registered (hereinafter in this article referred to as "the registered owner") a certificate of registration, which shall include the foregoing particulars and the date on which the certificate was issued:

Provided that the Authority shall not be required to furnish a certificate of registration if the registered owner is the holder of an aircraft dealer's certificate granted under this Order who has made to the Authority and has not withdrawn a statement of his intention that the aircraft is to fly only in accordance with the conditions set forth in Part C of Schedule 1 to this Order, and in that case the aircraft shall fly only in accordance with those conditions.

(9) The Authority may grant to any person qualified as aforesaid an aircraft dealer's certificate if it is satisfied that he has a place of business in the United Kingdom for buying and selling aircraft.

(10) Subject to paragraphs (4) and (5) of this article, if at any time after an aircraft has been registered in the United Kingdom an unqualified person becomes entitled to a legal or beneficial interest by way of ownership in the aircraft or a share therein, the registration of the aircraft shall thereupon become void and the certificate of registration shall forthwith be returned by the registered owner to the Authority.

(11) Any person who is the registered owner of an aircraft registered in the United Kingdom shall forthwith inform the Authority in writing of:

   (a) any change in the particulars which were furnished to the Authority upon application being made for the registration of the aircraft;

   (b) the destruction of the aircraft, or its permanent withdrawal from use;

   (c) in the case of an aircraft registered in pursuance of paragraph (5) of this article, the termination of the demise charter.

(12) Any person who becomes the owner of an aircraft registered in the United Kingdom shall within 28 days inform the Authority in writing to that effect.

(13) The Authority may, whenever it appears to it necessary or appropriate to do so for giving effect to this Part of this Order or for bringing up to date or otherwise correcting the particulars entered on the register, amend the register or, if it thinks fit, may cancel the registration of the aircraft, and shall cancel that registration if it is satisfied that there has been a change in the ownership of the aircraft.

(14) The Secretary of State may, by regulations, adapt or modify the foregoing provisions of this article as he deems necessary or expedient for the purpose of providing for the temporary transfer of aircraft to or from the United Kingdom register, either generally or in relation to a particular case or class of cases.

(15) In this article references to an interest in an aircraft do not include references to an interest in an aircraft to which a person is entitled only by virtue of his membership of a flying club and the reference in paragraph (11) of this article to the registered owner of an aircraft includes in the case of a deceased person, his legal personal representative, and in the case of a body corporate which has been dissolved, its successor.

(16) Nothing in this article shall require the Authority to cancel the registration of an aircraft if in its opinion it would be inexpedient in the public interest to do so.

(17) The registration of an aircraft which is the subject of an undischarged mortgage entered in the Register of Aircraft Mortgages kept by the Authority pursuant to an Order

in Council made under section 86 of the Civil Aviation Act 1982 shall not become void by virtue of paragraph (10) of this article, nor shall the Authority cancel the registration of such an aircraft pursuant to this article unless all persons shown in the Register of Aircraft Mortgages as mortgagees of that aircraft have consented to the cancellation.

Nationality and registration marks

5.—(1) An aircraft (other than an aircraft permitted by or under this Order to fly without being registered) shall not fly unless it bears painted thereon or affixed thereto, in the manner required by the law of the country in which it is registered, the nationality and registration marks required by that law.

(2) The marks to be borne by aircraft registered in the United Kingdom shall comply with Part B of Schedule 1 to this Order.

(3) An aircraft shall not bear any marks which purport to indicate:
  (a) that the aircraft is registered in a country in which it is not in fact registered; or
  (b) that the aircraft is a State aircraft of a particular country if it is not in fact such an aircraft, unless the appropriate authority of that country has sanctioned the bearing of such marks.

SCHEDULE 1

PART A. TABLE OF GENERAL CLASSIFICATION OF AIRCRAFT

Col. 1	Col. 2	Col. 3	Col. 4
Aircraft	Lighter than air aircraft	Non-power driven	Free Balloon / Captive Balloon
		Power driven	Airship
	Heavier than air aircraft	Non-power driven	Glider / Kite
		Power driven (flying machines)	Aeroplane (Landplane) / Aeroplane (Seaplane) / Aeroplane (Amphibian) / Aeroplane (Self-launching Motor Glider) / Rotorcraft { Helicopter / Gyroplane }

PART B. NATIONALITY AND REGISTRATION MARKS OF AIRCRAFT REGISTERED IN THE UNITED KINGDOM (Article 5(2))

1. The nationality mark of the aircraft shall be the capital letter "G" in Roman character and the registration mark shall be a group of four capital letters in Roman character assigned by the Authority on the registration of the aircraft. The letters shall be without ornamentation and a hyphen shall be placed between the nationality mark and the registration mark.

2. The nationality and registration marks shall be displayed to the best advantage,

taking into consideration the constructional features of the aircraft and shall always be kept clean and visible.

3. The nationality and registration marks shall also be inscribed, together with the name and address of the registered owner of the aircraft, on a fireproof metal plate affixed—

(a) in the case of an aeroplane having an empty weight not exceeding 150 kg. either in accordance with paragraph (b) or in a prominent position to the wing,

(b) in the case of any other aircraft in a prominent position on the fuselage or car or basket, as the case may be, and near to the main entrance to the aircraft.

4. The nationality and registration marks shall be painted on the aircraft or shall be affixed thereto by any other means ensuring a similar degree of permanence in the following manner—

I. Position of marks

(a) *Flying Machines and Gliders*

(i) *Horizontal Surfaces of the Wings or Fuselage (or equivalent structure):*

(aa) On aircraft having a fixed wing surface, the marks shall appear on the lower surface of the wing structure, and shall be on the left half of the lower surface of the wing structure unless they extend across the whole surface of both wings. So far as possible the marks shall be located equidistant from the leading and trailing edges of the wings. The tops of the letters shall be towards the leading edge of the wing.

(bb) On aircraft having no fixed wing surface and when owing to the structure of the aircraft the greatest height reasonably practicable for the marks on the vertical surface of the fuselage (or equivalent structure) is less than 15 centimetres the marks shall also appear on the lower surface of the fuselage on the line of symmetry and shall be placed with the tops of the letters towards the nose.

(ii) *Vertical Surfaces of the Tail or Fuselage (or equivalent structure):* The marks shall also be on each side of the aircraft either on the fuselage or on the upper halves of the vertical tail surfaces. On aircraft having a fixed wing surface, the marks, if placed on the fuselage (or equivalent structure), shall be between the horizontal tail surfaces and the wing. When on a single vertical tail surface, the marks shall be on both sides. When there is more than one vertical tail surface, the marks shall be on the outer sides of the outboard vertical tail surfaces.

(b) *Airships and Free Balloons*

(i) *Airships:* The marks shall be on each side of the airship. They shall be placed horizontally either on the hull near the maximum cross-section of the airship or on the lower vertical stabiliser.

(ii) *Free Balloons:* The marks shall be in two places diametrically opposite.

(iii) In the case of all airships and free ballons the side marks shall be so placed as to be visible both from the sides and from the ground.

II. Size of Marks

(a) *Flying Machines and Gliders*

(i) *Wings:* The letters constituting each group of marks shall be of equal height. The height of the letters shall be at least 50 centimetres.

(ii) *Fuselage (or equivalent structure) or Vertical Tail Surfaces:* The marks on the fuselage (or equivalent structure) shall not interfere with the visible outlines of the fuselage (or equivalent structure). The marks on the vertical tail surfaces shall be such as to leave a margin of at least 5 centimetres along each side of the vertical tail surface. The letters shall be of equal height. The height of the letters constituting each group of marks shall be at least 30 centimetres. Where marks are required to be carried on the lower surface of aircraft having no fixed wing surface the height of the marks shall be at least 50 centimetres.

Provided that where owing to the structure of the aircraft the appropriate height specified in this sub-paragraph (ii) is not reasonably practicable the height of the marks shall be the greatest height reasonably practicable in the circumstances consistent with compliance with Section III of this Part of this Schedule.

(b) *Airships and Free Balloons*

The letters constituting each group of marks shall be of equal height. The height of the letters shall be at least 50 centimetres.

III. *Width and Spacing of Marks*

(a) The width of each letter (except the letter I) and the length of the hyphen between the nationality mark and registration mark shall be two-thirds of the height of a letter.

(b) The letters and hyphen shall be formed by solid lines and shall be of a colour clearly contrasting with the background on which they appear. Thickness of the lines shall be one-sixth of the height of a letter.

(c) Each letter shall be separated from the letter which it immediately precedes or follows by a space equal to half the width of a letter. A hyphen shall be regarded as a letter for this purpose.

MORTGAGING OF AIRCRAFT ORDER 1972[1]

Citation and Commencement

1. This Order may be cited as the Mortgaging of Aircraft Order 1972 and shall come into operation on 1st October 1972.

Interpretation

2.—(1) The Interpretation Act 1889 applies for the interpretation of this Order as it applies for the interpretation of an Act of Parliament.

(2) In this Order:

"appropriate charge" means the charge payable under section 9 of the Civil Aviation Act 1971;

"the Authority" means the Civil Aviation Authority;

"mortgage of an aircraft" includes a mortgage which extends to any store of spare parts for that aircraft but does not otherwise include a mortgage created as a floating charge;

"owner" means the person shown as the owner of a mortgaged aircraft on the form of application for registration of that aircraft in the United Kingdom nationality register;

"United Kingdom nationality register" means the register of aircraft maintained by the Authority in pursuance of an Order in Council under section 8 of the Civil Aviation Act 1949.

Mortgage of Aircraft

3. An aircraft registered in the United Kingdom nationality register or such an aircraft together with any store of spare parts for that aircraft may be made security for a loan or other valuable consideration.

Registration of Aircraft Mortgages

4.—(1) Any mortgage of an aircraft registered in the United Kingdom nationality register may be entered in the Register of Aircraft Mortgages kept by the Authority.

(2) Applications to enter a mortgage in the Register shall be made to the Authority by or on behalf of the mortgagee in the form set out in Part I of Schedule 1 hereto, and shall be accompanied by a copy of the mortgage, which the applicant shall certify to be a true copy and the appropriate charge.

---

1. S.I. 1972 No. 1268.

5.—(1) A notice of intention to make an application to enter a contemplated mortgage of an aircraft in the Register (hereinafter referred to as "a priority notice") may also be entered in the Register.

(2) Applications to enter a priority notice in the Register shall be made to the Authority by or on behalf of the prospective mortgagee in the form set out in Part II of Schedule 1 hereto, and shall be accompanied by the appropriate charge.

6.—(1) Where two or more aircraft are the subject of one mortgage or where the same aircraft is the subject of two or more mortgages, separate applications shall be made in respect of each aircraft or of each mortgage, as the case may be.

(2) Where a mortgage is in a language other than English, the application to enter that mortgage in the Register shall be accompanied not only by a copy of that mortgage but also by a translation thereof, which the applicant shall certify as being, to the best of his knowledge and belief, a true translation.

7.—(1) When an application to enter a mortgage or priority notice in the Register is duly made, the Authority shall enter the mortgage or the priority notice, as the case may be, in the Register by placing the application form therein and by noting on it the date and the time of the entry.

(2) Applications duly made shall be entered in the Register in order of their receipt by the Authority.

(3) The Authority shall by notice in its Official Record specify the days on which and hours during which its office is open for registering mortgages and priority notices. Any application delivered when the office is closed for that purpose shall be treated as having been received immediately after the office is next opened.

(4) The Authority shall notify the applicant of the date and time of the entry of the mortgage or the priority notice, as the case may be, in the Register and of the register number of the entry and shall send a copy of the notification to the mortgagor and the owner.

Amendment of entries in the Register

8.—(1) Any change in the person appearing in the Register as mortgagee or as mortgagor or in the name or address of such person or in the description of the mortgaged property shall be notified to the Authority by or on behalf of the mortgagee, in the form set out in Part III of Schedule 1 hereto.

(2) On receipt of the said form, duly completed and signed by or on behalf of the mortgagor and the mortgagee and on payment of the appropriate charge, the Authority shall enter the notification in the Register and shall notify the mortgagor, the mortgagee and the owner that it has done so.

Discharge of Mortgages

9.—(1) Where a registered mortgage is discharged the mortgagor shall notify the Authority of the fact in the form set out in Part IV of Schedule 1 hereto.

(2) On receipt of the said form, duly completed and signed by or on behalf of the mortgagor and the mortgagee and of a copy of the mortgage with a discharge or receipt for the mortgage money duly endorsed thereon, or of any other document which shows, to the satisfaction of the Authority, that the mortgage has been discharged and on payment of the appropriate charge, the Authority shall enter the said form in the Register and mark the relevant entries in the Register "Discharged", and shall notify the mortgagee, the mortgagor and the owner that it has done so.

Rectification of the Register

10. Any of the following courts, that is to say the High Court of Justice in England, the Court of Session in Scotland and the High Court of Justice in Northern Ireland may order such amendments to be made to the Register as may appear to the court to be necessary or expedient for correcting any error therein. On being served with the order the Authority shall make the necessary amendment to the Register.

Inspection of Register and copies of entries

11.—(1) On such days and during such hours as the Authority may specify in its Official Record, any person may, on application to the Authority and on payment to it of the appropriate charge inspect any entry in the Register specified in the application.

(2) The Authority shall, on the application of any person and on payment by him of the appropriate charge, supply to the applicant a copy, certified as a true copy, of the entries in the Register specified in the application.

(3) The Authority shall, on the application of any person and on payment by him of the appropriate charge, notify the applicant whether or not there are any entries in the Register relating to any aircraft specified in the application by reference to its nationality and registration marks.

(4) A document purporting to be a copy of an entry in the Register shall be admissible as evidence of that entry if it purports to be certified as a true copy by the Authority.

(5) Nothing done in pursuance of paragraph (2) or (3) of this Article shall affect the priority of any mortgage.

Removal of aircraft from the United Kingdom Nationality Register

12. The removal of an aircraft from the United Kingdom nationality register shall not affect the rights of any mortgagee under any registered mortgage and entries shall continue to be made in the Register in relation to the mortgage as if the aircraft had not been removed from the United Kingdom nationality register.

Register as notice of facts appearing in it

13. All persons shall at all times be taken to have express notice of all facts appearing in the Register, but the registration of a mortgage shall not be evidence of its validity.

Priority of Mortgages

14.—(1) Subject to the following provisions of this article, a mortgage of an aircraft entered in the Register shall have priority over any other mortgage of or charge on that aircraft, other than another mortgage entered in the Register: provided that mortgages made before 1st October 1972, whether entered in the Register or not, shall up to and including 31st December 1972 have the same priority as they would have had if this Order had not been made.

(2) Subject to the following provisions of this article, where two or more mortgages of an aircraft are entered in the Register, those mortgages shall as between themselves have priority according to the times at which they were respectively entered in the Register:
Provided that:
    (i) mortgages of an aircraft made before 1st October 1972 which are entered in the Register before 31st December 1972 shall have priority over any mortgages of that aircraft made on or after 1st October 1972 and shall as between themselves have the same priority as they would have had if this Order had not been made;
    (ii) without prejudice to proviso (i), where a priority notice has been entered in the

Register and the contemplated mortgage referred to therein is made and entered in the Register within 14 days thereafter that mortgage shall be deemed to have priority from the time when the priority notice was registered.

(3) In reckoning the period of 14 days under the preceding paragraph of this article, there shall be excluded any day which the Authority has by notice in its Official Record specified as a day on which its office is not open for registration of mortgages.

(4) The priorities provided for by the preceding provisions of this article shall have effect notwithstanding any express, implied or constructive notice affecting the mortgagee.

(5) Nothing in this article shall be construed as giving a registered mortgage any priority over any possessory lien in respect of work done on the aircraft (whether before or after the creation or registration of the mortgage) on the express or implied authority of any persons lawfully entitled to possession of the aircraft or over any right to detain the aircraft under any Act of Parliament.

Mortgage not affected by bankruptcy

15. A registered mortgage of an aircraft shall not be affected by any act of bankruptcy committed by the mortgagor after the date on which the mortgage is registered, notwithstanding that at the commencement of his bankruptcy the mortgagor had the aircraft in his possession, order or disposition, or was reputed owner thereof, and the mortgage shall be preferred to any right, claim or interest therein of the other creditors of the bankrupt or any trustee or assignee on their behalf.

Application of Bills of Sale Acts and registration provisions of the Companies Acts

16.—(1) The provisions of the Bills of Sale Acts 1878 and 1882 and the Bills of Sale (Ireland) Acts 1879 and 1883 insofar as they relate to bills of sale and other documents given by way of security for the payment of money shall not apply to any mortgage of an aircraft registered in the United Kingdom nationality register, which is made on or after 1st October 1972.

(2) Section 95(2)(h) of the Companies Act 1948, section 106A (2)(d) of that Act as set out in the Companies (Floating Charges) (Scotland) Act 1961 or any re-enactment thereof and section 93(2)(h) of the Companies Act (Northern Ireland) 1960 shall have effect as if after the word "ship" where it first occurs in each case there were inserted the words "or aircraft":

Provided that nothing in this paragraph shall render invalid as against the liquidator or creditor of the company, any mortgage or charge created by a company before the date on which this Order comes into force which would not have been invalid against the liquidator or such a creditor if this Order had not been made.

False Statement and Forgery

17.—(1) If, in furnishing any information for the purpose of this Order, any person makes any statement which he knows to be false in a material particular, or recklessly makes any statement which is false in a material particular, he shall be guilty of an offence.

(2) Any person guilty of an offence under paragraph (1) of this article shall:—
  (a) on summary conviction be liable to a fine not exceeding £400;
  (b) on conviction on indictment be liable to a fine of such amount as the court think fit or to imprisonment for a term not exceeding 2 years or to both such a fine and such imprisonment.

(3) Without prejudice to any rule of the law of Scotland relating to forging and

uttering, the Forgery Act 1913 shall apply in relation to documents forwarded to the Authority in pursuance of this Order as if such documents were included in the list of documents in section 3(3) of that Act.

Indemnity

18.—(1) Subject to paragraph (2) of this article, any person who suffers loss by reason of any error or omission in the Register or of any inaccuracy in a copy of an entry in the Register supplied pursuant to Article 11(2) of this Order or in a notification made pursuant to Article 11(3) of this Order shall be indemnified by the Authority.

(2) No indemnity shall be payable under this article:

(a) where the person who has suffered loss has himself caused or substantially contributed to the loss by his fraud or has derived title from a person so committing fraud;

(b) on account of costs or expenses incurred in taking or defending any legal proceedings without the consent of the Authority.

Application to Scotland

19. The provisions of Schedule 2 to this Order shall have effect for the purpose of the application of this Order to Scotland.

SCHEDULE 1. FORMS

PART I. REGISTER OF AIRCRAFT MORTGAGES (ARTICLE 4(2))

Entry of Aircraft Mortgage

To be completed by Applicant:—

I hereby apply for the mortgage, particulars of which are given below, to be entered in the Register of Aircraft Mortgages.

1. Date of mortgage.

2. Description of the mortgaged aircraft (including its type, nationality and registration marks and aircraft serial number) and of any store of spare parts for that aircraft to which the mortgage extends.
(The description of the store of spare parts must include an indication of their character and approximate number and the place or places where they are stored must be given[1]).

3. The sum secured by the mortgage.[2]

4. Does the mortgage require the mortgagee to make further advances? If so, of what amount?

5. Name and address and, where applicable, company registration number of the mortgagor.

6. Register number of priority notice, if any.

Signed ....

Name in block capitals ....

On behalf of[3] ....
(insert name and, where applicable, company registration number of mortgagee)

of ....
(insert address of mortgagee)

---

1. The description of the mortgaged property may, if necessary, be continued on a separate sheet, which shall be signed by the applicant.
2. Where the sum secured is of a fluctuating amount, this should be stated and the upper and lower limits, if any, should be set out.
3. Delete where inapplicable.

PART II. REGISTER OF AIRCRAFT MORTGAGES (ARTICLE 5(2))

Entry of Priority Notice

To be completed by Applicant:—

I hereby give notice that I am contemplating entering into a mortgage, particulars of which are given below, and that if I do enter into the said mortgage I shall apply for it to be entered in the Register of Aircraft Mortgages. I hereby apply for this notice to be entered in the said Register.

1. Description of the aircraft which is the subject of the contemplated mortgage (including its type, nationality and registration marks and aircraft serial number) and of any store of spare parts for that aircraft to which it is contemplated that the mortgage will extend.[1]

2. The sum to be secured by the contemplated mortgage.[2]

3. Is it contemplated that the mortgage will require the mortgagee to make further advances? If so, of what amount?

4. Name and address and, where applicable, company registration number of the prospective mortgagor.

Signed ....

Name in block capitals ....

On behalf of[3] ....
(insert name and, where applicable, company registration number of mortgagee)

of ....
(insert address of mortgagee)

1. The description of the property which is the subject of the contemplated mortgage may, if necessary, be continued on a separate sheet which shall be signed by the applicant.
2. Where the sum to be secured is of a fluctuating amount, this should be stated and the upper and lower limits, if any, should be set out.
3. Delete where inapplicable.

PART III. REGISTER OF AIRCRAFT MORTGAGES (ARTICLE 8(1))

Change in Particulars

We hereby give notice that the particulars shown on the Register of Aircraft Mortgages under Register number .... should be amended as follows:—

(*a*) Signed ....

Name in block capitals ....

on behalf of[1] ....
(insert name of mortgagee)

(*b*) Signed ....

Name in block capitals ....

on behalf of[1] ....
(insert name of person shown in the Register as the mortgagee)[2]

(*c*) Signed ....

Name in block capitals ....

on behalf of[1] ....
(insert name of mortgagor)

1. Delete where inapplicable.
2. Applicable only where the change in particulars is a change in the person appearing in the Register as mortgagee.

PART IV. REGISTER OF AIRCRAFT MORTGAGES (ARTICLE 9(1))

Discharge of registered mortgage

I hereby give notice that the mortgage entered in the Register of Aircraft Mortgages under register number .... has been discharged.

Signed ....

Name in block capitals ....

on behalf of * ....
(insert name of mortgagor)

I agree that the aforesaid mortgage has been discharged.

Signed ....

Name in block capitals ....

on behalf of * ....
(insert name of mortgagee)

---

* Delete where inapplicable.

SCHEDULE 2

PART I. APPLICATION OF THE ORDER TO SCOTLAND (ARTICLE 19)

1. (a) In this Schedule—

"act of bankruptcy" has the meaning assigned to it in subparagraph (b)(ii) of this paragraph;

"aircraft mortgage" has the meaning assigned to it in paragraph 2 of this Schedule;

"mortgagee" means the creditor in an aircraft mortgage;

"mortgagor" means the person in security of whose indebtedness or obligation the aircraft mortgage is granted;

and references to an aircraft which is the subject of an aircraft mortgage include, where the mortgage so extends, a reference to a store of spare parts designated or appropriated to that aircraft.

(b) In the application of this Order to Scotland—

(i) in Article 14 there shall be added the following paragraph—

"6. Subject to paragraph 5 of this article, an aircraft mortgage may contain provisions regulating the order in which that mortgage shall rank with any other mortgage of that aircraft or any floating charge within the meaning of the Companies (Floating Charges) (Scotland) Act 1961 or any re-enactment thereof."

(ii) in Article 15 the words "act of bankruptcy" shall mean—

(a) in the case of a company, a winding-up order, or a resolution for voluntary winding-up (other than a members' voluntary winding-up) or the taking of possession, by or on behalf of the holders of any debentures secured by a floating charge, of any property of the company comprised in or subject to the charge;

(b) in the case of any other person, his notour bankruptcy, the execution of a trust deed for behoof of, or the making of a composition contract or arrangement with his creditors or in the event of his death, the appointment of a judicial factor under section 163 of the Bankruptcy (Scotland) Act 1913 to divide his insolvent estate among his creditors, or the making of an order for the administration of his estate according to the law of bankruptcy under section 130 of the Bankruptcy Act 1914 or the administration of his estate in accordance with the rules set out in Part I of Schedule 1 to the Administration of Estates Act 1925.

2. A security created in Scotland under Article 3 of this Order for a loan or other obligation shall be constituted by a mortgage in, or as nearly as may be in, the form specified in Part II of this Schedule which shall be known as an aircraft mortgage.

3. A mortgage registered under this Order shall have effect without any requirement of law that delivery of the aircraft shall be made to the mortgagee.

4. A mortgage so registered may be transferred, in whole or in part, by the mortgagee by a transfer in, or as nearly as may be in, the form specified in Part III of this Schedule.

5. An aircraft mortgage may be discharged, in whole or in part, by the mortgagee by a discharge in, or as nearly as may be in, the form specified in Part IV of this Schedule or by a receipt for the mortgage money duly endorsed on the aircraft mortgage.

6. The provisions of paragraphs 7 to 11 of this Schedule, with such variations as may have been agreed by the parties, shall regulate the rights and powers of parties under an aircraft mortgage.

7. Where the mortgagor, or the owner, is in default within the meaning of paragraph 8 of this Schedule, the mortgagee may exercise such of the rights conferred upon him by the following provisions of this Schedule as he may consider appropriate, and any such right shall be in addition to, and not in derogation from, any other remedy arising from the aircraft mortgage or any other agreement between the parties.

8. The mortgagor or the owner shall be in default if—
   (a) the mortgagee has required the discharge or performance of the debt or obligation to which the aircraft mortgage relates and the mortgagor fails to meet that requirement, or
   (b) the mortgagor or the owner has failed to comply with any other condition of the aircraft mortgage, or
   (c) the mortgagor or the owner has committed an act of bankruptcy.

9. Where default as aforesaid has occurred the mortgagee may sell the mortgaged aircraft in accordance with the following provisions of this paragraph:—
   (a) The mortgagee who intends to sell the aircraft shall give not less than 60 days notice in writing of that intention to the mortgagor, the owner and every person shown in the Register as holding a mortgage over the aircraft, but the said period of notice may be dispensed with or shortened with the consent of all the persons to whom notice is required to be given.
   (b) On the expiry of, or the dispensing with, the period of notice, or, as the case may be, of the reduced period of notice, the mortgagee may sell the aircraft with the consent in writing of every other mortgagee shown in the Register as holding a mortgage over the aircraft.
   (c) In the event of any mortgagee withholding his consent the mortgagee who has served the notice may apply to the Court of Session for a warrant to sell the aircraft; any such application shall be served upon any mortgagee who has withheld his consent and may be granted by the Court, subject to such conditions as it thinks reasonable in all the circumstances.

10. Moneys received by a mortgagee from the sale of the mortgaged aircraft shall be held by him in trust to be applied in accordance with the following order of priority:—
   (a) first, in payment of all expenses properly incurred by him in connection with the sale, or any prior attempted sale, of the aircraft;
   (b) secondly, in payment of the whole amount of principal and interest due under any prior aircraft mortgage to which the sale is not made conditional;
   (c) thirdly, in payment of the whole amount of principal and interest due under his aircraft mortgage and in payment in due proportion of the whole amount due under an aircraft mortgage, if any, ranking *pari passu* with his own mortgage;

(d) fourthly, in payment of any amounts of principal and interest due under any duly registered mortgages over the aircraft, the ranking of which is postponed to that of his own mortgage; and

(e) fifthly, in payment of any amount of principal and interest due under any mortgages over the aircraft ranked in accordance with the priorities provided for in Article 14 of this Order where the holder of any such mortgage has lodged in the hands of the mortgagee a claim in writing countersigned by the mortgagor,

and any residue of the moneys so received shall be paid to the owner or to any person authorised by the owner to give receipts therefor.

11.—(1) Where default as aforesaid has occurred the mortgagee may apply to the Court of Session for a warrant for possession of the mortgaged aircraft, and the application shall be served upon the mortgagor, the owner and every person shown in the Register as holding a mortgage over the aircraft and upon the owner or occupier of the land or premises where the aircraft is for the time being situated.

(2) Upon such an application being made the Court may—

(a) grant warrant to the applicant to take interim possession of the aircraft pending further consideration of the application,

(b) on further consideration grant the application for possession subject to such conditions as it shall consider reasonable in all the circumstances.

(3) Subject to any conditions imposed by the Court a warrant for possession shall empower the applicant to enter at any reasonable time on any land or into any premises where the mortgaged aircraft, or any part thereof, may be, and to remove the aircraft or part, to manage the aircraft and to receive all income accruing from freights or charter fees, to pay insurance premiums and expenses of such management, to effect repairs and make replacements of parts and to recover all expenses, payments and disbursements incurred by him in relation to the exercise of these powers as sums due under his mortgage with interest thereon at the rate stipulated therein from the respective dates of payment or disbursement.

(4) A mortgagee who has obtained a warrant for possession may at any time thereafter sell the mortgaged aircraft after giving not less than 30 days notice in writing of his intention to do so to the mortgagor, the owner and every person shown in the Register as holding a mortgage over the aircraft, provided that the said period of notice may be dispensed with or shortened with the consent of all the persons to whom notice is required to be given.

12. The Court of Session shall have jurisdiction to grant an application by a mortgagee in any mortgage of an aircraft registered in the United Kingdom for a warrant for possession or sale of the aircraft while the aircraft is situated in Scotland as if the mortgage had been an aircraft mortgage created in Scotland.

13. The provisions of section 16 of the Administration of Justice (Scotland) Act 1933 (power to regulate procedure, etc. by Act of Sederunt) shall apply to the provisions of this Order as it applies to the provisions of an Act of Parliament.

PART II. AIRCRAFT MORTGAGE

Particulars of Aircraft

Where registered
Nationality and registration marks
Type
    (a) Manufacturer's description
    (b) Aircraft serial number

(c) Any other relevant details appearing in the United Kingdom nationality register.
————————————

We,

hereby in security of (specify the nature of the debt or obligation for which the mortgage is granted and the instrument by which it is constituted) hereby grant a mortgage in favour of the said

over the Aircraft above particularly described of which we are the Owners, [and the store of spare parts for the said Aircraft of which we are the Owners wheresoever they are situated (or otherwise as the case may be)] And we covenant with the said

that we have power to mortgage in the manner aforesaid the said Aircraft [and its store of spare parts] and that the same is [are] free from encumbrances save as appears in the Register of Aircraft Mortgages.

[To be attested]

PART III. AIRCRAFT MORTGAGE

Transfer of Mortgage

We
in consideration of
paid to us by
hereby transfer to the said
the benefit of an Aircraft Mortgage granted in our favour [or in favour of ....
.....................................] dated
and registered in the Register of Aircraft Mortgages on ....
under Register No ....

[To be attested]

Note: This Transfer may be endorsed on the original of the Aircraft Mortgage or may be a separate document.

PART IV. AIRCRAFT MORTGAGE

Discharge of mortgage

We
acknowledge to have received the sum of
in [partial] discharge of an Aircraft Mortgage granted by
in our favour [or in favour of ....]
dated .... and registered in the Register of Aircraft Mortgages
on .... under Register No ....
[to which we acquired right by Transfer by the said ....
(or as the case may be) in our favour dated ....
and registered in the said Register on ....]

[To be attested]

Note: This Discharge may be endorsed on the original Aircraft Mortgage or may be a separate document.

INTERNATIONAL CONVENTION FOR THE UNIFICATION OF CERTAIN RULES OF LAW RELATING TO MARITIME LIENS AND MORTGAGES 1926[1]

Article 1

Mortgages, hypothecations, and other similar charges upon vessels, duly effected in accordance with the law of the Contracting State to which the vessel belongs, and registered in a public register either at the port of the vessel's registry or at a central office, shall be regarded as valid and respected in all other contracting countries.

Article 2

The following give rise to maritime liens on a vessel, on the freight for the voyage during which the claim giving rise to the lien arises, and on the accessories of the vessel and freight accrued since the commencement of the voyage:

(1) Law costs due to the State, and expenses incurred in the common interest of the creditors in order to preserve the vessel or to procure its sale and the distribution of the proceeds of sale; tonnage dues, light or harbour dues, and other public taxes and charges of the same character; pilotage dues; the cost of watching and preservation from the time of the entry of the vessel into the last port;

(2) Claims arising out of the contract of engagement of the master, crew, and other persons hired on board;

(3) Remuneration for assistance and salvage, and the contribution of the vessel in general average;

(4) Indemnities for collision or other accident of navigation, as also for damage caused to works forming part of harbours, docks, and navigable ways; indemnities for personal injury to passengers or crew; indemnities for loss of or damage to cargo or baggage;

(5) Claims resulting from contracts entered into or acts done by the master, acting within the scope of his authority, away from the vessel's home port, where such contracts or acts are necessary for the preservation of the vessel or the continuation of its voyage, whether the master is or is not at the same time owner of the vessel, and whether the claim is his own or that of ship-chandlers, repairers, lenders, or other contractual creditors.

Article 3

The mortgages, hypothecations, and other charges on vessels referred to in Article 1 rank immediately after the secured claims referred to in the preceding article.

National laws may grant a lien in respect of claims other than those referred to in the said last-mentioned article, so, however, as not to modify the ranking of claims secured

1. Signed at Brussels 10 April 1926.

by mortgages, hypothecations, and other similar charges, or by the liens taking precedence thereof.

Article 4

The accessories of the vessel and the freight mentioned in Article 2, mean:
   (1) Compensation due to the owner for material damage sustained by the vessel and not repaired, or for loss of freight;
   (2) General average contributions due to the owner, in respect of material damage sustained by the vessel and not repaired, or in respect of loss of freight;
   (3) Remuneration due to the owner for assistance and salvage services rendered at any time before the end of the voyage, any sums allotted to the master or other persons in the service of the vessel being deducted.

The provision as to freight applies also to passage money, and, in the last resort, to the sums due under Article 4 of the Convention on the limitation of shipowner's liability.

Payments made or due to the owner on policies of insurance, as well as bounties, subventions, and other national subsidies are not deemed to be accessories of the vessel or of the freight.

Notwithstanding anything in the opening words of Article 2, (2), the lien in favour of persons in the service of the vessel extends, to the total amount of freight due for all voyages made during the subsistence of the same contract of engagement.

Article 5

Claims secured by a lien and relating to the same voyage rank in the order in which they are set out in Article 2. Claims included under any one heading share concurrently and rateably in the event of the fund available being insufficient to pay the claims in full.

The claims mentioned under Nos. 3 and 5 in that article rank, in each of the two categories, in the inverse order of the dates on which they came into existence.

Claims arising from one and the same occurrence are deemed to have come into existence at the same time.

Article 6

Claims secured by a lien and attaching to the last voyage have priority over those attaching to previous voyage.

Provided that claims, arising on one and the same contract of engagement extending over several voyages, all rank with claims attaching to the last voyage.

Article 7

As regards the distribution of the sum resulting from the sale of the property subject to a lien, the creditors whose claims are secured by a lien have the right to put forward their claims in full, without any deduction on account of the rules relating to limitation of liability; provided, however, that the sum apportioned to them may not exceed the sum due having regard to the said rules.

Article 8

Claims secured by a lien follow the vessel into whatever hands it may pass.

Article 9

The liens cease to exist, apart from other cases provided for by national laws, at the expiration of one year, and, in the case of liens for supplies mentioned in No. 5 of Article 2, shall continue in force for not more than six months.

The periods for which the lien remains in force in the case of liens securing claims in respect of assistance and salvage run from the day when the services terminated, in the case of liens securing claims in respect of collision and other accidents and in respect of bodily injuries from the day when the damage was caused; in the case of liens for the loss of or damage to cargo or baggage from the day of the delivery of the cargo or baggage or from the day when they should have been delivered; for repairs and supplies and other cases mentioned in No. 5 of Article 2 from the day the claim originated. In all the other cases the period runs from the enforceability of the claim.

The fact that any of the persons employed on board, mentioned in No. 2 of Article 2 has a right to any payment in advance or on account does not render his claim enforceable.

As respects the cases provided for in the national laws in which a lien is extinguished, a sale shall extinguish a lien only if accompanied by formalities of publicity which shall be laid down by the national laws. These formalities shall include a notice given in such form and within such time as the national laws may prescribe to the authority charged with keeping the registers referred to in Article 1 of this Convention.

The grounds upon which the above periods may be interrupted are determined by the law of the court where the case is tried.

The High Contracting Parties reserve to themselves the right to provide by legislation in their respective countries, that the said periods shall be extended in cases where it has not been possible to arrest the vessel to which a lien attaches in the territorial waters of the state in which the claimant has his domicile or his principal place of business, provided that the extended period shall not exceed three years from the time when the claim originated.

Article 10

A lien on freight may be enforced so long as the freight is still due or the amount of the freight is still in the hands of the master or the agent of the owner. The same principle applies to a lien on accessories.

Article 11

Subject to the provisions of this Convention, liens established by the preceding provisions are subject to no formality and to no special condition of proof.

This provision does not affect the right of any State to maintain in the legislation provisions requiring the master of a vessel to fulfil special formalities in the case of certain loans raised on the security of the vessel, or in the case of the sale of its cargo.

Article 12

National laws must prescribe the nature and the form of documents to be carried on board the vessel in which entry must be made of the mortgages, hypothecations, and other charges referred to in Article 1; so, however, that the mortgagees requiring such entry in the said form be not held responsible for any omission, mistake, or delay in inscribing the same on the said documents.

Article 13

The foregoing provisions apply to vessels under the management of a person who operates them without owning them or to the principal charterer, except in cases where the owner has been dispossessed by an illegal act or where the claimant is not a *bona fide* claimant.

Article 14

The provisions of this Convention shall be applied in each Contracting State in cases in which the vessel to which the claim relates belongs to a Contracting State, as well as in any other cases provided for by the national laws.

Nevertheless the principle formulated in the preceding paragraph does not affect the right of the Contracting States not to apply the provisions of this Convention in favour of the nationals of a non-contracting State.

Article 15

This Convention does not apply to vessels of war, nor to government vessels appropriated exclusively to the public service.

Article 16

Nothing in the foregoing provisions shall be deemed to affect in any way the competence of tribunals, modes of procedure or methods of execution authorized by the national law.

Article 17

After an interval of not more than two years from the day on which the Convention is signed, the Belgian Government shall place itself in communication with the Governments of the High Contracting Parties which have declared themselves prepared to ratify the Convention, with a view to deciding whether it shall be put into force. The ratifications shall be deposited at Brussels at a date to be fixed by agreement among the said Governments. The first deposit of ratifications shall be recorded in a process verbal signed by the representatives of the powers which take part therein and by the Belgian Minister for Foreign Affairs.

The subsequent deposits of ratifications shall be made by means of a written notification, addressed to the Belgian Government, and accompanied by the instrument of ratification.

A duly certified copy of the process verbal relating to the first deposit of ratifications, of the notification referred to in the previous paragraph, and also of the instruments of ratification accompanying them, shall be immediately sent by the Belgian Government through the diplomatic channel to the powers who have signed this Convention or who have acceded to it. In the cases contemplated in the preceding paragraph the said Government shall inform them at the same time of the date on which it received the notification.

Article 18

Non-signatory States may accede to the present Convention whether or not they have been represented at the international Conference at Brussels.

A State which desires to accede shall notify its intention in writing to the Belgian Government, forwarding to it the document of accession which shall be deposited in the archives of the said Government.

The Belgian Government shall immediately forward to all the states which have signed or acceded to the Convention a duly certified copy of the notification and of the act of accession, mentioning the date on which it received the notification.

Article 19

The High Contracting Parties may at the time of signature, ratification, or accession declare that their acceptance of the present Convention does not include any or all of the

self-governing dominions, or of the colonies, overseas possessions, protectorates, or territories under their sovereignty or authority, and they may subsequently accede separately
on behalf of any self-governing dominion, colony, overseas possession, protectorate or
territory excluded in their declaration. They may also denounce the Convention separately in accordance with its provision in respect of any self-governing dominion, or any
colony, overseas possession, protectorate, or territory under their sovereignty or authority.

Article 20

The present Convention shall take effect, in the case of the states which have taken
part in the first deposit of ratifications, one year after the date of the process verbal
recording such deposit. As respects the states which ratify subsequently or which accede,
and also in cases in which the convention is subsequently put into effect in accordance
with article 19, it shall take effect six months after the notifications specified in article 17,
§ 2, and article 18, § 2, have been received by the Belgian Government.

Article 21

In the event of one of the Contracting States wishing to denounce the present Convention, the denunciation shall be notified in writing to the Belgian Government, which
shall immediately communicate a duly certified copy of the notification to all the other
states informing them of the date on which it was received.

The denunciation shall only operate in respect of the state which made the notification, and on the expiration of one year after the notification has reached the Belgian
Government.

Article 22

Any one of the Contracting States shall have the right to call for a new conference with
a view to considering possible amendments.

A State which would exercise this right should give one year advance notice of its
intention to the other states through the Belgian Government, which would make
arrangements for convening the conference.

PROTOCOL OF SIGNATURE

In proceeding to the signature of the International Convention for the unification of
certain rules relating to maritime liens and mortgages, the undersigned Plenipotentiaries
have adopted the present Protocol, which will have the same force and the same value as
if the provisions were inserted in the text of the Convention to which it relates:

I. It is understood that the legislation of each state remains free
   (1) to establish among the claims mentioned in No. 1 of article 2, a definite order of
       priority with a view to safeguarding the interests of the Treasury;
   (2) to confer on the authorities administering harbours, docks, lighthouses, and
       navigable ways, who have caused a wreck or other obstruction to navigation to
       be removed, or who are creditors in respect of harbour dues, or for damage
       caused by the fault of a vessel, the right, in case of non-payment, to detain the
       vessel, wreck, or other property, to sell the same, and to indemnify themselves
       out of the proceeds in priority to other claimants, and
   (3) to determine the rank of the claimants for damages done to works otherwise
       than as stated in Article 5 and in Article 6.

II. There is no impairment of the provisions in the national laws of the Contracting States conferring a lien upon public insurance associations in respect of claims arising out of the insurance of the personnel of vessels.

Done at Brussels, in a single copy, April 10th, 1926.

INTERNATIONAL CONVENTION FOR THE UNIFICATION OF CERTAIN RULES RELATING TO MARITIME LIENS AND MORTGAGES 1967[1]

The contracting parties,

Having recognized the desirability of determining by agreement certain rules relating to maritime liens and mortgages.

Have resolved to conclude a convention for this purpose, and thereto agreed as follows:

Article 1

Mortgages and "hypothèques" on sea-going vessels shall be enforceable in Contracting States provided that:

(a) such mortgages and "hypothèques" have been effected and registered in accordance with the law of the State where the vessel is registered;

(b) the register and any instruments required to be deposited with the registrar in accordance with the law of the State where the vessel is registered are open to public inspection, and that extracts of the register and copies of such instruments are obtainable from the registrar, and

(c) either the register or any instruments referred to in paragraph (b) above specifies the name and address of the person in whose favour the mortgage or "hypothèque" has been effected or that it has been issued to bearer, the amount secured and the date and other particulars which, according to the law of the State of registration, determine the rank as respects other registered mortgages and "hypothèques".

Article 2

The ranking of registered mortgages and "hypothèques" as between themselves and, without prejudice to the provisions of this Convention, their effect in regard to third parties shall be determined by the law of the State of registration; however, without prejudice to the provisions of this Convention, all matters relating to the procedure of enforcement shall be regulated by the law of the State where enforcement takes place.

Article 3

1. Subject to the provisions of Article 11, no contracting state shall permit the de-registration of a vessel without the written consent of all holders of registered mortgages and "hypothèques".

2. A vessel which is or has been registered in a contracting state shall not be eligible for registration in another contracting state, unless:

1. Done at Brussels on 27 May, 1967.

(a) a certificate has been issued by the former State to the effect that the vessel has been deregistered, or

(b) a certificate has been issued by the former State to the effect that the vessel will be deregistered on the day when such new registration is effected.

Article 4

1. The following claims shall be secured by maritime liens on the vessel:

    (i) wages and other sums due to the master, officers and other members of the vessel's complement in respect of their employment on the vessel;

    (ii) port, canal and other waterway dues and pilotage dues;

    (iii) claims against the owner in respect of loss of life or personal injury occurring, whether on land or on water, in direct connection with the operation of the vessel;

    (iv) claims against the owner, based on tort and not capable of being based on contract, in respect of loss of or damage to property occurring, whether on land or on water, in direct connection with the operation of the vessel;

    (v) claims for salvage, wreck removal and contribution in general average.

The word "owner" mentioned in this paragraph shall be deemed to include the demise or other charterer, manager or operator of the vessel.

2. No maritime lien shall attach to the vessel securing claims as set out in paragraph 1 (iii) and (iv) of this Article which arise out of or result from the radioactive properties or a combination of radioactive properties with toxic, explosive or other hazardous properties of nuclear fuel or of radioactive product or waste.

Article 5

1. The maritime liens set out in Article 4 shall take priority over registered mortgages and "hypothèques", and no other claim shall take priority over such maritime liens or over mortgages and "hypothèques" which comply with the requirements of Article 1, except as provided in Article 6(2).

2. The maritime liens set out in Article 4 shall rank in the order listed, provided however that maritime liens securing claims for salvage, wreck removal and contribution in general average shall take priority over all other maritime liens which have attached to the vessel prior to the time when the operations giving rise to the said liens were performed.

3. The maritime liens set out in each of sub-paragraphs (i), (ii), (iii) and (iv) of paragraph (1) of Article 4 shall rank *pari passu* as between themselves.

4. The maritime liens set out in sub-paragraph (v) of paragraph (1) of Article 4 shall rank in the inverse order of the time when the claims secured thereby accrued. Claims for contribution in general average shall be deemed to have accrued on the date on which the general average act was performed; claims for salvage shall be deemed to have accrued on the date on which the salvage operation was terminated.

Article 6

1. Each contracting state may grant liens of rights of retention to secure claims other than those referred to in Article 4. Such liens shall rank after all maritime liens set out in Article 4 and after all registered mortgages and "hypothèques" which comply with the provisions of Article 1; and such rights of retention shall not prejudice the enforcement of maritime liens set out in Article 4 or registered mortgages or "hypothèques" which comply with the provisions of Article 1, nor the delivery of the vessel to the purchaser in connection with such enforcement.

2. In the event that a lien or right of retention is granted in respect of a vessel in possession of
(a) a shipbuilder, to secure claims for the building of the vessel, or
(b) a ship repairer, to secure claims for repair of the vessel affected during such possession,
such lien or right of retention shall be postponed to all maritime liens set out in Article 4, but may be preferred to registered mortgages or "hypothèques". Such lien or right of retention may be exercisable against the vessel notwithstanding any registered mortgage or "hypothèque" on the vessel, but shall be extinguished when the vessel ceases to be in the possession of the shipbuilder or ship repairer, as the case may be.

Article 7

1. The maritime liens set out in Article 4 arise whether the claims secured by such liens are against the owner or against the demise or other charterer, manager or operator of the vessel.
2. Subject to the provisions of Article 11, the maritime liens securing the claims set out in Article 4 follow the vessel notwithstanding any change of ownership or of registration.

Article 8

1. The maritime liens set out in Article 4 shall be extinguished after a period of one year from the time when the claims secured thereby arose unless, prior to the expiry of such period, the vessel has been arrested, such arrest leading to a forced sale.
2. The one year period referred to in the preceding paragraph shall not be subject to suspension or interruption, provided however that time shall not run during the period that the lienor is legally prevented from arresting the vessel.

Article 9

The assignment of or subrogation to a claim secured by a maritime lien set out in Article 4 entails the simultaneous assignment of or subrogation to such maritime lien.

Article 10

Prior to the forced sale of a vessel in a contracting state, the competent authority of such State shall give, or cause to be given at least thirty days written notice of the time and place of such sale to:
(a) all holders of registered mortgages and "hypothèques" which have not been issued to bearer;
(b) such holders of registered mortgages and "hypothèques" issued to bearer and to such holders of maritime liens set out in Article 4 whose claims have been notified to the said authority;
(c) the registrar of the register in which the vessel is registered.

Article 11

1. In the event of the forced sale of the vessel in a contracting state all mortgages and "hypothèques", except those assumed by the purchaser with the consent of the holders, and all liens and other encumbrances of whatsoever nature shall cease to attach to the vessel, provided however that:
(a) at the time of the sale, the vessel is in the jurisdiction of such contracting state, and

(b) the sale has been effected in accordance with the law of the said State and the provisions of this Convention.

No charterparty or contract for the use of the vessel shall be deemed a lien or encumbrance for the purpose of this Article.

2. The cost awarded by the court and arising out of the arrest and subsequent sale of the vessel and the distribution of the proceeds shall first be paid out of the proceeds of such sale. The balance shall be distributed among the holders of maritime liens, liens and rights of retention mentioned in paragraph 2 of Article 6 and registered mortgages and "hypothèques" in accordance with the provisions of this Convention to the extent necessary to satisfy their claims.

3. When a vessel registered in a contracting state has been the object of a forced sale in a contracting state, the court or other competent authority having jurisdiction shall, at the request of the purchaser, issue a certificate to the effect that the vessel is sold free of all mortgages and "hypothèques", except those assumed by the purchaser, and all liens and other encumbrances, provided that the requirements set out in paragraph 1, subparagraphs (a) and (b) have been complied with, and that the proceeds of such forced sale have been distributed in compliance with paragraph 2 of this Article or have been deposited with the authority that is competent under the law of the place of the sale. Upon production of such certificate the registrar shall be bound to delete all registered mortgages and "hypothèques", except those assumed by the purchaser, and to register the vessel in the name of the purchaser or to issue a certificate of deregistration for the purpose of re-registration, as the case may be.

Article 12

1. Unless otherwise provided in this Convention, its provisions shall apply to all seagoing vessels registered in a contracting state or in a non contracting state.

2. Nothing in this Convention shall require any rights to be conferred in or against, or enable any rights to be enforced against any vessel owned, operated or chartered by a State and appropriated to public non-commercial services.

Article 13

For the purposes of Articles 3, 10 and 11 of this Convention, the competent authorities of the contracting states shall be authorised to correspond directly between themselves.

Article 14

Any contracting party may at the time of signing, ratifying or acceding to this Convention make the following reservations:
1. to give effect to this Convention either by giving it the force of law or by including the provisions of this Convention in its national legislation in a form appropriate to that legislation;
2. to apply the International Convention relating to the limitation of the liability of owners of seagoing ships, signed at Brussels on October 10, 1957.

Article 15

Any dispute between two or more contracting parties concerning the interpretation or application of this Convention which cannot be settled through negotiation, shall, at the request of one of them, be submitted to arbitration. If within six months from the date of the request for arbitration the parties are unable to agree on the organisation of the arbitration, any one of those parties may refer the dispute to the International Court of Justice by request in conformity with the Statute of the court.

Article 16

1. Each contracting party may at the time of signature or ratification of this Convention or accession thereto, declare that it does not consider itself bound by Article 15 of the Convention. The other contracting party shall not be bound by this Article with respect to any contracting party having made such a reservation.

2. Any contracting party having made a reservation in accordance with paragraph 1 may at any time withdraw this reservation by notification to the Belgian Government.

Article 17

This Convention shall be open for signature by the States represented at the twelfth session of the Diplomatic Conference on Maritime Law.

Article 18

This Convention shall be ratified and the instruments of ratification shall be deposited with the Belgian Government.

Article 19

1. This Convention shall come into force three months after the date of the deposit of the fifth instrument of ratification.

2. This Convention shall come into force in respect of each signatory State which ratified it after the deposit of the fifth instrument of ratification, three months after the date of the deposit of the instrument of ratification.

Article 20

1. States, Members of the United Nations or Members of the specialised agencies, not represented at the twelfth session of the Diplomatic Conference on Maritime Law, may accede to this Convention.

2. The instruments of accession shall be deposited with the Belgian Government.

3. The Convention shall come into force in respect of the acceding State three months after the date of deposit of the instrument of accession of that State, but not before the date of entry into force of the Convention as established by Article 19(1).

Article 21

Each contracting party shall have the right to denounce this Convention at any time after the coming into force thereof in respect of such contracting party. Nevertheless, this denunciation shall only take effect one year after the date on which notification thereof has been received by the Belgian Government.

Article 22

1. Any contracting party may at the time of signature, ratification or accession to this Convention or at any time thereafter declare by written notification to the Belgian Government which, among the territories under its sovereignty or for whose international relations it is responsible, are those to which the present Convention applies.

The Convention shall three months after the date of the receipt of such notification by the Belgian Government, extend to the territories named therein.

2. Any contracting party which has made a declaration under paragraph (1) of this Article may at any time thereafter declare by notification given to the Belgian Government that the Convention shall cease to extend to such territories.

This denunciation shall take effect one year after the date on which notification thereof has been received by the Belgian Government.

Article 23

The Belgian Government shall notify the States represented at the twelfth session of the Diplomatic Conference on Maritime Law, and the acceding States to this Convention, of the following:

1. The signatures, ratifications and accessions received in accordance with Articles 17, 18 and 20.
2. The date on which the present Convention will come into force in accordance with Article 19.
3. The notifications with regard to Articles 14, 16 and 22.
4. The denunciations received in accordance with Article 21.

Article 24

Any contracting party may three years after the coming into force of this Convention, in respect of such contracting party, or at any time thereafter request that a Conference be convened in order to consider amendments to this Convention.

Any contracting party proposing to avail itself of this right shall notify the Belgian Government which, provided that one-third of the contracting parties are in agreement, shall convene the Conference within six months thereafter.

Article 25

In respect of the relations between States which ratify this Convention or accede to it, this Convention shall replace and abrogate the International Convention for the unification of certain rules relating to Maritime Liens and Mortgages and Protocol of signature, signed at Brussels on April 19, 1926.

In witness whereof the undersigned plenipotentiaries, duly authorised, have signed this Convention.

Done at Brussels, this 27th day of May 1967, in the French and English languages, both texts being equally authentic, in a single copy, which shall remain deposited in the archives of the Belgian Government, which shall issue certified copies.

INDEX